MARCUS CORNELIUS FRONTO

I

THE CORRESPONDENCE OF
MARCUS CORNELIUS FRONTO

WITH MARCUS AURELIUS ANTONINUS, LUCIUS VERUS, ANTONINUS PIUS, AND VARIOUS FRIENDS

EDITED AND FOR THE FIRST TIME TRANSLATED
INTO ENGLISH BY

C. R. HAINES, M.A., F.S.A.

IN TWO VOLUMES

I

CAMBRIDGE, MASSACHUSETTS
HARVARD UNIVERSITY PRESS
LONDON
WILLIAM HEINEMANN LTD
MCMLXXXII

American ISBN 0-674-99124-9
British ISBN 0-434-99112-0

First printed 1919
Revised and reprinted 1928, 1955, 1962, 1982

Printed in Great Britain
by Fletcher & Son Ltd, Norwich

CONTENTS

PREFACE

THIS, the first edition of Fronto in English, has been a work of more than ordinary difficulty. Before a satisfactory translation could be attempted a new text had to be formed based on the labours of Studemund, Brakman, and Hauler. The single MS., which alone is available, is part of a palimpsest in two volumes made up of leaves from various old MSS., the Fronto leaves being arranged anyhow, besides being incomplete, full of lacunae and erasures, and generally difficult, sometimes impossible, to decipher. A first-hand acquaintance with the original, which is partly at Milan and partly at Rome, has been impossible, and the facsimile of the Vatican portion will be seen, by anyone who inspects it, to be of small use to an editor.

Little could have been done for a fundamental improvement of Naber's standard text without Dr. Hauler's numerous contributions to its recension, based upon his laborious examination of the Codex,

PREFACE

and I cannot but acknowledge my very great debt
to him in that regard. Much help has also been
given me by J. W. E. Pearce, M.A. Oxon., and
Miss M. D. Brock, Litt.D. Dublin.

C. R. HAINES.

PETERSFIELD,
February, 1919.

INTRODUCTION

Time has not dealt kindly with Fronto. For more
than a millennium and a half his name stood high in
the lists of fame. On the strength of ancient testimony he was looked upon as the Cicero of his age;
if not indeed his equal, yet as an Isocrates to a
Demosthenes. Eumenius,[1] writing late in the third
century, described him as " not the second but the
alternative glory of Roman eloquence." A century or
more later he is singled out by Macrobius[2] as the
representative of the plain, precise, matter-of-fact
style, contrasted with the copious, in which Cicero is
supreme, the laconic, which is the province of Sallust,
and the rich and florid, in which Pliny the Younger
and Symmachus luxuriate.

Jerome[3] about the same time, speaks of the
subtleties of Quintilian, the fluency of Cicero, the
serious dignity of Fronto, and the smooth periods of
Pliny. A little later Claudius Mamertus[4] recommends Plautus for elegance, Cato for *gravitas*, Gracchus

---

[1] *Paneg. Const.* 14 : *Romanae eloquentiae non secundum sed
alterum decus.*

[2] *Saturnalia*, v. 1. He says *tenuis quidam et siccus et sobrius
amat quandam dicendi frugalitatem*, and he ascribes the *siccum
genus* to Fronto, as an orator, no doubt. This was the style
of Lysias.

[3] *Epist.* 12 : *gravitatem Frontonis.*   [4] *Ep. ad Sepandum.*

for pungency, Chrysippus for dialectical skill, Cicero for eloquence, and Fronto for splendour (*pompa*). Sidonius Apollinaris[1] attributes *gravitas* to Fronto and *pondus* to Apuleius.

Though Fronto's reputation stood so high for 300 years after his death, scarcely a line of his works had survived, as it seemed, to modern times, until in 1815 Cardinal Mai discovered in the Imperial Library at Milan a palimpsest MS. containing many of his letters, the existence of which in classical times had indeed been occasionally intimated, though little was known of their contents.

When deciphered the work proved to consist mostly of his educational correspondence with his royal pupils, afterwards the joint Emperors Marcus Antoninus and Lucius Verus. There were included, however, one or two letters between Fronto and their adoptive father, the Emperor Pius, and some, chiefly commendatory, letters to the orator's friends, of whom the only one whose answer is preserved was the historian Appian. Some of the letters are in Greek. In judging this correspondence it should not be forgotten that Fronto disclaims the habit of letter-writing, and declares that no one could be a worse correspondent than himself.[2]

It would, therefore, not be fair to estimate Fronto's eminence as an orator from these letters alone, though, of course, they throw light on his

[1] *Epist.* iv. 3.   [2] *Ad Amicos*, i. 18.

mind and powers in general, and his theory of
rhetorical art in particular. They labour under the
limitation of having been mostly written to pupils,
and chiefly in connexion with their studies. They
are of a private, domestic, and professional nature,
and coloured by the relationship between a courtly
master and his royal scholars.

The early editors of the book, who were disappointed with the nature and contents of the work,
had no good word to say for it or its author, but
their indignation and contempt were certainly not
justified.[1] The volume was well worth recovering,
and is here presented to the English reader for the
first time.

On discovering the MS. in 1815, Mai, the librarian
of the Ambrosian Library at Milan, lost no time in
producing his first edition of it. But the work
was done too hastily and carelessly. He also seems to
have injured the MS. by a too free use of reagents to
bring out the faded characters.[2]

Becoming librarian of the Vatican library a few
years later, Mai found a second volume containing
more leaves of the original Fronto Codex. These he
published with the previous portion in 1823. The
Vatican leaves being in better condition than the

---

[1] See Hauler, *Wien. Stud.* (1912), 24. p. 259; Fröhner, *Phil.*
v. 1889; and Brock, *Studies in Fronto*, p. 5, for a much more
favourable view.
[2] Hauler, *Wien. Stud.* 12 and 31 (p. 267), and Naber,
Proleg. viii., xiv. But Stud. *Epist. ad Klussm.* p. 6, seems
to differ on this point.

INTRODUCTION

Ambrosian ones, and the editor besides being now more skilful in deciphering the palimpsest, and having taken more pains with his work, the result was more satisfactory. Moreover, the older portion was somewhat improved through a fresh inspection of the MS. by Peter Mazuchelli at Milan, and also because Mai availed himself freely of the critical labours of Niebuhr, Heindorf, and Buttmann on the moiety already published. In their edition of 1816 they had sometimes divined, without seeing the MS., the correct reading, which Mai had missed with it under his eyes.

The old Codex of Fronto must have been dismembered and its leaves mixed with others of the same kind before being used for a second writing upon them. For the two volumes of the *Acta Concilii* of the first Council of Chalcedon, in 451 A.D., in which the Fronto fragments are found, contain besides the Fronto leaves, which are the most numerous, parts of seven speeches of Symmachus, a portion of Pliny's *Panegyric,* some scholia on Cicero, Moeso-Gothic notes on St. John's Gospel, fragments of a tract on the Arian Controversy, and a single page apiece of Juvenal and Persius. The monks in using the leaves for a second script have generally turned them upside down. When this is not the case, the writing is more difficult to read.

On the first page of both volumes is found the inscription, *Liber S. Columbani e Bobio.* Bobbio lies in

xii

a secluded valley of the Pennine Alps, near the scene of the battle of the Trebia, where Saint Columban founded a monastery at the beginning of the seventh century, and formed a good library containing not only Latin works in Saxon characters but many classical authors in their own script, such as Cicero, Juvenal, Persius, and Fronto. The Fronto Codex was, we may suppose, purchased by Columban in Italy. In the same library there was another book of Fronto's, entitled *Cornelii Frontonis Elegantiae Latinae*, which was extant as late as 1494.[1] It was lexicographically arranged. Possibly it was one of the works of Fronto mentioned below.

The Vatican volume (No. 5750), contains a Latin version of the *Acta* of the Council of Chalcedon to nearly the end of the first session, written about the tenth century. The volume contained 292 leaves of which two are missing at the beginning and four at the end.

The Ambrosian volume (E. 147) is larger and had 480 pages of which are now wanting twelve at the opening and sixteen at the close. There must have been a third volume of the *Acta*, somewhat smaller than the others, possibly of about 230 pages, the whole work thus comprising with the other two volumes about 1000 leaves.

The Fronto part of the Vatican volume, as we have it, is 106 leaves, of the Ambrosian, 282. The thirty-

[1] See Raphael Maffaeus Volaterranus, *Geogr.* iv. *ad finem.*

four pages missing from these two volumes would probably have contained about twenty Fronto leaves. As the Fronto leaves are more numerous in the Ambrosian volume than in the Vatican according to the proportion $\frac{106}{286} : \frac{282}{452}$, it is likely that in the third volume there would have been a corresponding increase of them. The whole might therefore have contained about 580 Fronto leaves. But the quaternion marks, still visible in the margin of the MS., show that there were at least $42\frac{1}{2}$ quaternions or 680 pages, in the original Fronto Codex.[1] Even if the third volume were forthcoming, we should still be about one-seventh part short of the Fronto Codex. What we have contains something like four-sevenths of the whole work, but some part of this has not been deciphered, and not a little is obliterated for ever.

Dr. Hauler, of Vienna, has been engaged upon the study of the MS. for more than twenty years, and we must wait for the final word on our author until his edition is published. It will certainly revolutionize the text. He has been given unusual facilities by the Italian authorities in his work, and the leaves of the Vatican MS. have been especially washed, cleaned and pressed for the purpose of photographing it in facsimile.

As far as possible the new readings which Dr. Hauler has made public in various periodicals have been incorporated in this work, together with

[1] The speeches of Fronto must have been in a separate Codex, if in the Bobbio library at all.

the important, if rather hastily compiled, notes of a fresh collation of the MS. by the Dutch scholar, Professor Brakman. In spite of Dr. Hauler's keen eyesight and prodigious industry, certain of his restorations do not command complete confidence, especially in cases where we find the other inspectors of the Codex, Mai, du Rieu, and Brakman supporting an entirely different reading.

The original Fronto Codex has two columns of writing to each page, each column containing twenty-four lines of fifteen to twenty-one letters each.[1]

As the Greek in the Codex is written without accents, the MS. must have been produced before the seventh century, and probably in the sixth. The alterations made by the reviser of the copy show that the copyist was a careless one ; nor did the corrector notice all the errors. Some letters are given twice over,[2] as if a second exemplar had been used.

A few of the Fronto leaves seem themselves to have had a previous writing on them,[3] and these must themselves have been palimpsests before being

---

[1] The Fronto leaves in the Vat. volume are numbered 1–4, 13–16, 29, 30, 79–128, 131, 132, 137, 138, 141–160, 165, 168, 173, 180, 185–190, 227, 228, 241, 242 ; in the Ambrosian, 55–76, 81–110, 133–138, 143–152, 155–158, 161–163, 179, 182, 195–198, 213–262, 287–308, 311–314, 319–356, 373–408, 411–414, 417–436, 443–446.

[2] *e.g. Epist. Graec.* 1 is found in Ambr. 56, Vat. 166, 165, and Ambr. 157, 158, 163, 164.

[3] See Hauler, *Vers. d. deut. Phil.* 41, 1895, p. 85. He thinks a speech of Hadrian's underlay a page of the *Principia Historiae* in the Fronto Codex.

used for the *Acta Concilii*. Moreover, our Codex of Fronto was revised and annotated by a certain Caecilius. Besides correcting mistakes, and adding various readings from at least two other exemplars,[1] he gives explanatory glosses and occasionally suggests emendations.[2] Further, to our manifest advantage, he used the margins, which are free from the second writing, for setting down numerous words or passages, that struck him, sometimes verbatim, sometimes in an abbreviated or paraphrased form. The writing of the text and the corrections are in uncial letters, the marginal additions in sloping cursive. Caecilius endorsed each separate section of the work except the *Epistulae Graecae* and (apparently by inadvertence) *Ad Verum Imp.* i.

Indices were probably prefixed to all the separate books of letters, of which are extant only those to *Ad M. Caes.* iv., v; *Ad Anton. Imp.* i.; *Ad Pium*; *Ad Amicos* i., ii. They are valuable as supplying the opening words of letters that are lost, but they do not in all cases seem to correspond with the succeeding letters.

From Fronto to Marcus as Caesar there are fifty-six letters or parts of letters, and nine to him as Emperor, besides the four *De Eloquentia*. From Marcus seventy-one and seven respectively. To Verus as Emperor eight, and six from him, and six to Pius

---

[1] There are over forty of these *variae lectiones*.

[2] The corrector did not revise the Greek letters, but there is a remarkable gloss at the beginning of *Ep. Graec.* 1.

with two answers. There are forty letters to friends, two being in Greek, and one answer (from Appian) ; two in Greek to the mother of Marcus ; the set piece on Arion ; the two specimens of *nugalia,* the *De Bello Parthico,* the *Principia Historiae,* and the Greek λόγος ἐρωτικός.

There are few traces of Fronto's letters in such subsequent writers as have descended to us. It is certain that Minucius Felix, who was probably a fellow-countryman of Fronto's, knew something of him, for in his *Octavius* he quotes his declamation against the Christians, and calls him *Cirtensis noster.*[1] Capitolinus,[2] or his authority Marius Maximus, probably had an eye on what Fronto says, when he mentions the habit that Marcus had of reading in the theatre, and where he calls him *durus.* However that may be, it can hardly be doubted that Nazarius[3] in his Panegyric on Constantine recalls, though in a confused way, what Fronto says about the Parthian king and Verus in his *Principia Historiae.* Symmachus too, another orator of the same century, shews some signs of being acquainted with Fronto. Augustine, himself an African, is supposed in a letter to the *Cirtenses* to refer to the mention of Polemo by Fronto.[4]

---

[1] Mai, Pref. to ed. 1823, p. xxxiii., and Schanz, *Rhein. Mus.* 1895, p. 133, adduce certain supposed parallelisms. If there is anything in them, the *Octavius* could not have been written before 166 at least.

[2] *Vit. Mar.* xv. and xxii. 5 ; see below, p. 206.

[3] He speaks of *Antoninus,* but he means Lucius Verus.

[4] *Epist.* 144 : *et nos ex illis litteris recordamur.*

INTRODUCTION

Servius, the fifth-century commentator on Vergil, quotes Fronto for one or two usages, but his quotations cannot be identified with any passages in our extant letters. A contemporary grammarian, Charisius,[1] however, undoubtedly quotes from Fronto's letters as we have them. P. Consentius, another grammarian of the same period, quotes a sentence referring to Rheims, which may very possibly come from a lost letter to Victorinus. Niebuhr thought that Sidonius Apollinaris, a learned and eloquent bishop of the fifth century, imitated Fronto here and there.

The last author to refer to Fronto was John of Salisbury in the twelfth century. He quotes an obscure remark of his concerning Seneca, that " he was so successful in abolishing error that he seemed almost to create again an age of gold and call down the Gods from heaven to live among men." But Fronto, as we know him, has no word of praise for Seneca.

We cannot tell who made and published this collection of letters, but it is impossible to subscribe to the view of Mommsen that it was Fronto himself.[2] Several letters are misplaced : one that was certainly to the Emperor with his answer appears under the heading *Ad M. Caesarem* ; and some that are related to one another are widely separated.

---

[1] See Index. He also quotes from Fronto's speech, *Pro Ptolemaeensibus*.

[2] *Hermes*, viii. p. 201.

INTRODUCTION

Mommsen considered that the letters were in the main arranged chronologically, but this can only be allowed with large deductions. For instance, some of the earliest letters come quite at the end of the book. The correspondence with Pius is put after that with his successors. But there is obviously some attempt at systematic arrangement. The letters that belong to the year of Fronto's consulship are grouped together and placed first. In more than one case several letters bearing on a single subject are found placed in juxtaposition in their proper order, as with the letters relating to Herodes.[1] In the separate books the letters are arranged, with obvious exceptions however, in some chronological order ; but the letters of a second book, for instance, do not follow those of the first, but begin a new series. The various ailments, also, of Marcus and Fronto are a guide in some cases. Some letters can be dated by means of the speeches of Marcus alluded to in them. As for instance the mention of his Caesar speech by Marcus in *Ep. Graec.* 6 (p. 18) dates this letter as written in 139–140. The speech referred to in *Ad M. Caes.* iii. 7 (p. 34) is probably a speech of thanks for his first consulship in 140, and the one in v. 1, 2, that for his second consulship in 145 or for the *Trib. Potestas* in 147.[2]

[1] See pp. 58 f.
[2] For further discussion of this subject, see article by C. R. Haines, " On the Chronology of the Fronto Correspondence," in the *Classical Quarterly* for April, 1914, vol. viii., pp. 113 ff.

The only letters which can be dated to a precise year, except those which mention Fronto's consulship, are *Ad M. Caes.* i. 8, written when Marcus was twenty-two, and *Ad M. Caes.* iv. 13,[1] written when he was twenty-four. The latter forms a sort of turning point, not only in the correspondence but also in the life of Marcus. To Fronto's infinite chagrin he broke with rhetoric and betook himself wholly to philosophy, at about the time (147 A.D.) when he became in reality, though not in name, co-emperor. At all events, whether from a slight coolness in their relations or owing to increasing ill-health on the part of Fronto and increasing duties on that of Marcus, the character of the correspondence changes with Book V. Most of the letters are short, some being mere messages, and many of a quite trivial character. The illnesses and ailments of master and pupil figure largely in them. Fronto's rheumatism, for it was this and not gout, had become chronic by that time.

On the accession of Marcus and Lucius the correspondence resumes some of its former character. There are no letters to Lucius earlier than 161, when he became Emperor, but Fronto must have written to him often enough before. But only the later ones were preserved, as the main object of the publication seems to have been to shew Fronto's intimate relations with the Court. We could wish

1 See pp. 37, 217.

for more correspondence with Pius, but two of Fronto's letters to him are among the best of the series.

Fronto became tutor to Marcus after his adoption by Hadrian in 138. None of the letters we have can be dated before 139, when Marcus became Caesar. The marriage of Marcus, which took place most probably in 145, and the various births of his children enable us to give approximate dates to many of the letters in Book V. The letters *Ad Amicos* can only be dated with reference to the proconsulships or other governorships of the recipients, many of them being letters commendatory, recommending friends to the notice of the governor of a province.

The more important oratorical and historical pieces, with the letters on the Alsian holiday and the death of Fronto's grandson, a characteristic and interesting piece, fall between 161 and 166, in which year or the next Fronto probably died.

Excluding Fronto himself, who could have collected and published the correspondence ? The only person in a position to do this seems to be Aufidius Victorinus, the life-long friend of Marcus and Fronto's son-in-law. We have evidence that Fronto kept copies of some of his letters, and Victorinus, as Fronto's heir and one of the leading men in the reign of Commodus, was in a specially favourable position for acting as his father-in-law's literary executor.

The object of the compilation was not only to bring into prominence the position of Fronto as

Magister and *Amicus* to the Imperial Brothers, but also to put on record his views on oratorical and literary style, in fact his whole theory of rhetoric, which there is no reason to think he ever formulated in any special treatise.

The letters are valuable not only for what they tell us of Fronto and the light they shed on the literary tendencies of the age, but also for their picture of the young Marcus, whose character and rule will always have an interest for mankind. As Pater has said, these letters recall for us "the long buried fragrance of a famous friendship of the ancient world." We find here a young man and an older one, with a genuine affection for one another, exchanging kindly thoughts on their children, their health, the art of rhetoric, and the ancient writers of their country, while here and there we get a glimpse into the *penetralia* of the imperial court, or read a page from country life at Lorium or a visit to the seaside.[1]

A hundred years ago Mai[2] expressed a confident expectation that one day the letters would be arranged in their approximate chronological order. A first attempt has here been made to do this.[3]

---

[1] For some interesting and attractive items, see pp. 58–66, 150, 174–184, the *De Fer. Als.*, the *De Nepote Amisso*, etc.

[2] Pref. to ed. of 1823, p. xviii.

[3] For various views on the chronology, see Mommsen in *Herm.* viii. pp. 198 ff.; Brakman in *Frontoniana*, ii. pp. 24–42; Pauly-Wissowa under "Fronto"; Naber, *Proleg.* xx.–xxxi.

FRONTO, THE ORATOR AND THE MAN

Almost all that we know of Fronto is drawn from the book before us. The probable date of his birth is 100 A.D., and in any case before 113 A.D. He was born at Cirta, now Constantine, in Numidia. This was a Roman colony, and his name being Cornelius, he was doubtless of Roman descent, though he jestingly calls himself " a Libyan of the nomad Libyans." His brother, who is mentioned several times in the *Letters,* was named Quadratus.[1] Of his youth we are told nothing, but he no doubt studied at Alexandria, for at a later time he had numerous friends there. He mentions as his *parens* and *magister* the philosopher Athenodotus, but it was not philosophy, which he disliked, that he learnt from him, but an inordinate fondness for similes, or as he calls them, εἰκόνες.[2] Another master named by him is Dionysius the rhetor, whose fable on *The Vine and the Holm-Oak* he quotes. He tells us that he took late to the study of Latin literature, in which he afterwards came to be such an adept.

---

[1] See inscription (*C.I.L.* xv. 7438) on conduit pipes from the Esquiline hill, where his *Horti Maecenatiani* (see Index) were situated.   [2] See Index and pp. 131 ff.

FRONTO, THE ORATOR AND THE MAN

An inscription found at Calamae (Guelma) in Numidia,[1] of which city, as of Cirta, he was a *patronus,* gives us the earlier part of his *cursus honorum,* from which we learn his father's name Titus, the name of his tribe Quirina, and that he was successively *triumvir capitalis,* quaestor in Sicily, plebeian aedile, and praetor. The office of quaestor gave him a place in the Senate.

In 143, under Pius, he became *consul suffectus* for July and August, the *consul ordinarius* for which year was Herodes the eminent Athenian rhetorician, himself like Fronto a tutor to the young princes. Fronto's lesser honour gave occasion for the jesting allusion of Ausonius [2] to the consuls in whose consulship Fronto was consul.

From his place in the Senate he tells us that he extolled Hadrian *studio impenso et propenso* in speeches that were still read many years later.[3] But he confesses that in this he courted rather than loved him. His great reputation,[4] but no doubt his character also, induced Pius on his accession to choose him as the instructor of his adopted sons in Latin and oratory.

---

[1] *Corp. Inscr. Lat.* viii. 5350.

[2] " Unica mihi amplectenda est Frontonis imitatio : quem tamen Augusti magistrum sic consulatus ornavit, ut praefectura non cingeret. Sed consulatus ille cuiusmodi ? Ordinario suffectus, bimestri spatio interpositus, in sexta anni parte consumptus, quaerendum ut reliquerit tantus orator, quibus consulibus gesserit consulatum." *In Gratiarum Actione, ad med.*   [3] See p. 110.

[4] Dio, lxix. 8 ; Lucian, *De Conscr. Hist.* 21, ἀοίδιμος ἐπὶ λόγων δυνάμει.

He remained for the rest of his life on the most intimate and affectionate terms with the court, and there is no evidence that he abused his position in any way. He was not, however, above flattering his royal pupils on occasion, for he could scarcely have believed himself, when he attributed to Marcus the abilities of the great Julius or to Lucius the military genius of a Marius or a Vespasian. Still at times he could tell Marcus some home truths, and at all events impressed both his charges with his sincerity and love of truth.[1] It was more excusable in Marcus to overrate, as he did, Fronto's oratorical gifts, and to set him beside Cato, Gracchus, Sallust, and Cicero, asserting that he alone of present-day orators talked Latin.[2]

When the time came for Fronto to receive a provincial appointment, the lot gave him Asia. He made preparations to take up his duties there, but a more than usually serious attack of illness supervened, and he was obliged to beg off his appointment.

His political life being now ended, Fronto devoted his remaining years to his profession of eloquence and to literature. Aulus Gellius[3] gives us a picture of him as one of the recognized leaders in the intellectual salons of the time, where questions of literature and archaeology were habitually discussed. He is there seen surrounded by all the great authors

---

[1] *Ad M. Caes.* iii. 12, *Ad Verum,* ii. 2 (*verique amorem*).
[2] *Ad M. Caes.* ii. 13 ; *Ad Ant.* i. 4.
[3] *Noctes Atticae,* ii. 26, xiii. 23, xix. 8, 10, 13.

and critics of Rome, and regarded as an oracle on linguistic and grammatical questions, and in his letters we find him always inculcating a careful precision in the use of words and a deference to the authority of older writers.

How far was his great reputation as orator and pleader justified? Unfortunately we have no specimen, even approximately complete, of his oratory, whether forensic or epideictic, on which to base a verdict. The longest extract extant is from a speech respecting oversea wills, possibly delivered before the Emperor's Court of Appeal. There is besides the well-known fragment of an indictment of the Christians,[1] preserved by Minucius Felix in his *Octavius*, which reads like a set declamation, or an episode in a speech on behalf of some client. But we do not know how far the writer has given Fronto's words verbatim.

The interesting and important letter to Arrius Antoninus on behalf of Volumnius Quadratus[2] is an example of legal *causidicatio*. There remain besides a few sentences quoted by the orator himself[3] from his speech of thanks to Pius in 143, and a simile, perhaps from the same speech, quoted by Eumenius,

[1] *Octavius*, ix. It seems probable that the section immediately preceding this, and describing the "Thyestean feasts" attributed to the Christians, also comes from the same speech. Some think the whole of the anti-Christian polemic of the *Octavius* is drawn from a Frontonian source. See Schanz, *Rhein. Mus.* 1895, 114–36.
[2] *Ad Amicos*, ii. 7.　　[3] *Ad M. Caes.* i. 8, pp. 118 ff.

where the success of the Roman arms in Britain is
referred to.[1] Moreover we have, preserved on a
palimpsest in the Palatine Library, a few concluding
words of a speech of thanks for the Carthaginians,
some years later.[2] It was evidently one of his
pompaticae orationes.

Of other speeches we have a mere mention: the
Pro Ptolemaeensibus, from which Charisius preserves a
single grammatical form; a speech against Herodes
in 142, of which we do not know the title; one *Pro
Demostrato Petitiano*; several in behalf of Saenius
Pompeianus and other friends;[3] and speeches on
behalf of the Cilicians and Bithynians, the latter in
its revised form giving details of his past life, the
loss of which is to be regretted.[4] His most famous
effort, according to Sidonius Apollinaris, was the
speech against Pelops, probably a physician of
Pergamus, mentioned by Galen.

It will be seen from this short summary that we
have really no material for judging Fronto's capacity
either as advocate in the courts or as orator in the
Senate. Dirksen[5] denies his juristic competence,
but few will believe that he was not perfectly con-
versant with Roman Law. How otherwise could he
have gained his commanding position at the bar in
an age which produced such eminent jurists and was

[1] See below. He made many speeches in praise of Pius.
[2] On the occasion of Pius's liberality to the city after a
great fire. See Capit. *Vit. Pii,* ix.   [3] See pp. 232, 238.
[4] For the mention of these, see Index.
[5] *Opp.* 1, pp. 243 ff. and 277 ff.

almost the heyday of Roman Law. Not but that Fronto was, first and foremost, an orator, whose object is not justice but persuasion. It cannot be denied that in the extract from the speech on wills he indulges in fancy pictures and ignores obvious and material facts. Still his presentment of the case is certainly not without point and vigour, though it is over-elaborated and smacks too much of the art of rhetoric.

The letters on Matidia's will and the Falcidian Law are in their mutilated condition too ambiguous to assist us in our enquiry as to Fronto's legal attainments.

Fronto's ideals in oratory were high. The most difficult test of an orator seemed to him to be that he should please without sacrificing the true principles of eloquence. Smooth phrases for tickling the ears of the hearers must not be such as are offensive to good taste, a feebleness in form being preferable to a coarseness of thought.[1] In spite of his insistence on style and the choice of words, Fronto knows well enough and affirms that noble thoughts are the essential thing in oratory, for the want of which no verbal dexterity or artistic taste will compensate. It was his deficiency in "high thought's invention" that forced Fronto to concentrate his attention on the form and eke out the matter with the manner. Needless to say he has at his fingers' ends all the tropes and

[1] P. 37.

figures and devices of the art of rhetoric, and his knowledge of the Roman language and literature was profound.

It has too hastily been assumed that he slighted the great writers of the best age, except Cicero and Sallust, and totally ignored the silver age authors except Lucan and Seneca. But he constantly imitates Terence, recognizes the literary eminence of Caesar and quotes him with approval,[1] calls Lucretius sublime, quotes him, and ranks him with his prime favourites, quotes Horace, whom he calls *memorabilis*, more than once, shows an intimate knowledge of Vergil,[2] and borrows from Livy. He also shows some acquaintance with Quintilian, Tacitus and Juvenal.

Fronto has been repeatedly called a pedant, but he was a true lover of his own language and guarded it jealously from unauthorized innovations and ignorant solecisms. His aim seemed to have been to shake the national speech out of the groove into which the excessive and pedantic purism of Cicero, Caesar and their followers had confined it. To do this effectually it was necessary to call in the aid of the great writers of an earlier age, such as Plautus and Ennius and Cato. But this sort of archaism was nothing novel. Thucydides was a thorough archaist, and so was Vergil, and Sallust was eminently one.[3] As the cramping

---

[1] Aul. Gell. xix. 8.   [2] Aul. Gell. ii. 26.

[3] Bacon " spangled his speech with unusual words," and Ben Jonson says that Spenser "in affecting the ancients writ no language."

effects of the Ciceronian tradition tended more and more to squeeze the life out of the language, the ingrained feeling that "the old is better" gradually spread among the leaders of literary thought. An immense impetus was given to this tendency by the versatile *littérateur* Hadrian, who openly preferred Ennius to Vergil and Cato to Cicero.

But Fronto, fond as he was of old words and ancient locutions, insisted that such must be not only old but more expressive and appropriate than modern ones, or they must not be preferred. He himself confesses that he used only ordinary and commonplace words. No one in his opinion has a right to invent expressions—he calls such words counterfeit coin. He availed himself of old and established words, that were genuine Latin and had all the charm of novelty without being unintelligible, drawing largely on the vocabulary and idiom of Plautus, Ennius, Cato, and Gracchus, and interspersing his familiar letters with quotations from Naevius, Accius, Pacuvius, and Laberius. But this was not an affected or repellent archaism, such as Seneca and Lucian mock at.[1] Fronto's attitude somewhat resembled that of Rossetti, who declares that " he has been reading early English ballads in search of stunning old words."[2] It is of such words that Fronto is thinking when he speaks of words that must be hunted out with toil and care and watchfulness and

[1] Seneca, *Ep.* 114 ; Lucian, *Demonax*, 26.
[2] See Brock, *Studies in Fronto*, p. 103n.

by the treasuring up of old poems in the memory.[1]
He explains that he has in mind the " inevitable "
word, for which, if withdrawn, no substitute equally
good could be found. Some old words would
certainly have no modern equivalent, as for instance
in English the word " hansel." " The best words in
the best places " would be Fronto's definition of
oratory, as it was Coleridge's of poetry.

It is a prevalent but mistaken idea that Fronto
disparages or underrates Cicero. He may personally
prefer Cato or Sallust, but he recognizes the pre-emin-
ence of Cicero's genius. It is quite possible that if we
had the works of the older writers, we also should
prefer their simple dignity and natural vigour even
to the incomparable finish and opulence of Tully.
However that may be, Fronto credits Cicero with
almost every conceivable excellence except the due
search for the precise word.[2] He calls him the greatest
mouthpiece of the Roman language, the head and
source of Roman eloquence, master on all occasions
of the most beautiful language, and deficient only
in unlooked for words.[3] He candidly confesses his
own inferiority.[4] Of his letters he says " nothing
can be more perfect." He calls them *tullianae* and
remissiores, and seems to envy their careless ease.[5]
But in practice he disavows the structure of the
Ciceronian sentence and the arrangement of its

[1] P. 7. [2] P. 4. [3] *Ad Amicos*, i. 14.
[4] When he bids Victorinus compare his *Pro Bithynis* with
Cicero's *Pro Sulla. Ad Amicos,* i. 14. [5] See p. 122.

words. He breaks up the flowing periods of Ciceronian prose and introduces new and abrupter rhythms. For older cadences he substitutes cadences of his own, though he occasionally prides himself on imitating the Tullian mannerisms.[1] Where he affects the staccato style, and the historic present, as in *Arion*, the result is as unpleasing as it is in modern English. In some cases, for forensic speeches, he recommends a deliberate roughness and studied negligence at the end of sentences; but in epideictic displays everything must be neatly and smoothly finished off.[2] Circumlocution and inversions he utterly condemns.[3] Next to the choice of words their natural and perspicuous arrangement counts most with him. This makes his work easy reading. Such difficulties as we find are chiefly due to the mutilated condition of the text in our copy. We have often not only to interpret but to divine what was written.

It has been supposed that Fronto set himself purposely to renovate and remodel the language by recalling old words and obsolete idioms,[4] and by transferring into the literary language colloquialisms from the common speech. But the *novella elocutio* of which he speaks seems rather to mean a fresher, more vivacious diction, and a more individual form of expression: in fact originality of style. The

---

[1] Brock, *Studies in Fronto*, p. 141, and Droz, *De Frontonis institutione oratoria*, p. 64; and see p. 110 below, and *Ad Anton.* i. 2.   [2] P. 40.   [3] *De Orationibus, ad fin.*
[4] *cp.* Horace, *Ars Poet.* 70.

patina of antiquity which he wished to give his
work need not necessarily be thought to disfigure
it ; and his minute accuracy in the use of words is
surely more deserving of praise than of blame.   He
prided himself on distinguishing the nice shades of
meaning in allied words, and insisted that his pupil
should be exact in his use of words, knowing well
that clearness of thought is dependent on definite-
ness of expression.   The extracts from Aulus Gellius
given at the end of the book show us the care
with which Fronto distinguished the meaning of
words, of which there is further evidence in the *De
Differentiis Vocabulorum*,[1] if that work is his, as it
may well be.   It was possibly written for the use
of his pupils, that they might not misuse words
apparently synonymous, such as the various terms
for sight and perception.   In this connexion it
may be noted that Fronto set great store by the
careful use of synonyms, and they abound in his
correspondence, but are seldom so colourless as, for
instance, our " tied and bound," " let and hinder,"
" many a time and oft " or so run to death as
" by leaps and bounds " or " in any shape or form."

   Eloquence was to Fronto the only thing that
mattered in the universe.   It was the real sovereign
of the human race.   Philosophy he disliked and even

---

   [1] Printed in Mai's edition of Fronto, with another work
attributed to Fronto, the *Exempla Elocutionum*. This consists
of phrases from Terence, Vergil, Cicero, and Sallust.   We
know that he made extracts from Cicero, *Ad Anton.* ii. 5.

despised, though he admitted that it inspired great thoughts, which it was for eloquence to clothe.[1] Philosophy and rhetoric contended for the soul of Marcus in the persons of the austere Rusticus,[2] the domestic chaplain of Marcus in the Stoic creed, and the courtly Fronto. But the result was a foregone conclusion. Marcus before he was twelve had already made his choice;[3] and though he tried loyally to please his master and learn all the tricks of rhetoric, yet his heart was always far from the wind-flowers of eloquence.[4] He aroused his master's ire by asserting that, when he had said something more than usually brilliant, he felt pleased, and therefore shunned eloquence. Fronto pertinently rejoined, "You feel pleasure, when eloquent; then, chastise yourself, why chastise eloquence?" Again when Marcus in his ultra-conscientiousness avows a distaste for the obliquities and insincerities of oratory, Fronto is clearly nettled, and counters smartly with a reference to the irony of Socrates.

In spite of all Fronto's efforts Marcus in his twenty-fourth year finally declared his decision. He could no longer consent to argue on both sides of a question, as the art of oratory would have him do. There is no doubt that his master was bitterly

---

[1] *De Eloqu.* i. *ad finem.*

[2] Under him as *Praef. Urbi*, about 163, Justin Martyr and his companions were condemned.

[3] Capit. *Vit. Mar.* ii. 6.

[4] *Thoughts*, **i. 7 ; i. 17, § 4.**

disappointed, as he honestly believed he could make
a consummate orator of Marcus.

A few words require to be said now as to Fronto's
method of instruction. He began by taking his
pupil through a course of old farces, comedies,
ancient orators and poets, and Marcus was en-
couraged to make extracts from the authors that
were read. Cato, Gracchus, Ennius, Sallust, and
Cicero were especially studied. The first was Marcus's
favourite, but Fronto preferred Sallust before all.
In letter-writing Cicero was recognized as supreme,
and the "tullian" style of his more familiar letters
was looked upon as worthy of imitation.

Verse-making was regularly practised as an aid
towards oratory. Only hexameters are mentioned
in this connexion, and Vergil, who is both archaistic
and intensely rhetorical, was no doubt the model.
Horace was apparently read but Marcus took a
dislike to him.[1]

Similes, or εἰκόνες, formed an important part of
Fronto's oratorical armoury. He always had numbers
at command on every conceivable subject, some
appropriate, and many ingenious, but others far-
fetched and out of place. He clearly regarded them
as indispensable, and gives elaborate instructions as
to their use.[2] They could scarcely have been of
much use in his forensic speeches, one would think.

The next step was to use the *Commonplaces of*

---

[1] P. 140.   [2] P. 36.

Theodorus for the manufacture of maxims or γνῶμαι.
One aphorism a day was the allotted task. The
object was to strike out some neat epigrammatic
sententia, such as are characteristic of Sallust, and to
turn the same thought freely and boldly in various
ways, often from one language to another. Truth to
say, Fronto is himself extraordinarily deficient in
sayings of pith and moment. He imitates the
panem et Circenses of Juvenal and perhaps the *cupido
gloriae novissima exuitur* [1] of Tacitus, but the most
striking of his own maxims are noticeable chiefly for
their rhythm, such as *pleraque propria venustate carentia gratiam sibimet alienam extrinsecus mutuantur,* and
*longeque praestat secundo gentium rumore iniuriam
neglegere quam adverso vindicare.* We do not know
which maxim of Marcus it was that Fronto declared
worthy of Sallust,[2] but this is a not unsuccessful
one : *turpe alioqui fuerit diutius vitium corporis quam
animi studium ad reciperandam sanitatem posse durare.*[3]

Translation from one language to another forms
part of the curriculum. Original composition in
history was also recommended by Fronto, and Marcus
himself seems to have had some aspirations in that
direction. Too much stress was laid upon the out-
ward trappings of rhetoric, such as alliteration, oxy-
moron, antithesis, paronomasia, paraleipsis, and every
variety of trope or figure. And in the use of these

---

[1] Tac. *Hist.* iv. 6, and *De Eloqu.* i. *ad med.* below.
[2] P. 12.   [3] *Ad M. Caes.* iv. 8.

for his rhetorical flights Fronto is ever urging Marcus to "be bold, be bold, and evermore be bold." [1]

Finally came the writing of themes and *controversiae*, in which the pros and cons of any question, historical or fictitious, are discussed as by a forensic speaker.

Whether after all this study Marcus became a really accomplished speaker is not known. We have too little to judge by. But at all events he had mastered thoroughly the principles of the art,[2] and that he was straightforward, sensible, and practical in his official orations is certain. The Senate, the soldiers, and the people alike heard him with eagerness.[3]

There are several passages in this work where Fronto tries his hand at descriptive narrative, and two in which he essays the rôle of historian. But his view of history, and how it should be written, was thoroughly mistaken. His eyes are not on the facts, but on the best way to show his rhetorical skill in commonplace or panegyric. His efforts therefore in this direction are useless as history and of no account as literature. The descriptive passages are more successful, the best being the apologue on sleep, translated by Pater in his *Marius the Epicurean*. A favourable specimen is the mutilated passage referring to Orpheus at the beginning of *Ad Marcum*, iv, p.70. *Arion*

---

[1] Ennius, see p. 10.
[2] Dio, lxxi. 35, § 1. He shows his skill in rhetoric even in the Greek of the *Meditations*.   [3] *Ad Anton.* i. 2.

is technically skilful but lacks distinction, and the *Ring of Polycrates* is decidedly tame. The *Praises of Smoke and Dust* and *Negligence* are mere *tours de force*, but they throw light on his theory of rhetoric.

After so long and close an intimacy as these letters reveal we are surprised to find so meagre a mention of Fronto in the gallery of Worthies, from whom he learnt enduring lessons, which Marcus sets at the head of his *Thoughts*. It is nothing but this:

" From Fronto, to note the envy, the subtlety, and the dissimulation, which are habitual to a tyrant; and that as a general rule those amongst us who rank as patricians are somewhat wanting in natural affection." [1]

We find no trace in these letters of the former part of this obligation but there are references to φιλοστοργία, in which Fronto says that the patricians are wholly deficient.[2] He was himself a notable exception. Marcus calls him *philostorgus*.[3] His devotion to his wife and daughter, and to Victorinus, her husband, and their children, shows him to us in a very amiable light. He was very fond of children, and his love for Marcus and Lucius was deep and abiding.

We cannot help liking the old man for his honest, kindly disposition, and his loyalty to a high ideal of friendship.[4] He always showed the greatest affection

---

[1] *Thoughts*, i. 11.   [2] *Ad Verum*, ii. 7.   [3] *De Fer. Als.* 4.
[4] See his letter to Pius about his friend Censorius and the letter to Appian.

for the young pupils who from time to time lived under his roof, and readiness to help them in their careers. He was the centre of a large literary coterie, and his personal friends were devoted to him, while his services as advocate had attached to him many influential friends in the provinces, especially in Cilicia and Africa.

Though not really wealthy compared with many other patricians of his time, and very far behind his rival Herodes in this respect, he had by his profession and by taking pupils and also through good management, aided by legacies, gathered a competence sufficient not only for his own wants but for the helping of his friends. He owned one or more villas near Rome and probably estates in Africa. His *Horti Maecenatiani* on the Esquiline could have been no mean residence, and he was able on one occasion to spend as much as £3000 on new baths there.[1]

The family life of Fronto was a singularly happy one in the mutual affection of its surviving members, though death deprived him of five out of his six children (all daughters) in their infancy. The sole surviving daughter, Gratia, married Aufidius Victorinus, one of the best and most capable men of his age, who afterwards committed suicide under Commodus. One child of this union died, aged three, in Germany, where Victorinus was governor, about

---

[1] Aul. Gell. xix. 10.

165 A.D. One son certainly, and possibly a second, survived to manhood. The former, M. Aufidius Victorinus Fronto, was brought up in Fronto's house and lived to be consul in 199, and in an inscription [1] to his son at Pisaurum recalled his grandfather as " orator, consul, and master of Marcus and Lucius." We hear of an eloquent descendant of Fronto's, Leo by name, in the fifth century at Toulouse. [2]

Mommsen and others have supposed that Fronto lived till the year 175 at least, and possibly longer, because in the *De Orationibus* he mentions coins of Commodus, but it is necessary to explain the allusion in some other way than as implying the date of Commodus's participation in the Empire. For it is certain that no letter in this correspondence, as we have it, can be dated later than 166, and we find Fronto's health getting worse and worse, and the loss of his wife and grandchild in 165 also affected him greatly. There can be little doubt that he predeceased Verus and died in 166 or 167. His grateful pupil Marcus rewarded his love and fidelity with equal affection, and on his death obtained permission from the Senate to set up his statue in the Senate-house and kept his bust among his household gods. [3] No representation of him has come down to us.

He founded a school of disciples who imitated his methods in oratory and language, and he playfully alludes to his *secta*. [4] The Frontonian tradition had

---

[1] *Corp. Inscr. Lat.* xi. 6334.   [2] Sidon. Apoll. *Ep.* iv. 21.
[3] Capit. *Vit. Mar.* ii. § 5.   [4] *Ad Anton.* i. 2.

a vogue of a least 300 years, as Sidonius Apollinaris mentions the Frontoniani in an obscure passage.[1]

The great service that Fronto did to his country-men was to leave their language a freer and more plastic instrument of speech than he found it, by reinforcing it with those elements which were in danger of atrophy for want of use, or were being wasted by being left outside the pale of good literature. Moreover by minute accuracy in the use of words and careful definition of their meaning, he gave precision and clarity to the language, which was a work well worth doing, and deserving of credit.

To the reader his style is easy and perspicuous, and far less abnormal and fantastic than that of his fellow African Apuleius. Unfortunately Fronto lacked originality of thought, and his humour is rather heavy, but his fatal foible lay not in his leanings to archaism but in his faith in εἰκόνες, which disfigure even the real pathos of his dirge over the loss of his grandson, and lessen the force of his special plead-ing for Volumnius of Concordia, though in his

---

[1] *Ep.* i. 1. "Nor did Jul. Titianus picture Cicero's whole epistolary style in a worthy image (*by means of a series of fictitious letters*) under the names of noble women. On this account all *the Frontonians*, as rivals of their fellow-disciple, because he followed the languid (Ciceronian) style of speak-ing, called him the orators' ape." Here the style of Cicero's letters, which Fronto calls *remissior*, easy or careless, seems to be disparaged. See Barth, *Advers.* xlvii. 9, and Nieb., Introd. to his ed. of Fronto, p. xxiii. The word used by Sidonius is *veternosus*. How Cicero's style could be called *languid* or *senile* (*veternosus*) is incomprehensible.

criticism of Seneca they find an effective place. He never grasped the fact that *comparatio* is not *ratio*. Whether he was proof against the seductive powers of the simile in the speeches which earned for him the epithets *gravis* and *siccus* we do not know, but the fragment on overseas wills is not free from this favourite device. One thing seems highly probable, that, if the bulk of Fronto's speeches should ever be recovered, we should form a much higher opinion of his abilities. As it is we can say of him, and this is surely much, that he was *vir bonus dicendi peritus.*

BIBLIOGRAPHY

1. *M. Cornelii Frontonis Opera inedita cum Epistulis item ineditis Antonini Pii, M. Aurelii, L. Veri, et Appiani, necnon aliorum fragmentis. Invenit et commentario praevio notisque illustravit Angelus Maius. Pars prior. Pars altera, cui adduntur seu edita seu cognita eiusdem Frontonis opera: Mediolani, regiis typis,* 1815, 4to.[1]

This first edition only contained the Fronto leaves from the Ambrosian Codex with a facsimile page of the MS., followed by the two works previously attributed to Fronto, viz. *De Differentiis Vocabulorum* and *Exempla Elocutionum*, together with the passages in Aulus Gellius where Fronto is mentioned. Republished in 1816 at Frankfort, without second part.

2. *M. Cornelii Frontonis Reliquiae ab Angelo Maio primum editae: meliorem in ordinem digestas suisque et Ph. Buttmanni, L. F. Heindorfii ac selectis a Maii animadversionibus instructas iterum edidit B. G. Niebuhrius, C.F. Accedunt Liber de Differentiis Vocabulorum et ab eodem a Maio primum edita Q. Aurelii Symmachi octo orationum fragmenta: Berolini,* MDCCCXVI.

This was a great advance on Mai's edition, many of his erroneous readings being corrected, the text itself emended in various places, the dislocated fragments better arranged, and valuable notes added.

3. *M. Cornelii Frontonis et M. Aurelii Imperatoris Epistulae: L. Veri et Antonini Pii et Appiani Epistularum reliquiae: Fragmenta Frontonis et Scripta Grammatica. Editio prima Romana plus centum epistulis aucta ex codice rescripto bibliothecae pontificiae Vaticanae, curante Angelo Maio: Romae,* MDCCCXXIII.

---

[1] One of three copies only on thick bluish paper, is in the Cambridge University Library. It contains Mai's autograph.

This, besides the same facsimile and supplements as the Milan edition, has a second facsimile page of the Vatican MS., the Caecilius signature, and a few lines of the Palatine palimpsest, containing part of Fronto's *Actio Gratiarum pro Carthaginiensibus*, the whole of which fragment, as far as it is decipherable, is given at the end of the volume.

4. *Lettres inédites de Marc Aurèle et de Fronton retrouvées sur les palimpsestes de Milan et de Rome : traduites avec le texte latin en regard et des notes par M. Armand Cassan* : 2 vols., Paris, 1830.

This is a most disappointing edition.[1] No improvements are made in the text and the translation evades or omits all the difficulties. But the notes, with their numerous illustrative passages from the older Roman writers, are useful.

5. In 1832 the Vatican portion of Mai's Roman edition was published at Zell by Schultz. It had no new features.

6. In 1867 S. A. Naber brought out the serviceable edition, from which everyone has since derived his knowledge of Fronto. Its title was : *M. Cornelii Frontonis et M. Aurelii Imperatoris Epistulae : L. Veri et T. Antonini Pii et Appiani Epistularum Reliquiae : post Angelum Maium cum codicibus Ambrosiano et Vaticano iterum contulit G. N. du Rieu : recensuit Samuel Adrianus Naber : Lipsiae*, 1867.

This was a great improvement on previous editions, the text being based on a fresh inspection of the MS. by du Rieu in 1858. But it left a great deal still to be desired. Owing to certain perverse ideas, especially about the date of Marcus's marriage, the editor went far astray in his chronology of the correspondence. The main indices, taken almost entirely from Mai, are totally inadequate.

The following translations of selected letters from the correspondence have appeared in English :—

(a) *Selections from Fronto's Letters*, translated into English : Rome, 1824. By J. McQuige. This contains paraphrases rather than translations of some twenty-three of the letters.

---

[1] A. Pierson, in his edition of Marcus Aurelius, 1843, has reproduced seventy of these letters, with trifling alterations.

BIBLIOGRAPHY

(b) Dr. W. H. D. Rouse, in an Appendix to his edition of Meric Casaubon's translation of the *Meditations* of Marcus Aurelius, published in 1900, has given us an excellent version of some entire letters and parts of many others.

(c) Miss M. D. Brock, Litt.D. Dubl., in her *Studies in Fronto and his Age*, published in 1911, has translated more than thirty letters, mostly in full, with the text opposite. Her rendering gives a very good idea of the original, and the whole book is most helpful to the student of Fronto and his literary claims.

Besides the above, P. B. Watson, in his *Life of Marcus Aurelius*, London, 1884, gives versions of several passages from the Correspondence, but he is an unsafe guide as to Fronto's meaning, his knowledge of Latin being inadequate.

A more scholarly contribution to the same subject is that of Hastings Crossley in his *Fourth Book of the Meditations of Marcus Aurelius*, London, 1882, an appendix to which contains a number of select passages from the letters admirably Englished with a running comment.

Finally, Robinson Ellis published at Oxford in 1904 a lecture on *The Correspondence of Fronto and Marcus Aurelius.* It translates a considerable number of passages from various parts of the work with connecting comments.

The more important contributions to the study of Fronto beside the above are as follows :—

Alan, H., *Coniecturae et Animadversiones* : Dublin, 1841. *Observationes in Frontonem* : Dublin, 1863, 1867.

Anon., *Index Phil. Leutschianus*, i. 60 ff.

Bährens, E., *Fleckh. Jahrbuch*, 105, pp. 632–4 (1872).

Beck, J .W., *De Different. Script. Latinis* (on the *Le Nominum Verborumque Differentiis* of Fronto (?)) ; *Mnem.* x. 9 : review of Brakman's work.

Becker, G., *Jenaer Lit. Ztg.* 1874, p. 631.

Beer, Rud., *Anz. d. philos.-hist. Kl. der k. Akad. d. Wiss.* : Vienna, 1911, nr. xi. " Über den aeltesten Handschriftenbestand des Klosters Bobbio."

Beltrami, Ach., *Le tendenze letterarie negli scritti di Frontone* : Milan, 1907. "Il ' numerus ' e Frontone," in *Riv. di fil.* 36, 1906. See also *Berl. Phil. Woch.* xxx. 1 ; *Bibl. Phil. klass.* 1908, p. 61 ; *Classici e Neolatini*, v. 1.

BIBLIOGRAPHY

Blase, H., *Archiv f. latein. Lexicographie* (Wölfflin), **9**, p. 491 (1896).

Boissonade, *Biographie Universelle*, xvi. 121 ff. : article "Fronton." See also Cassan's translation of Fronto, ii. p. 382.

Brakman, C., *Frontoniana*, Series i., ii.: Utrecht, 1902.

Bursian-Miller, *Jahresbericht über die Fortschritte der klass. Alterthumswissenschaft.* Berlin, 1873 : 2, 1320 ; 7, 172 ; 18, 172 ; 27, 8 ; 40, 232 ; 55, 238–240 ; 84, 189, 192, 196–203.

Cobet, C. G., *Mnem.* 3, p. 305 (1875) and 5, p. 232.

Cornelissen, J. J., *Mnem.*, N.S. 1, pp. 91–6 (1873) ; 13, pp. 115 ff. (1885).

Crossley, H., *Hermathena*, 5, p. 67. See also above.

Crutwell, C. T., *History of Roman Literature*, pp. 463–5, Lond. 1887.

Daunon, *Journ. d. Sav.* Sept. 1816, pp. 27 ff.: review of Mai's edition (1815).

Dareste, A. C., *De rhetore Ael. Aristide*, 1843.

Desrousseaux, A. M., *Rev. de Phil.* 10, pp. 149 ff. (1886).

Dircksen, H. E., *Opp.* 1, pp. 243–253, 276–280.

Dobson, J. F., *Classical Quarterly*, Jan. 1912.

Droz, E., *De M. Cornelii Frontonis institutione oratoria.*

Ebert, Ad., "De Frontonis Syntaxi," *Acta Semin. phil. Erlangensis*, ii. 311–354 (1881) : *Bl. f. d. bayr. Gymn.-wes.* xix. 527–30 (1883).

Eckstein, F. A., *Allgemeine Encyclopädie* (J. S. Ersch and J. G. Grüber), Section 1, Pt 51, pp. 442 ff. See also Naber's edit. p. xxxiv.

Egger, E., *Fragmenta ad Stoicorum et rhetorum historiam congruentia*, 1852.

Ehrenthal, L., *Quaestiones Frontonianae :* Königsberg, 1881.

Eickstadt, *Cornelii Frontonis Operum nuper in lucem protractorum notitia et specimen*, Jenae, 1846. See also Niebuhr's edit. pp. 293–4.

Ellis, Robinson, *Journal of Phil.* i pp. 15 ff. (1868) ; **xxix.** (1902), and see above, p. xlv.

Eussner, Ad., *Fleckh. Jahrb.* 107, pp. 522–3 (1873) ; pp. 766 ff. (1875) ; *Rhein. Mus.* 25, pp. 541–7 (1870); *Liter. Centralbl* 43 (1871).

Freytag, F. G., *Ex antiqua historia literaria de M. Corn. Frontine et Frontonianorum secta rhetorica*, Nuremberg, 1732.

BIBLIOGRAPHY

Friedländler, L., *Darstellungen aus d. Sittengeschichte Roms.*
    ii. 127 ff. Leipzig, 1901.
Fröhner, W., *Philol. Suppl.* 5, pp. 49–52 (1889).
Greef, A., *Philol.* 1876, pp. 682 ff.
Haines, C. R., *Classical Quarterly*, Apr. 1914, "On the
    Chronology of the Fronto Correspondence"; and *ibid.*.
    Jan. 1915, "On the text of Fronto."
Hauler, Edm.

    Verh. d. 41 *Vers. d. deut. Phil. in Köln* (1895), pp. 78–88,
    338. "Vortrag über das Ergebnis der neuen Unter-
    suchungen der Mailänder Frontoreste" : Leipzig, 1896 ;
    ibid. 59 in Graz : Vienna, 1909 (*Wiener Eranos*). "Zum
    Sendschreiben des Catulus und über die *Consilia* des
    Asinius Pollio."

    Serta Harteliana, pp. 263–269 : Vienna, 1896.

    Archiv. f. lateinische Lexicographie, x. 145 : Leipzig,
    1898 ; xv. 106–112 (1908). "Lepturgus and Chirur-
    gus."

    Rhein. Mus. 54, Pt. 2, pp. 161–170 (1899).

    Festschrift Theod. Gomperz, pp. 392, 393 : Vienna, 1902.

    Zeitsc. f. d. oesterr. Gymn. 54, pp. 32–37 (1903) ; 61,
    pp. 673–684 : Vienna, 1910.

    Mélanges Boissier, pp. 243 ff.: Paris, 1903.

    Mitteil. d. könig. deutsch. archaeol. Instit. Rom. Abteil 19,
    pp. 317–321 : Rome, 1904. "Fronto über Protogenes
    und Nealkes."

    Ver. d. 48 *Versam. d. Philol. in Hamburg*, pp. 51–53
    (1905) : Leipzig, 1906. "Bericht über dem Stand der
    Fronto Aufgabe."

    Miscellanea Ceriani, pp. 501–510 : Milan, 1909.

    Wien. Studien, 22, pp. 140, 318 (1900).

      ,,   ,,   23, p. 238 (1901).
      ,,   ,,   24, Pt. 1, pp. 232, 519–22 (1902).
      ,,   ,,   25, Pt. 1, pp. 162–4, 331 (1903).
      ,,   ,,   26, p. 344 (1904).
      ,,   ,,   27, Pt. 1, p. 146 (1905).
      ,,   ,,   27, Pt. 2, p. 304 (1905).
      ,,   ,,   28, Pt. 1, pp. 169, 170 (1906).
      ,,   ,,   29, Pt. 1, pp. 172, 328 (1907).
      ,,   ,,   29, Pt. 2, p. 328 (1907).
      ,,   ,,   31, Pt. 1, pp. 179, 180, 259, 268–270 (1909).
      ,,   ,,   32, Pt. 1, p. 160 (1910).
      ,   ,,   32, Pt. 2, pp. 325, 326 (1910).

BIBLIOGRAPHY

Hauler, Edm. (*cont.*)

    Wien. Studien, 33, Pt. 1, pp. 173–176 (1911).
      ,,   ,,   33, Pt. 2, p. 338 (1911).
      ,,   ,,   34, Pt. 1, pp. 253–259 (1912).
      ,,   ,,   35, pp. 398, 399 (1913).
      ,,   ,,   36, pp. 342, 343 (1914).
      ,,   ,,   37, pp. 187, 188 (1915).
      ,,   ,,   38, Pt. 1, pp. 166–175 (1916).
      ,,   ,,   38, Pt. 2, pp. 379–381 (1916).
      ,,   ,,   39, pp. 132–134, 173–176 (1917).
      ,,   ,,   39, Pt. 2, pp. 193 ff. (1917).
      ,,   ,,   40, Pt. 1, p. 195 (1918).
    Festschrift Bormanni, pp. 287–290 (1902).
    Mélanges Emile Chatelain, pp. 622–627 (1910).
    Bibl. phil.-klass., p. 56 (1910) : see *Woch. f. klass. Phil.*
    36, p. 979 (1910). "Neues aus dem Fronto-palim-
    psest."

Haupt, M., *Index Lectionum Berolin.* pp. 3 ff.: Berlin, 1867 ;
    Hermes, v. pp. 190, 191 (1871) ; viii. p. 178 (1874) ;
    Opusc. ii. pp. 346–357 ; iii. pp. 316, 563, 616, 619.

Havet, L., *Rev. de Phil.* 10, p. 189 (1886). "Le Reviseur du
    MS. de Fronton."

Heinrich, C. F., *Auctuarium emendationum in Frontonis*
    reliquias ex edit. Berolin. 1817, Kiel.

Hertz, M., *Renaissance und Rococo in der röm. Litteratur* :
    Berlin, 1865 ; *Fleckh. Jahrbuch*, 93, pp. 579, 580 (1866) ;
    Rhein. Mus. 1874, pp. 29, 367 ; *Vindiciae Gellii Alterae*,
    p. 23 adn. 52, 53 ; Program. Vratislav. 1873, *De ludo*
    talario ; *Philol.* 1876, p. 757.

Herwerden, N. van, *Mnem.* N.S. 1, pp. 223, 292–294 (1873) ;
    ibid. 31, p. 210.

Hirschfield, O., *apud* Studemund, *Epist. ad Klussm.* xxxii.

Jacobs, Fr., *Wolfii Analecta*, i. pp. 108 ff.; ii. pp. 246 ff.: Berlin,
    1817–1818 ; Zimmermann, *Diar. Antiq.*, p. 1019 (1838).

Jahn, O., *Rhein. Mus.* 3, p. 156 ; *Berl. Sächs. Gesellsch.* 1851,
    pp. 360 ff.

Jordan, H., *Herm.* 6, pp. 68–81 (1872). "Catulus de Con-
    sulatu ; Ad Catonem, p. xcviii."

Kaemmel, H., *Ann. Paedag.* 1870, pp. 13 ff.

Kessler, K. C. G., *De locis qui in Frontonis Epistulis litura*
    corrupti deprehenduntur coniectura sarciendis, Progr.
    Gymn. Rosslebiensis, 1828.

BIBLIOGRAPHY

Kiehl, E. J., *Mnem.* 2, pp. 225–227 (1874).

Kiessling, Ad., *ap.* Studemund, *Epist. ad Klussm.* p. xxxiii.

Klussmann, E., *Philol.* 27, p. 240.

Klussmann, R., *Emendationum Frontoniarum particula*: Göttingen, 1871; *Emendat. Frontonianae cum Epistula Critica Gulielmi Studemundi ad R. Klussmann*: Berlin, 1874. *Fleck. Jahrbuch*, 109, pp. 636–638 (1874); *Progr. Gymn.* Gerensis, 1877, *Curae Africanae*: Gera, 1883; *Archiv. f. lat. Lexicographie* (Wölfflin), 1893, pp. 134, 135.

Kretschmer, Jul., *De Gellii Fontibus* (Arion), p. 103: Posen, 1860.

Krüger, P., *ap.* Studemund, *Epist. ad Klussm.* pp. iii., iv.

Kübler, B., *Archiv. f. lat. Lexicographie*, vii. pp. 593 ff.; viii. pp. 161 ff.

Mackail, J. W., *Latin Literature*, Pt. 3, ch. 5, pp. 232–238.

Madvig, J. N., *Adversaria Critica*, ii., pp. 613 ff.: Copenhagen, 1873.

Mähly, J., *Philol.* 17, pp. 176 ff. (1861); 19, pp. 159 ff. (1863).

Meyer, H., *Fragments of Roman Oratory*, pp. 609 ff.: Zurich, 1842.

Mommsen, Th., *Herm.* viii. pp. 198–217 (1874). "Die Chronologie der Briefe Frontonis."

Müller, C. F. W., *Fleck. Jahrbuch*, 93, pp. 487 ff., 1866; 100, p. 350 (1873); *Progr.* Landsbergian., pp. 9 ff. (1865); *Rhein. Mus.* 20, p. 156.

Müller, Er., *Marc. Aurel. in seinen Briefen an Fronto*: Program, Ratibor, 1869 (*Festschr. z. hundertjährigen Stiftungsfeier d. könig. evang. Gymn.*).

Naber, S. A., *Mnem.* 2, pp. 225–227 (1874); *ibid.* 24, p. 396 (1896).

Niebuhr, B. G., *Scripta Minora*, ii. pp. 50–72.

Novák, R., *Wien. Stud.* 19, pp. 242–257 (1897). *Listy filol.* 1886, pp. 202 ff.

Orelli, J. C., "Chrestomathia Frontoniana": Appendix to Tacitus, *Dialogus*, pp. 115 ff.: Zurich, 1830.

Pater, W., *Marius the Epicurean*, 2 vols.: London, 1885.

Pauly-Wissowa, *Real-Encyclopädie*, "Fronto."

Pellini, S., "Frontone, Marco Aurelio e Lucio Vero"; *Classici e Neolatini*, 1 (1912), 2, pp. 220–248; Continuazione, *ibid.* 8 (1912), 3, pp. 442–475; "Aulo Gellio e Frontone," *Classici e Neolatini*, 8 (1912), 2, pp. 415–425.

BIBLIOGRAPHY

Peter, H., "Der Brief in der römischen Literatur" : *Abh. d. Philol. hist.-klass. d. Königl. Sächs. Gesellschaft d. Wissensch.* 20 : Leipzig, 1901.

Philibert-Soupé, A., *De Frontonis reliquiis* : Amiens, 1851.

Pierron, A., *Hist. de la Littér. Latin*, 1852, pp. 58, 60, 306, 345, 608.

Priebe, C., *De Frontone imitationem prisci sermonis Latini adfectante :* Gymn. Progr. des Stadt-gymnasiums zu Stettin, 1885.

Rasi, P., *Riv. d. filol.*, 38, 4, pp. 545–7 ; *Bollet. d. filol. class.* xv. 7, pp. 3, 157–9. See also *Woch. f. klass. phil.* xxvi. 38, 1012–15.

Reinhardt, L., *De retractatione fabularum Plautinarum*, Diss. inauguralis.

Roth, F., *Bemerkungen über die Schriften des M. Corn. Fronto und über das Zeitalter der Antonine* : Munich, 1817 (*Sammlung etlicher Vorträge*, pp. 12–76 : Munich, 1851).

du Rieu, G. N., *Schedae Vaticanae*, 1868.

Schäfer, Arn., *Philol.* 26, pp. 574 ff. (1867) ; "De locis non nullis Ciceronis, Plinii, Frontonis," *Progr. Gymn. Vizthumiani Dresd.*, pp. 12–16, 1844.

Schanz, M.von, *Geschichte der römischen Literatur*, iii. Fronto : Munich, 1890.

Schenkl, K., *Zeitschr. f. d. oest. Gymn.*, 26, pp. 30–34, 1875.

Schneidewin, F. W., *Philol.* 10, p. 321 (1885).

Schopen, L., *Emendationes Frontonianae*, Pts. 1, 2 : Bonn, 1830, 1841.

Schwierczina, Th., *Frontoniana* : Breslau, 1883.

Sheppard, J. T., *Wochenschrift f. klass. Phil.*, Feb. 1914 : Berlin.

Simcox, G. A., *History of Latin Literature* : London, 1867.

Smiley, C. N., *Latinitas and Ἑλληνισμός* : Bulletin of the University of Wisconsin : Madison, Wisconsin, 1906.

Steele, R. B., "Chiasmus in the Epistles of Cicero, Seneca, Pliny and Fronto" ; *Studies in honour of B. Gildersleeve* : Baltimore, 1902. Ablative absolute in the same writers : *American Journ. of Phil.*, 25, pp. 315–327 (1904).

Still, K., "Archaismus" : *Comment. Wolfflinianae*, pp. 407 ff.

Studemund, W., *Epistula ad R. Klussmann* : Berlin, 1874, and *passim* throughout the latter's *Emendat. Frontonianae* ; *Annales Livian.*, 1873, p. 11 : Leipzig ; *Annal. Philol.* (= *Fleckh. Jahrbuch*), 1868, p. 549 ; *Wien. Stud.*, 31,

BIBLIOGRAPHY

Pt. i., p. 259 (1909).   See also Hauler **above** (*Verh. d.*
48 *Versam. d. Phil.*, 1905).

Talbot, E., *De ludicris apud veteres laudationibus*, 1850.

Teuffel, W. S., *Geschichte der römischen Literatur*, ii. § 355,
pp. 212-218.   English translation by G. C. W. Warr,
1900.

Usener, Herm., *Fleckh. Jahrb.*, 91, pp. 267, 268 (1865).

Vahlen, J., *Zeitsch. f. d. oest. Gymn.*, 19, p. 10 (1868) ;
Hermes, 1876, p. 458 ; *Cn. Naevii reliquiae*, pp. 6 ff. ; *Ad
Ennium*, p. xix. f.

Vallaurius, Th., *Critica Latinarum litterarum historia* :
Zurich, 1851.

Valmaggi, L., *Quaestiones Frontonianae* : Ivrea, 1889 ; *I pre-
cursori di Frontone* : Ivrea, 1887 ; *Riv. di fil.* 36, p. 312,
April, 1908 (review of Beltrami's *Le tendenze* etc., see
above).

Volkmann, R., *Die Rhetorik der Griechen und Römer*, pp. 354,
427 : Leipzig, 1885.

Warren, Minton, "On a literary judgment of Fronto" ;
Trans. and *Proceed. Amer. Phil. Assoc.*, 43 : Boston,
1894.

Westermann, A., *Geschichte der Beredsamkeit in Griechenland
und Rom*, 2 Parts : Leipzig, 1833-5.

W., C., *Berl. Wochenschrift f. klass. Phil.*, 1900 and 1904.

Wer kann dieses lesen (viz. that the Fronto Letters had been
found by Mai), der den Antonin kennt, und vor Begierde
nicht brennen? So manches von diesem Manne noch
ungedruckt, aus dessen Munde kein wort auf die Erde
hälte fallen mussen? der vollends keine Sylbe gesch-
rieben haben, die nach jetzt mit Motte et Moder Kämfte.
Lessing, *Opp.* xiv. 223.

BIBLIOGRAPHICAL ADDENDUM (1982)

Hauler, Edmund, Hauler's adversaria (conveniently listed in the following item, pp. lxxxviff) continued to pour out until 1940 but he never lived to produce the edition he had been planning for a lifetime.

Van Den Hout, M. P. J., *M. Cornelii Frontonis Epistulae*, volume 1 (Prolegomena, text, index nominum)—volume 2, planned to contain commentary, never appeared—Leiden, 1954.

Marache, R., *La critique littéraire de langue latine et le développement du goût archaisant au IIe siècle de notre ère*, Paris, 1952.

Marache, R., *Mots nouveaux et mots archaïques chez Fronton et Aulu-Gelle*, Paris, 1957.

Portalupi, Felicità, *Marco Cornelio Frontone*, Turin, 1961.

Bowersock, G. W., *Greek Sophists in the Roman Empire*, Oxford, 1969.

Champlin, Edward, *Fronto and Antonine Rome*, Cambridge, Mass. 1980; contains an updated chronology of the letters, slightly modified from his earlier "The Chronology of Fronto," *JRS* 64 (1974), 136–159.

CHRONOLOGICAL TABLE

CHRONOLOGICAL TABLE

CHRONOLOGICAL TABLE

SIGLA

< > Conjectural additions.

[   ] Words which should be omitted.

†   Doubtful readings.

(   ) Additions in the English translation, or explanatory
words.

THE CORRESPONDENCE OF
M. CORNELIUS FRONTO

M. CORNELII FRONTONIS

ET M. AURELII, L. VERI, ALIORUMQUE EPISTULAE

Ad M. Caesarem et invicem, iv. 3 (Naber, p. 61).

Cod. Vat
180, col. 2
ad med.

| DOMINO meo Fronto.

1. Omnium artium, ut ego arbitror, imperitum et indoctum omnino esse praestat quam semiperitum ac semidoctum. Nam qui sibi conscius est artis expertem esse minus adtemptat, eoque minus praecipitat; diffidentia profecto audaciam prohibet. At Vat. 179 ubi quis leviter quid cognitum pro comperto | ostentat, falsa fiducia multifariam labitur. Philosophiae quoque disciplinas aiunt satius esse numquam adtigisse quam leviter et primoribus, ut dicitur, labiis delibasse, eosque provenire malitiosissimos, qui in vestibulo artis obversati prius inde averterint quam penetraverint. Tamen est in aliis artibus ubi interdum delitescas et peritus paulisper habeare quod nescias. In verbis vero eligendis conlocandisque ilico dilucet, nec verba dare diu quis[1] potest, quin se ipse

---

[1] Klussmann for Cod. *diutius.*

---

[1] Certainly an early letter, possibly the earliest preserved (see § 4). In a subsequent letter to Marcus, as Emperor, it seems to be referred to as *prima illa longiuscula epistula* (see

2

THE CORRESPONDENCE OF

M. CORNELIUS FRONTO

Fronto to Marcus Aurelius as Caesar

Fronto to my Lord.[1]   ? 139 A.D.

1. In all arts, as I think, total inexperience and
ignorance are preferable to a semi-experience and a
half-knowledge. For he who is conscious that he
knows nothing of an art aims at less, and consequently comes less to grief: in fact, diffidence ex-
cludes presumption. But when anyone parades a
superficial knowledge as mastery of a subject, through
false confidence he makes manifold slips. They say,
too, that it is better to have kept wholly clear of the
teachings of philosophy than to have tasted them
superficially and, as the saying goes, with the tips of
the lips; and that those turn out the most knavish
who, going about the precincts of an art, turn aside
or ever they have entered its portals. Yet in other
arts it is possible, sometimes, to escape exposure,
and for a man to be deemed, for a period, proficient
in that wherein he is an ignoramus. But in the
choice and arrangement of words he is detected
instantly, nor can anyone make a pretence[2] with

Ad Ant. i. 2). Marcus became consul in 140, and this fact
could scarcely have been ignored in § 6.

[2] The Latin phrase *verba dare alicui* means " to use mere
words to a person," *i.e.* to deceive him. It is difficult to
reproduce the subtle play on the words.

3

indicet verborum ignarum esse, eaque male probare et temere existimare et inscie contrectare, neque modum neque pondus verbi internosse.

2. Quam ob rem rari admodum veterum scriptorum in eum laborem studiumque et periculum verba industriosius quaerendi sese commisere. Oratorum post homines natos unus omnium M. Porcius eiusque frequens sectator C. Sallustius; poetarum maxime Plautus, multo maxime Q. Ennius, eumque studiose aemulatus L. Coelius, nec non Naevius, Lucretius, Accius etiam, Caecilius, Laberius quoque. Nam praeter hos partim scriptorum animadvertas particulatim elegantes, Novium et Pom|ponium et id genus in verbis rusticanis et iocularibus ac ridiculariis, Attam in muliebribus, Sisennam in lascivis,[1] Lucilium in cuiusque artis ac negotii propriis.

Vat. 146

3. Hic tu fortasse iamdudum requiras quo in numero locem M. Tullium, qui caput atque fons Romanae eloquentiae cluet. Eum ego arbitror usquequaque verbis pulcherrimis elocutum et ante omnes alios oratores ad ea, quae ostentare vellet, ornanda magnificum fuisse. Verum is mihi videtur a quaerendis scrupulosius verbis procul afuisse vel magnitudine animi vel fuga laboris vel fiducia, non quaerenti etiam sibi, quae vix aliis quaerentibus subvenirent, praesto adfutura. Itaque comperisse videor, ut qui eius scripta omnia studiosissime lectitarim, cetera eum genera verborum copiosissime uber-

---

[1] Mai for Cod. *lasciviis.*

words for long without himself betraying that he is ignorant of them, that his judgment of them is incorrect, his estimate of them haphazard, his handling of them unskilful, and that he can distinguish neither their propriety nor their force.

2. Wherefore few indeed of our old writers have surrendered themselves to that toil, pursuit, and hazard of seeking out words with especial diligence. M. Porcius alone of the orators of all time, and his constant imitator C. Sallustius, are among these; of poets Plautus especially, and most especially Q. Ennius and his zealous rival L. Coelius, not to omit Naevius and Lucretius, Accius too, and Caecilius, also Laberius. Besides these, certain other writers are noticeable for choiceness in special spheres, as Novius, Pomponius and their like in rustic and jocular and comic words, Atta in women's talk, Sisenna in erotics, Lucilius in the technical language of each art and business.

3. At this point, perhaps, you will have long been asking in what category I should place M. Tullius, who is hight the head and source of Roman eloquence. I consider him on all occasions to have used the most beautiful words, and to have been magnificent above all other orators in embellishing the subject which he wished to display. But he seems to me to have been far from disposed to search out words with especial care, whether from greatness of mind, or to escape toil, or from the assurance that what others can scarcely find with careful search would be his at call without the need of searching. And so, from a most attentive perusal of all his writings, I think I have ascertained that he has with the utmost copiousness and opulence handled all

rimeque tractasse, verba propria translata simplicia
composita et, quae in eius scriptis ubique dilucent,
verba honesta, saepenumero etiam amoena: quom
tamen in omnibus eius orationibus paucissima admodum reperias insperata atque inopinata verba, quae
non nisi cum studio atque cura atque vigilia atque
multa veterum carminum memoria indagantur. | In-
speratum autem atque inopinatum verbum [1] appello,
quod praeter spem atque opinionem audientium aut
legentium promitur, ita ut, si subtrahas atque eum
qui legat quaerere ipsum iubeas, nullum aut non ita
significando adcommodatum verbum aliud reperiat.
Quam ob rem te magno opere conlaudo, quod ei rei
curam industriamque adhibes, ut verbum ex alto
eruas et ad significandum adcommodes. Verum, ut
initio dixi, magnum in ea re periculum est, ne minus
apte aut parum dilucide aut non satis decore, ut a
semidocto, conlocetur, namque multo satius est volg-
aribus et usitatis quam remotis et requisitis uti, si
parum significet.[2]

4. Haud sciam an utile sit demonstrare quanta
difficultas, quam scrupulosa et anxia cura in verbis
probandis adhibenda sit, ne ea res animos adulescentium retardet aut spem adipiscendi debilitet. Una
plerumque littera translata aut exempta aut immut-
ata vim verbi ac venustatem commutat et elegantiam
vel scientiam [3] loquentis declarat. Equidem te anim-
adverti, quom mihi scripta tua relegeres, atque ego

---

[1] Studemund for Cod. *vero*.   [2] Schopen reads *significent*.
[3] Haupt, *inscientiam*.

6

other kinds of words—words literal and figurative, simple and compound and, what are conspicuous everywhere in his writings, noble words, and oftentimes also exquisite ones : and yet in all his speeches you will find very few words indeed that are unexpected and unlooked for, such as are not to be hunted out save with study and care and watchfulness and the treasuring up of old poems in the memory. By an unexpected and unlooked-for word I mean one which is brought out when the hearer or reader is not expecting it or thinking of it, yet so that if you withdrew it and asked the reader himself to think of a substitute, he would be able to find either no other at all or one not so fitted to express the intended meaning. Wherefore I commend you greatly for the care and diligence you shew in digging deep for your word and fitting it to your meaning. But, as I said at first, there lies a great danger in the enterprize lest the word be applied unsuitably or with a want of clearness or a lack of refinement, as by a man of half-knowledge, for it is much better to use common and everyday words than unusual and far-fetched ones, if there is little difference in real meaning.[1]

4. I hardly know whether it is advisable to shew how great is the difficulty, what scrupulous and anxious care must be taken, in weighing words, for fear the knowledge should check the ardour of the young and weaken their hopes of success. The transposition or subtraction or alteration of a single letter in many cases changes the force and beauty of a word and testifies to the taste or knowledge of the speaker. I may say I have noticed, when you were reading over to me what you had written

[1] Or "if the word be inadequate," cp. p. 220.

de verbo syllabam per|mutarem, te id neglegere nec multum referre arbitrari. Nolim igitur te ignorare syllabae unius discrimen quantum referat. Os *colluere* dicam, pavimentum autem in balneis *pelluere*, non colluere; lacrimis vero genas *lavere* dicam, non pelluere neque colluere, vestimenta autem *lavare*, non lavere; sudorem porro et pulverem *abluere*, non lavare; sed maculam elegantius *eluere* quam abluere. Si quid vero magis haeserit nec sine aliquo detrimento exigi possit, Plautino verbo *elavere* dicam. Tum praeterea mulsum *diluere*, fauces *proluere*, ungulam iumento *subluere*.

5. Tot exemplis unum atque idem verbum syllabae atque litterae commutatione in varium modum ac sensum[1] usurpatur: tam hercule quam faciem medicamento *litam*, caeno corpus *conlitum*, calicem melle *delitum*, mucronem veneno *<inlitum>*, radium visco *oblitum* rectius dixerim.

6. Haud sciam an quis roget *namquis me prohibet vestimenta lavere potius quam lavare, sudorem lavare potius quam abluere dicere?* Tibi vero nemo in ea re intercedere aut modificari iure ullo poterit qui sis

liber | liberis prognatus et equitum censum praetervehare,[2] et in senatu sententiam rogere; nos vero qui doctorum auribus servituti serviendae nosmet

---

[1] C. F. W. Müller for Cod. *adcensum* (= ἀξιωθέν, Ellis).
[2] Fronto may have in mind here Hor. *Ars Poet.* 382-4.

[1] *i.e.* "to rinse the mouth."
[2] *i.e.* "to swab the flagged floor in the baths."
[3] "To bathe the cheeks in tears."

and I altered a syllable in a word, that you paid no attention to it and thought it of no great consequence. I should be loth, therefore, for you not to know the immense difference made by one syllable. I should say *Os colluere*,[1] but *in balneis pavimentnm pelluere*,[2] not *colluere*; I should, however, say *lacrimis genas lavere*,[3] not *pelluere* or *colluere*; but *vestimenta lavare*,[4] not *lavere*; again, *sudorem et pulverem abluere*,[5] not *lavare*; but it is more elegant to say *maculam eluere* than *abluere*; if, however, the stain had soaked in and could not be taken out without some damage, I should use the Plautine word *elavere*.[6] Then there are besides *mulsum diluere*,[7] *fauces proluere*,[8] *ungulam iumento subluere*.[9]

5. So many are the examples of one and the same word, with the change of a syllable or letter, being used in various ways and meanings; just as, by heaven, I should speak with a nicer accuracy of a face, painted with rouge, a body splashed with mud, a cup smeared with honey, a sword-point dipped in poison, a stake daubed with bird-lime.

6. Someone maybe will ask, Who, pray, is to prevent me saying *vestimenta lavere* rather than *lavare*, *sudorem lavare* rather than *abluere*? As for you, indeed, no one will have any right to interfere with or prescribe for you in that matter, as you are a free man born of free parents, and have more than a knight's income, and are asked your opinion in the Senate; we, however, who have dedicated ourselves in dutiful service to the ears of the cultured must

---

4 "To wash clothes."
5 "To wash off sweat and dust."   6 "To scour out."
7 "To water mead."   8 "To gargle the throat."
9 "To scrub out a horse's frog."

dedimus, necesse est tenuia quoque ista et minuta
summa cum cura persequamur. Verba prorsus alii
vecte et malleo ut silices moliuntur, alii autem caelo
et marculo ut gemmulas exculpunt; te aequius erit
ad quaerenda sollertius verba quod correctus sis
meminisse, quam quod deprehensus detrectare aut
retardari. Nam si quaerendo desistes, numquam
reperies; si perges quaerere, reperies.

7. Denique visus etiam es mihi insuper habuisse,
quom ordinem verbi tuum[1] immutassem, uti ante
tricipitem diceres quam *Geryonam* nominares. Id quoque ne ignores; pleraque in oratione ordine immut-
ato vel rata verba fiunt vel supervacanea. *Navem*
triremem rite dixerim; *triremem navem* supervacaneo
addiderim. Neque enim periculum est ne quis lecti-
culam aut redam aut citharam triremem dici arbitre-
tur. Tum praeterea quom commemorares, cur Parthi
manuleis laxioribus uterentur, ita, opinor, scripsisti,
intervallis vestis aestum ut *suspendi* di/ceres. Ain
tandem quo pacto aestus suspenditur? Neque id
reprehendo, te verbi translatione audacius progres-
sum, quippe qui Ennii sententia *oratorem audacem*
esse debere censeam. Sit sane audax orator, ut Ennius
postulat: sed a significando quod volt eloqui nusquam digrediatur. Igitur voluntatem quidem tuam
magno opere probavi laudavique, quom verbum

[1] Cod. m[2] for *tui*.

---

[1] As it happens, it might mean one or two other things in
English.

needs with the utmost care study these nice distinctions and minutiae. Some absolutely work at their words with crowbar and maul as if they were flints; others, however, grave them with burin and mallet as though they were little gems. For you it will be better, for greater deftness in searching out words, to take it to heart when corrected, than to demur or flag when detected in a fault. For if you give up searching you will never find; if you go on searching you will find.

7. Finally, you seemed even to have thought it a work of supererogation when I changed your order of a word, so that the epithet *three-headed* should come before the name *Geryon*. Bear this, too, in mind: it frequently happens that words in a speech, by a change in their order, become essential or superfluous. I should be right in speaking of a *ship with three decks*, but *ship* would be a superfluous addition to *three-decker*. For there is no danger[1] of anyone thinking that by three-decker was meant a litter, a landau, or a lute. Then, again, when you were pointing out why the Parthians wore loose wide sleeves, you wrote, I think, to this effect, that the heat was *suspended*[2] by the openings in the robe. Can you tell me, pray, how the heat is suspended? Not that I find fault with you for pushing out somewhat boldly[3] in the metaphorical use of a word, for I agree with Ennius his opinion that "an orator should be bold." By all means let him be bold, as Ennius lays down, but let him in no case deviate from the meaning which he would express. So I greatly approved and applauded your intention when you

[2] Used in the sense of *supprimo*, "checked."
[3] *cp.* below, *Ad Caes*, ii. 5, *Ad Ant.* i. 2, *ad med.*

quaerere adgressus es; indiligentiam autem quaesiti verbi, quod esset absurdum, reprehendi. Namque manuleorum intervallis, quae interdum laxata videmus atque fluitantia, *suspendi* aestus non potest: potest aestus per vestis intervalla *depelli,* potest *degi,* potest *demeare,* potest *circumduci,* potest *interverti,* potest *eventilari*—omnia denique potius potest quam [posse] suspendi, quod verbum superne quid[1] sustineri, non per laxamenta deduci significat.

8. Post ista monui quibus studiis, quoniam ita velles, te historiae scribundae praeparares. Qua de re quom longior sit oratio, ne modum epistulae egrediar, finem facio. Si tu de ea quoque re scribi ad te voles, etiam atque etiam admonebis.

Ad M. Caes. et invicem, iii. 11 (Naber, p. 48).

Vat. 114, end of col. | DOMINO MEO.

Gratia ad me heri nocte venit. Sed pro Gratia mihi fuit quod tu gnomas egregie convertisti, hanc quidem quam hodie accepi prope perfecte, ut poni in libro Sallustii possit, nec discrepet aut quicquam decedat. Ego beatus hilaris sanus iuvenis denique fio, quom tu ita proficis. Est grave quod postulabo;

---

[1] Cod. *quit* (Mai): Brakm. reads the word as *volt.*

---

[1] Marcus (see *Thoughts*, iii. 14) possibly wrote some sort of *History of the Greeks and Romans,* which Nicephorus

set about seeking for a word; what I found fault with was the want of care shewn in selecting a word which made nonsense. For by openings in sleeves, which we occasionally see to be loose and flowing, heat cannot be suspended: heat can be dispelled through the openings of a robe, it can be thrown off, it can radiate away, it can be given a passage, it can be diverted, it can be ventilated out—it can be almost anything, in fact, rather than be suspended, a word which means that a thing is held up from above, not drawn away through wide passages.

8. After that I advised you as to the preparatory studies necessary for the writing of history,[1] since that was your desire. As that subject would require a somewhat lengthy discussion, I make an end, that I overstep not the bounds of a letter. If you wish to be written to on that subject too, you must remind me again and again.

Fronto to Marcus Aurelius as Caesar

To my Lord.   ? 139 A.D.

Gratia[2] came home last night. But to me it has been as good as having Gratia, that you have turned your "maxims" so brilliantly; the one which I received to-day almost faultlessly, so that it could be put in a book of Sallust's without jarring or shewing any inferiority. I am happy, merry, hale, in a word become young again, when you make such progress. It is no light thing that I shall require; but

Callistus (iii. 31) may perhaps refer to. But Marcus in his *Thoughts*, i. 17 *ad fin.*, disclaims the study of histories.

[2] Gratia was Fronto's wife. He had also a daughter Gratia, who was married about 160, and so probably born between 140 and 145.

sed quod ipse mihimet profuisse memini non potest quin a te quoque postulem. Bis et ter eandem convertito, ita ut fecisti in illa gnome brevicula. Igitur Vat. 113 longiores quoque | bis ac ter converte naviter, audacter. Quodcumque ausus fueris cum isto ingenio, perficies: at enim cum labore[1] laboriosum quidem negotium concupisti, sed pulchrum et rectum et paucis impetratum. De . . . .[2] perfecte absolveris. Plurimum tibi in oratione facienda <proderit hic labor>: tum certe quidem cotidie <aliquas sententias excerpere> ex Iugurtha aut ex Catilina. Deis propitiis, quom Romam reverteris, exigam a te denuo versus diurnos. Dominam matrem tuam saluta.

Ad M. Caes. et invicem, iii. 12 (Naber, p. 49).

MAGISTRO meo.

Duas per id tempus epistulas tuas excepi. Earum altera me increpabas et temere sententiam scripsisse[3] arguebas, altera vero tueri studium meum laude nitebaris.[4] Adiuro tamen tibi meam, meae matris, tuam salutem mihi plus gaudii in animo coortum esse illis tuis prioribus litteris; meque saepius exclamasse inter legendum *O me felicem! Itane, dicet aliquis, felicem te, si est qui te doceat quomodo*

---

[1] Madvig would put a colon here and a comma after *perficies*.

[2] A few words are lost, of which Mai gives a dozen letters, one word probably being <*voc*> *abula*.

[3] Cod. m[2] *exscripsisse*.

[4] Brakman reads the MS. as *tuebare studium meum laude et levabas*.

what I remember to have been of service to myself,
I cannot but require of you also. You must turn
the same maxim twice or thrice, just as you have
done with that little one. And so turn longer
ones two or three times diligently, boldly. Whatever you venture on, such are your abilities, you will
accomplish : but, indeed, with toil have you coveted
a task that is truly toilsome, but fair and honourable
and attained by few . . . . you have got (it) perfectly out. This exercise will be the greatest help
to you in speech making; undoubtedly, too, the
excerpting of some sentences from the *Jugurtha* or
the *Catiline*. If the Gods are kind, on your return
to Rome I will exact again from you your daily quota
of verses. Greet my Lady, your mother.[1]

Marcus Aurelius to Fronto

To my master.   ? 139 a.d.

I have received two letters[2] from you at once.
In one of these you scolded me and pointed out that
I had written a sentence carelessly; in the other,
however, you strove to encourage my efforts with
praise. Yet I protest to you by my health, by my
mother's, and yours, that it was the former letter
which gave me the greater pleasure, and that, as I
read it, I cried out again and again *O happy that I
am! Are you then so happy*, someone will say, *for
having a teacher to shew you how to write a maxim more*

---

[1] Domitia Lucilla, the widow of Annius Verus. The
adopted mother of Marcus, the elder Faustina, wife of Pius,
died between July 140 and July 141.

[2] The second of these must be the preceding letter. The
other may possibly be the first letter given above.

γνώμην *sollertius dilucidius brevius politius scribas?* Non
hoc est quod me felicem nuncupo. Quid est igitur?
Quod verum dicere ex te disco. Ea res—verum|dic-
ere—prorsum deis hominibusque ardua : nullum
denique tam veriloquum oraculum est, quin aliquid
ancipitis in se vel obliqui vel impediti habeat, quo
imprudentior inretiatur, et[1] ad voluntatem suam
dictum opinatus captionem post tempus ac negotium
sentiat. Sed ista res lucrosa[2] est, et plane mos talia
tantum pio errore et vanitate ex<cus>are. At tuae
seu accusationes seu lora confestim ipsam viam ostendunt sine fraude et inventis verbis. Itaque deberem etiam gratias agere tibi si verum me dicere satius
simul et audire verum me doces. Duplex igitur
pretium solvatur, pendere quod ne valeam <ela-
bora>bis. Si resolvi vis[3] nil, quomodo tibi par pari
expendam nisi obsequio? Impius tamen mihi malui
te nimia motum cura . . . . die<s isti quom essent>
vacui, licuit me . . . . bene st<udere et multas
sententias> excerpere . . . . Vale mi bone et optime <magister. Te>, optime orator, sic m<ihi in
amicitiam> venisse gaudeo. | Domina mea te salutat.

---

[1] From here to *motum cura* is as read by Hauler (see
Mélanges Boissier, pp. 245-248). He reserves further additions to this letter for his forthcoming edition.

[2] Cod. m[2] for *via ludiosa* : m[2] also *praeterea* for *plane*, and
m[2] has *vel* for *tibi* after *agere* below.

[3] m[1] *si remiseris.*

deftly, more clearly, more tersely, more elegantly? No, that is not my reason for calling myself happy. What, then, is it? It is that I learn from you to speak the truth.[1] That matter—of speaking the truth—is precisely what is so hard for Gods and men : in fact, there is no oracle so truth-telling as not to contain within itself something ambiguous or crooked or intricate, whereby the unwary may be caught and, interpreting the answer in the light of their own wishes, realize its fallaciousness only when the time is past and the business done. But the thing is profitable, and clearly it is the custom to excuse such things merely as pious fraud and delusion. On the other hand, your fault-findings or your guiding reins, whichever they be, shew me the way at once without guile and feigned words. And so I ought to be grateful to you for this, that you teach me before all to speak the truth at the same time and to hear the truth. A double return, then, would be due, and this you will strive to put it beyond my power to pay. If you will have no return made, how can I requite you like with like, if not by obedience? Disloyal, however, to myself, I preferred that you, moved by excess of care . . . . since I had those days free, I had the chance . . . . of doing some good work and making many extracts . . . . Farewell, my good master, my best of masters. I rejoice, best of orators, that you have so become my friend. My Lady[2] greets you.

[1] His other pupil, Lucius Verus, also pays Fronto this compliment, see II. 118. But Marcus, in his tribute to Fronto in his *Thoughts* (i. 11), omits all mention of it.

[2] This title can stand for the mother of Marcus as it does in the previous letter, or for Faustina the elder, his adopted mother, or, after his marriage in 145, for his wife Faustina the younger.

Epist. Graecae, 6 (Naber, p. 252).

| HAVE mi magister optime.[1]

Si quid somni redit post vigilias, de quibus questus es, oro te, scribe mihi; et illud oro te primum, valetudini operam da. Tum *securim Tenediam,* quam[2] minaris, abde aliquo ac reconde, nec | tu consilium causarum agendarum dimiseris, aut tum simul omnia ora taceant.

Graece nescio quid ais te compegisse, quod[3] ut aeque pauca a te scripta placeat tibi. Tune es qui me nuper concastigaras,[4] quorsum Graece scriberem? Mihi vero nunc[5] potissimum Graece scribendum est. *Quam ob rem* rogas? Volo "periculum facere," an id quod non didici facilius obsecundet mihi, quoniam quidem illud, quod didici, deserit. Sed si me amares,[6] misisses mi istud novicium quod placere ais. Ego vero te vel invitum istic lego; et quidem hac re una vivo et resto.[7]

Materiam cruentam misisti mihi. Necdum[8] legi Coelianum excerptum quod misisti, nec legam prius quam sensus ipse venatus fuero. Sed me Caesaris oratio uncis unguibus adtinet. Nunc denique sentio quantum operis sit ternos vel quinos versus tornare,[9] et aliquid diu scribere. Vale, spiritus meus. Ego

---

[1] This letter is copied twice in the Codex, after iii. 8, Vat. and after *Epist. Graecae* 6, Ambr., possibly, as there are so many variations, from different exemplars.

[2] *qua* Vat.   [3] Vat. omits *quod* and reads *placeant.*

[4] Ambr. *concastigabas.*   [5] Ambr. *quid.*   [6] Ambr. *amas.*

[7] Ambr. has (says Naber) *una · egresu ·* (? *adquiesco*).

[8] Ambr. omits *dum.*   [9] Vat. *etornare.*

M. CORNELIUS FRONTO

MARCUS AURELIUS TO FRONTO

? 139 A.D.

HAIL my best of masters.

If any sleep comes back to you after the wakeful nights of which you complain, I beseech you write to me and, above all, I beseech you take care of your health. Then hide somewhere and bury that "axe of Tenedos,"[1] which you hold over us, and do not, whatever you do, give up your intention of pleading cases, or along with yours let all lips be dumb.

You say that you have composed something in Greek[2] which pleases you more than almost anything you have written. Are you not he who lately gave me such a castigation for writing in Greek? However, I must now, more than ever, write in Greek. Do you ask *why*? I wish to make trial whether what I have not learnt may not more readily come to my aid, since what I have learnt leaves me in the lurch. But, an you really loved me, you would have sent me that new piece you are so pleased with. However, I read you here in spite of yourself and indeed that alone is my life and stay.

It is a sanguinary theme you have sent me. I have not yet read the extract from Coelius which you sent, nor shall I read it until I, on my part, have hunted up my wits. But my Caesar-speech[3] grips me with its hooked talons. Now, if never before, I find what a task it is to round and shape[4] three or five lines and to take time over writing. Farewell, breath of my life. Should I not burn with

---

[1] A proverb for unflinching justice or determination.

[2] The *Discourse on Love* which follows.

[3] The speech of thanks to Pius in the Senate for being given the title of Caesar in the year 139 is probably meant.

[4] *cp.* Hor. *Ars Poet.* 441.

non ardeam tuo amore qui mihi hoc[1] scripseris!
Quid faciam? Non possum insistere. At mihi

anno | priore datum fuit hoc eodem loco eodemque
tempore matris desiderio peruri. Id desiderium hoc

anno tu mihi accendis. | Salutat te Domina mea.

Epist. Graecae, 8 (Naber, p. 255).

<Ἐρωτικὸς λόγος>

1. | Ὦ φίλε παῖ, τρίτον δή σοι τοῦτο περὶ τῶν αὐτῶν
ἐπιστέλλω, τὸ μὲν πρῶτον διὰ Λυσίου τοῦ Κεφάλου,
δεύτερον δὲ διὰ Πλάτωνος τοῦ σοφοῦ, τὸ δὲ δὴ τρίτον διὰ
τοῦδε τοῦ ξένου ἀνδρός, τὴν μὲν φωνὴν ὀλίγου δεῖν
βαρβάρου, τὴν δὲ γνώμην, ὡς ἐγῷμαι, οὐ πάνυ ἀξυνέτου.
γράφω δὲ νῦν οὐδέν τι τῶν πρότερον γεγραμμένων ἐφαπτ-
όμενος, μηδὲ ἀμελήσῃς τοῦ λόγου ὡς παλιλλογοῦντος.
εἰ δέ σοι δόξει τῶν προτέρων διὰ Λυσίου καὶ Πλάτωνος
ἐπεσταλμένων πλείω τάδε εἶναι, ἔστω σοι τεκμήριον ὡς
εὔλογα ἀξιῶ, ὅτι οὐκ ἀπορῶ λόγων. προσέχοις δ' ἂν τὸν
νοῦν, εἰ καινά τε ἅμα καὶ δίκαια λέγω.

2. Ἔοικας, ὦ παῖ, πρὸ τοῦ λό, ου παντὸς βούλεσθαι
μαθεῖν, τί δήποτέ γε μὴ ἐρῶν ἐγὼ μετὰ τοσαύτης σπουδῆς

[1] Ambr. *huc*.

---

[1] Possibly Lorium, twelve miles from Rome, where Pius
had a villa.

[2] If the preceding sentence can be taken to imply that his
mother Lucilla was away, this must refer to Faustina the
elder, wife of Pius.

love of you, who have written to me as you have!
What shall I do? I cannot refrain. Last year it
befell me in this very place,[1] and at this very time,
to be consumed with a passionate longing for my
mother. This year you inflame that my longing.
My Lady[2] greets you.

FRONTO TO MARCUS AURELIUS AS CAESAR

A Discourse on Love[3]　? 139 A.D.

1. This is the third letter, beloved Boy, that I am
sending you on the same theme, the first by the
hand of Lysias, the son of Kephalus, the second of
Plato, the philosopher,[4] and the third indeed by
the hand of this foreigner, in speech little short
of a barbarian, but as regards judgment, as I think,
not wholly wanting in sagacity. And I write now
without trenching at all upon those previous writings,
and so do not you disregard the discourse as saying
what has been already said. But if the present
treatise seem to you to be longer than those which
were previously sent through Lysias and Plato, let
this be a proof to you that I can claim in fair words
to be at no loss for words. But you must consider
now whether my words are no less true than new.

2. No doubt, O Boy, you will wish to know at the
very beginning of my discourse how it is that I, who
am not in love, long with such eagerness for the

[3] This is the piece referred to in the previous letter.
[4] He is alluding to the speeches of Lysias and Socrates in
Plato's *Phaedrus*. Philostratus (*Ep.* 6) sums up the opinions
expressed in them thus: τὸ μὲν μὴ ἐρῶντι χαρίζεσθαι, Λυσίου
δόξα· τῷ δὲ ἐρῶντι, δοκεῖ Πλάτωνι.

γλίχομαι τυχεῖν ὦνπερ οἱ ἐρῶντες. τοῦτο δή σοι φράσω
πρῶτον ὅπως τε ἔχει. οὐ μὰ Δία πέφυκεν ὁρᾶν ὀξύτερον
οὑτοσὶ ὁ πάνυ ἐραστὴς ἐμοῦ τοῦ μὴ ἐρῶντος, ἀλλ᾽ ἔγωγε
τοῦ σοῦ κάλλους αἰσθ<άν>ομαι οὐδενὸς ἧττον τῶν ἄλλων·
δυναίμην δ᾽ ἂν εἰπεῖν ὅτι τούτου καὶ πολὺ ἀκριβέστερον.
ὅπερ δὲ ἐπὶ τῶν πυρεττόντων καὶ τῶν εὖ μάλα ἐν παλ-
αίστρᾳ γυμνασαμένων ὁρῶμεν, οὐκ ἐξ ὁμοίας αἰτίας
ταὐτὸν συμβαίνειν. διψῶσιν μὲν γάρ, ὁ μὲν ὑπὸ νόσου,
ὁ δὲ ὑπὸ γυμνασιῶν· τοιάνδε τινὰ κἀμοὶ καμεῖν [1] <νόσον
ὑπ᾽ ἔρωτος συμβεβήκει> . . . . [2]

Ambr. 70 . . . . | . . . λειτον τε ἅμα καὶ ὄλισθον.

3. ᾽Αλλ᾽ οὐκ ἔμοιγε ἐπ᾽ ὀλέθρῳ πρόσει, οὐδὲ ἐπὶ
βλάβῃ τινὶ ὁμιλήσεις, ἀλλ᾽ ἐπὶ παντὶ ἀγαθῷ. καὶ
ὠφελοῦνται γὰρ καὶ διασῴζονται οἱ καλοὶ ὑπὸ τῶν μὴ
ἐρώντων μᾶλλον, ὥσπερ τὰ φυτὰ ὑπὸ τῶν ὑδάτων. οὐ
γὰρ ἐρῶσιν οὔτε πηγαὶ οὔτε ποταμοὶ τῶν φυτῶν, ἀλλὰ
παριόντες οὕτω δὴ καὶ παραρρέοντες ἀνθεῖν αὐτὰ καὶ
θάλλειν παρεσκεύασαν. χρήματα δὴ τὰ μὲν ὑπ᾽ ἐμοῦ
διδόμενα δικαίως ἂν καλοίης δῶρα, τὰ δὲ ὑπ᾽ ἐκείνου
λύτρα. μάντεων δὲ παῖδές φασιν καὶ τοῖς θεοῖς ἡδίους
εἶναι τῶν θυσιῶν τὰς χαριστηρίους ἢ τὰς μειλιχίους· ὧν
τὰς μὲν οἱ εὐτυχοῦντες ἐπὶ φυλακῇ τε καὶ κτήσει τῶν
ἀγαθῶν, τὰς δὲ οἱ κακῶς πράττοντες ἐπὶ ἀποτροπῇ τῶν
δεινῶν θύουσιν. τάδε μὲν περὶ τῶν συμφερόντων καὶ
τῶν σοί τε κἀκείνῳ ὠφελίμων εἰρήσθω.

4. Εἰ δὲ τοῦτο δίκαιός ἐστιν τυχεῖν τῆς παρὰ σοῦ
βοηθείας . . . . ἠρείσω σὺ τοῦτο . . . . αὐτῷ τὸν ἔρωτα
ἐτεκτήνω καὶ ἐμηχανήσω τὰς Θεττα<λὰς ἐπῳδάς> . . . .
ἀναίτιος . . . . τινος διὰ τὴν αὐτῷ κατάκο<ρον ἐπιθυμ-
Ambr. 69 ίαν> . . . . | πλὴν εἰ μή τι ὀφθεὶς ἠδίκηκας.[3]

[1] The Codex is said to have καμοι και καμοι. The last three
words are added by Dobson.

[2] At least two pages are lost.

[3] This mutilated passage covers eleven lines (Mai) or four-
teen lines (du Rieu) of the Codex.

very same things as lovers. I will tell you, therefore, first of all how this is. He who is ever so much a lover is, by heaven, gifted with no keener sight than I who am no lover, but *I* can discern your beauty as well as anyone else, aye, far more accurately, I might say, even than your lover. But, just as we see in the case of fever patients, and those who have taken right good exercise in the gymnasium, the same result proceeds from different causes. They are both thirsty, the one from his malady, the other from his exercise. It has been my lot also to suffer some such malady from love . . . .

3. But me you shall not come near to your ruin, nor associate with me to any detriment, but to your every advantage. For it is rather by non-lovers that beautiful youths are benefited and preserved, just as plants are by waters. For neither fountains nor rivers are in love with plants, but by going near them and flowing past them they make them bloom and thrive. Money given by me you would be right in calling a gift, but given by a lover a quittance. And the children of prophets say that to Gods also is the thank-offering among sacrifices more acceptable than the sin-offering, for the one is offered by the prosperous for the preservation and possession of their goods, the other by the wretched for the averting of ills. Let this suffice to be said on what is expedient and beneficial both for you and for him.

4. But if it is right that he should receive aid from you . . . . you set this on a firm basis . . . . you framed this love for him and devised Thessalian love-charms . . . . owing to his insatiable desire . . . . unless you have manifestly done wrong.

5. Μὴ ἀγνοεῖ δὲ καὶ ἀδικηθεὶς αὐτὸς καὶ ὑβριζόμενος οὐ μετρίαν ἤδη ταύτην ὕβριν, τὸ ἅπαντας εἰδέναι τε καὶ φανερῶς οὕτως διαλέγεσθαι, ὅτι σου εἴη ὅδε ἐραστής· φθάνεις δὲ καὶ πρίν τι τῶν τοιῶνδε πρᾶξαι τοὔνομα τῆς πράξεως ὑπομένων. καλοῦσί γ᾽ οὖν σε οἱ πλεῖστοι τῶν πολιτῶν τὸν τοῦδε ἐρώμενον· ἐγὼ δέ σοι διαφυλάξω τοὔνομα καθαρὸν καὶ ἀνύβριστον. καλὸς γάρ, οὐχὶ ὁ ἐρώμενος, τό γε κατ᾽ ἐμὲ ὀνομασθήσει. εἰ δὲ δὴ τούτῳ ὡς δικαίῳ τινὶ χρήσεται, ὅτι μᾶλλον ἐπιθυμεῖ, ἴστω ὅτι οὐκ ἐπιθυμεῖ μᾶλλον ἀλλὰ ἰταμώτερον. τὰς δὲ μυίας καὶ τὰς ἐμπίδας μάλιστα ἀποσοβοῦμεν καὶ ἀπωθούμεθα, ὅτι ἀναιδέστατα καὶ ἰταμώτατα ἐπιπέτονται. τοῦτο μὲν οὖν καὶ θηρία ἐπίσταται φεύγειν μάλιστα πάντων τοὺς κυνηγέτας, καὶ τὰ πτηνὰ τοὺς θηρευτάς. καὶ πάντα δὴ τὰ ζῷα τούτους μάλιστα ἐκτρέπεται τοὺς μάλιστα ἐνεδρεύοντας καὶ διώκοντας.

6. Εἰ δέ τις οἴεται ἐνδοξότερον καὶ ἐντιμότερον εἶναι τὸ κάλλος διὰ τοὺς ἐραστάς, τοῦ παντὸς διαμαρτάνει. κινδυνεύετε μὲν γὰρ οἱ καλοὶ περὶ τοῦ κάλλους τῆς ἐς τοὺς ἀκούοντας πίστεως διὰ τοὺς ἐρῶντας <διαμαρτάνειν>,[1] δι᾽ ἡμᾶς δὲ τοὺς ἄλλους βεβαιοτέραν τὴν δόξαν κέκτησθε. εἰ γοῦν τις τῶν μηδέπω σε ἑωρακότων πυνθάνοιτο, ὁποῖός τις εἴ]ης τὴν ὄψιν, ἐμοὶ μὲν ἂν πιστεύσαι ἐπαινοῦντι, μαθὼν ὅτι οὐκ ἐρῶ· τῷ δὲ ἀπιστῆσαι, ὡς οὐκ ἀληθῶς ἀλλ᾽ ἐρωτικῶς ἐπαινοῦντι. ὅσοις μὲν οὖν λώβη τις σώματος καὶ αἶσχος καὶ ἀμορφία πρόσεστιν, εὔξαιντο ἂν εἰκότως ἐραστὰς αὐτοῖς γένεσθαι· οὐ γὰρ ἂν ὑπ᾽ ἄλλων θεραπεύ-

Ambr. 84

[1] Heindorf.

---

[1] As your relations with him imply.

5. And do not ignore the fact that you are yourself wronged and subjected to no small outrage in this, that all men know and speak openly thus of you, that he is your lover; and so, by anticipation and before being guilty of any such things,[1] you abide the imputation of being guilty. Consequently the generality of the citizens call you the man's darling; but I shall keep your name unsullied and inviolate. For as far as I am concerned you shall be called *Beautiful*,[2] not *Darling*. But if the other use this name as his by right because his desire is greater, let him know that his desire is not greater, but more importunate. Yet with flies and gnats the especial reason why we wave them away and brush them off is because they fly at us most impudently and importunately. It is this, indeed, that makes the wild beast shun the hunter most of all, and the bird the fowler. And, in fact, all animals avoid most those that especially lie in wait for and pursue them.

6. But if anyone thinks that beauty is more glorified and honoured by reason of its lovers, he is totally mistaken. For you, the beautiful ones, through your lovers, run the risk of your beauty winning no credence with hearers, but through us non-lovers you establish your reputation for beauty on a sure basis. At any rate, if anyone who had never seen you were to enquire after your personal appearance, he would put faith in my praises, knowing that I am not in love; but he would disbelieve the other as praising not truthfully but lovingly. As many, then, as are maimed or ugly or deformed would naturally pray for lovers to be theirs, for they would find no others

[2] καλός was the recognised tribute to the victorious boy-athlete, and is constantly so used on vases. See also Aristoph. *Vespae*, 199.

οιντο ἢ τῶν κατ᾽ ἐρωτικὴν λύτταν καὶ ἀνάγκην προσιόν-
των· σὺ δὲ ἐν τῷ τοιῷδε κάλλει οὐκ ἔσθ᾽ ὅτι καρπώσει
πλέον ὑπ᾽ ἐρῶ<ν>τος. οὐδὲν γὰρ ἧττον δέονταί σου οἱ
μὴ ἐρῶντες. ἀχρεῖοι δὲ οἱ ἐρασταὶ τοῖς ὄντως καλοῖς
οὐδὲν ἧττον ἢ τοῖς δικαίως ἐπαινουμένοις οἱ κόλακες.
ἀρετὴ δὲ δὴ καὶ δόξα καὶ τιμὴ καὶ κέρδος <καὶ> κόσμος
θαλάττῃ μὲν ναῦται καὶ κυβερνῆται καὶ τριήραρχοι καὶ οἱ
ἔμποροι καὶ οἱ ἄλλως πλέοντες—οὐ μὰ Δία δελφῖνες, οἷς
ἀδύνατον τὸ ζῆν ὅτι μὴ ἐν θαλάττῃ—, καλοῖς[1] δὲ ἡμεῖς οἱ
τηνάλλως ἐπαινοῦντες καὶ ἀσπαζόμενοι, οὐκ ἐρασταί, οἷς
ἀβίωτον ἂν εἴη στερομένοις τῶν παιδικῶν. εὕροις δ᾽ ἂν
σκοπῶν πλείστης ἀδοξίας αἰτίους μὲν ὄντας τοὺς ἐραστάς·
ἀδοξίαν δὲ φεύγειν ἅπαντας μὲν χρὴ τοὺς εὐφρονοῦντας,
μάλιστα δὲ τοὺς νέους, οἷς ἐπὶ μακρότερον ἐγκείσεται τὸ
κακὸν ἐν ἀρχῇ μακροῦ βίου προσπεσόν.

7. Ὥσπερ οὖν ἱερῶν καὶ θυσίας, οὕτω καὶ τοῦ βίου,
Ambr. 83 τοὺς ἀρχομένους εὐλογίας | μάλιστα πρ<έπει ἐπιμελεῖ-
σθαι>[2] . . . . τοῖς τῶν . . . . εἰς ἐσχάτην ἀδοξίαν
ἀ<γόντων> . . . . τούτους δὴ τοὺς χρηστοὺς ἐραστὰς
ἔξον, εἰ καὶ . . . . πέντε καὶ . . . . χρῆμα ἐρασταῖς
. . . .[3] καὶ γὰρ οἱ ἐρῶντες
διὰ τῶν τοιῶνδε φορημάτων οὐκ ἐκείνους τιμῶσιν, ἀλλ᾽
Ambr. 74 αὐτοὶ ἀλα|ζονεύονταί τε καὶ ἐπιδείκνυνται, καὶ ὡς εἰπεῖν
ἐξορχοῦνται τὸν ἔρωτα. συγγράφει δέ, ὥς φασιν, ὁ σὸς
ἐραστὴς ἐρωτικά τινα περὶ σοῦ συγγράμματα, ὡς τούτῳ
δὴ μάλιστά σε δελεάσων καὶ προσαξόμενος καὶ αἱρήσων·

[1] Naber for Cod. κάλλους.
[2] Heindorf.
[3] The greater part of a page is lost.

to court them but those who approach them under
the madness and duress of love; but you, such is
your beauty, cannot reap any greater advantage from
a lover. For non-lovers have need of you no less
than they. And indeed, to those who are really
beautiful, lovers are as useless as flatterers to those
who deserve praise. It is sailors and steersmen and
captains of warships and merchants, and those that
in other ways travel upon it, who give excellence
and glory and honour and gain and ornament to the
sea—not, heaven help us, dolphins that can live only
in the sea: but for beautiful boys it is we who
cherish and praise them disinterestedly, not lovers,
whose life, deprived of their darlings, would be un-
livable. And you will find, if you look into it, that
lovers are the cause of the utmost disgrace. But all
who are right-minded must shun disgrace, the young
most of all, since the evil attaching to them at the
beginning of a long life will rest upon them the
longer.

7. As, then, in the case of sacred rites and sacrifices, so also of life, it behoves above all those who
are entering upon them to have a care for their
good name . . . .
. . . .
. . . . For indeed by such
adornments lovers do them no honour, but are themselves guilty of affectation and display, and, as it were,
dance away the mysteries[1] of love. Your lover,
too, as they say, composes some amatory writings
about you in the hope of enticing you with this bait,
if with no other, and attracting you to himself and

---

[1] *cp.* Lucian, *De Saltat.* 16: τοὺς ἐξαγορεύοντας τὰ μυστήρια
ἐξορχεῖσθαι λέγουσιν οἱ πολλοί.

τὰ δὲ ἔστιν αἴσχη καὶ ὀνείδη καὶ βοή τις ἀκόλαστος ὑπ'
οἴστρου προπεμπομένη, ὁποῖαι θηρίων ἢ βοσκημάτων ὑπὸ
ἔρωτος βρυχωμένων ἢ χρεμετιζόντων ἢ μυκωμένων ἢ
ὠρυομένων. τούτοις ἔοικεν τὰ τῶν ἐρώντων ᾄσματα. εἰ
γοῦν ἐπιτρέψαις σαυτὸν[1] τῷ ἐραστῇ χρῆσθαι ὅπου καὶ
ὅποτε βούλοιτο, οὔτ' ἂν καιρὸν περιμείνας ἐπιτήδειον οὔτε
σχολὴν οὔτε ἐρημίαν, ἀλλὰ θηρίου δίκην ὑπὸ λύττης εὐθύ
σε ἴοιτο[2] ἂν καὶ βαίνειν προθυμοῖτο μηδὲν αἰδούμενος.

8. Τοῦτο ἔτι προσθεὶς καταπαύσω τὸν λόγον, ὅτι πάντα
θεῶν δῶρα καὶ ἔργα, ὅσα ἐς ἀνθρώπων χρείαν τε καὶ
τέρψιν καὶ ὠφέλειαν ἀφῖκται, τὰ μὲν αὐτῶν πάνυ καὶ
πάντη θεῖα, γῆν φημὶ καὶ οὐρανὸν καὶ ἥλιον καὶ θάλατταν,
ὑμνεῖν μὲν καὶ θαυμάζειν πεφύκαμεν, ἐρᾶν δὲ οὔ· καλῶν δέ
τινων φαυλοτέρων καὶ ἀτιμοτέρας μοίρας τετυχηκότων,
τούτων ἤδη φθόνος καὶ ἔρως καὶ ζῆλος καὶ ἵμερος ἅπτεται.
Ambr 73 καὶ οἱ μέν τινες κέρδους ἐρῶσιν, οἱ δὲ ὄψων αὖ, οἱ | δὲ
οἴνου. ἐν δὴ τῷ τοιῷδε ἀριθμῷ καὶ μερίδι καθίσταται τὸ
κάλλος ὑπὸ τῶν ἐρώντων, ὅμοιον κέρδει καὶ ὄψῳ καὶ μέθῃ·
ὑπὸ δὲ ἡμῶν τῶν θαυμαζόντων μέν, μὴ ἐρώντων δέ, ὅμοιον
ἡλίῳ καὶ οὐρανῷ καὶ γῇ καὶ θαλάττῃ· τὰ γὰρ τοιαῦτα
παντὸς ἔρωτος κρείττω καὶ ὑπέρτερα.

9. Ἕν τί σοι φράσω πρὸς τούτοις, ὃ καὶ σὺ πρὸς τοὺς
ἄλλους λέγων παῖδας πιθανὸς εἶναι δόξεις. εἰκὸς δέ σε ἢ
παρὰ μητρὸς ἢ τῶν ἀναθρεψαμένων μὴ ἀνήκοον εἶναι ὅτι
τῶν ἀνθῶν ἐστίν τι ὃ δὴ τοῦ ἡλίου ἐρᾷ καὶ πάσχει τὰ τῶν

---

[1] The Codex has αὐτόν.
[2] Heindorf εὐθὺ σοῦ: Naber ἔχοιτο.

catching you; but such things are a disgrace and an insult and a sort of licentious cry, the outcome of stinging lust, such as those of wild beasts and fed cattle, that from sexual desire bellow or neigh or low or howl. Like to these are the lyrics of lovers. If, therefore, you submit yourself to your lover to enjoy where and when he pleases, awaiting neither time that is fitting nor leisure nor privacy, then, like a beast in the frenzy of desire, will he make straight for you and be eager to " go to it " nothing ashamed.

8. I will add but one thing before I conclude my discourse, that we are formed by nature to praise and admire, but not to love, all the gifts of the Gods and their works that have come for the use and delight and benefit of men—those indeed of them which are wholly and in every way divine, I mean the earth and sky and sun and sea—while in the case of some other beautiful things of less worth, and formed to fulfil a less comely part, these at once are the subject of envy and love and emulation and desire. And some are in love with wealth, others again with rich viands, and others with wine. In the number and category of such is beauty reckoned by lovers, like wealth and viands and strong drink; but by us, who admire, indeed, but love not, like sun and sky and earth and sea, for such things are too good for any love and beyond its reach.

9. One thing more will I tell you, and if you will pass it on to all other boys, your words will seem convincing. Very likely you have heard from your mother, or from those who brought you up, that among flowers there is one that is indeed in love with the sun and undergoes the fate of lovers, lifting

ἐρώντων, ἀνατέλλοντος ἐπαιρόμενον καὶ πορευομένου
καταστρεφόμενον, δύνοντος δὲ περιτρεπόμενον· ἀλλ' οὐδέν
γε πλέον ἀπολαύει,[1] οὐδὲ εὐμενεστέρου πειρᾶται διὰ τὸν
ἔρωτα τοῦ ἡλίου. ἀτιμότατον γοῦν ἐστὶν φυτῶν ·καὶ
ἀνθῶν οὔτε εἰς ἑορταζόντων θαλίας οὔτε στεφάνους θεῶν ἢ
ἀνθρώπων παραλαμβανόμενον. ἔοικας, ὦ παῖ, τὸ ἄνθος
τοῦτο ἰδεῖν ἐθέλειν, ἀλλ' ἔγωγέ σοι ἐπιδείξω, <εἰ ἔξω> τεί-
χους[2] πρὸς τὸν Ἰλισὸν ἅμα ἄμφω βαδίσαιμεν . . . .

Epist. Graecae, 7 (Naber, p. 253).

Ambr. 136
and Vat. 121
| HAVE mi magister optime.

1. Age perge, quantum libet, comminare et
argumentorum globis criminare : numquam tu tamen
erasten tuum, me dico, depuleris. Nec ego minus
amare me Frontonem praedicabo, minusque amabo,
quod tu tam variis tamque vehementibus sententiis
adprobaris minus amantibus magis opitulandum ac
largiendum esse. Ego hercule te ita amore depereo,
neque deterreor isto tuo dogmate, ac si magis eris
aliis non amantibus properus et promptus, ego tamen
vivus salvusque amabo.

Ceterum quod ad sensuum densitatem, quod ad
inventiones[3] argutiarum, quod ad aemulationis tuae
felicitatem adtinet, nolo quidem[4] dicere <te> multo
placentes illos sibi et provocantes Atticos anteven-

---

[1] Cod. ἀπόλλυσι.
[2] Naber reads εἰ εὐθὺς πρὸς for Cod. τιχους.

itself up when the sun rises, following his motions
as he runs his course, and when he sets, turning itself
about; but it takes no advantage thereby, nor yet,
for all its love for the sun, does it find him the
kinder.   Least esteemed, at any rate, of plants and
flowers, it is utilized neither for festal banquets nor
for garlands of Gods or men.   Maybe, O Boy, you
would like to see this flower.[1]   Well, I will shew it
you if we go for a walk outside the city walls as far
as the Ilissus . . . .

Marcus Aurelius to Fronto

Hail, my best of masters.   ? 139 A.D.

1. Go on, threaten as much as you please and
attack me with hosts of arguments, yet shall you
never drive your lover, I mean me, away; nor shall
I the less assert that I love Fronto, or love him the
less, because you prove with reasons so various and
so vehement that those who are less in love must be
more helped and indulged.   So passionately, by
heaven, am I in love with you, nor am I frightened off
by the law you lay down, and even if you shew yourself
more forward and facile to others, who are non-lovers,
yet will I love you while I have life and health.

For the rest, having regard to the close packing
of ideas, the inventive subtilties, and the felicity of
your championship of your cause, I hardly like, indeed, to say that you have far outstripped those
Atticists, so self-satisfied and challenging, and yet I

[1] Possibly the sunflower (*girasole*), or marigold ; see Shaks.
Sonnets, xxv. 6

---

[3] Cod. *inventionis*, which Buttm. keeps, and reads *argutiam*,
cp. p. 156.   [4] For Cod. *quicquam*.

isse, ac tamen nequeo quin dicam. Amo enim, et
hoc denique amantibus vere tribuendum esse censeo,
quod victoriis τῶν ἐρωμένων magis gauderent. Vici-
mus igitur, vicimus, inquam. Num . . . .[1] | prae-
stabilius[2] sub laquearibus quam sub platanis, intra
pomerium quam extra murum, sine deliciis quam
ipsa proxime adsistente habitanteve Lai disputari?
Nequeo reteiaclari utra re magis caveam, quod de
Lai[3] ista orator saeculi huius dogma<m> tulerit an
quod magister meus de Platone.

2. Illud equidem non temere adiuravero: Si quis
iste revera Phaeder fuit, si umquam is a Socrate
afuit, non magis Socratem Phaedri desiderio quam
me per istos dies, dies dico? menses inquam, tui ad-
spectus cupidine arsisse? . . . .[4] amet, nisi confestim
tuo amore corripitur. Vale mihi maxima res sub
caelo, gloria mea. Sufficit talem magistrum habuisse.
Domina mea mater te salutat.

Ad M. Caes. iii. 7 (Naber, p. 44).

| MAGISTRO meo.

Quom tu quiescis et quod commodum valetudini
sit tu facis, tum me recreas.[5] Et libenter et otiose
age. Sentio ergo: recte fecisti, quod brachio cur-

---

[1] A loss of two and a half lines.
[2] For Hauler's reconstruction of the following passage,
see *Wien. Stud.* 34, pt. i. pp. 253–259 (1912). He reads
delictis, for which J. T. Sheppard suggested *deliciis*. The
words *habitanteve Lai* are marked by Hauler as doubtful.

cannot but say so. For I am in love and this, if
nothing else, ought, I think, verily to be allowed to
lovers, that they should have greater joy in the
triumph of their loved ones. Ours, then, is the
triumph, ours, I say. Is it . . . . preferable to talk
philosophy under ceilings rather than under plane-
trees, within the city bounds than without its walls,
scorning delights than with Lais herself sitting at
our side or sharing our home? Nor can I "make a
cast" which to beware of more, the law which an
orator[1] of our time has laid down about this Lais,
or my master's dictum about Plato.

2. This I can without rashness affirm : if that
Phaedrus of yours ever really existed, if he was ever
away from Socrates, Socrates never felt for Phaedrus
a more passionate longing than I for the sight of you
all these days : days do I say? months I mean . . . .
unless he is straightway seized with love of you.
Farewell, my greatest treasure beneath the sky, my
glory. It is enough to have had such a master. My
Lady mother sends you greeting.

Marcus Aurelius to Fronto

Probably from Naples 139 A.D.

To my Master.

When *you* rest and when *you* do what is good
for your health, then am I, too, the better for it.
Humour yourself and be lazy. My verdict, then, is :
you have acted rightly in taking pains to cure your

---

[1] *Orator* and *master* seem both to refer to Fronto. We do
not know what he may have said about Lais.

---

[3] Sheppard suggests *Lysia*.   [4] One line missing.
[5] Brakman reads the Codex as *recreav<i>*.

ando operam dedisti. Ego quoque hodie a septima
in lectulo nonnihil egi, nam εἰκόνας decem ferme
expedivi. <In> nona te socium et optionem mihi
sumo, nam minus secunda fuit in persequendo mihi.
Est autem quod in insula Aenaria intus lacus est: in

eo lacu alia | insula est, et ea quoque inhabitatur.
Ἔνθε<νδε τι>νὰ εἰκόνα ποιοῦμεν. Vale, dulcissime
anima. Domina mea te salutat.

Ad M. Caes. iii. 8 (Naber, p. 45).

DOMINO meo.

1. Imaginem quam te quaerere ais, meque tibi
socium ad quaerendum et optionem sumis, num
moleste feres si in tuo atque in tui patris sinu id
fictum quaeram? Ut insula[1] in mari Ionio sive
Tyrrhenico sive vero potius in Hadriatico mari, seu
quod aliud est mare, eius nomen maris addito—
igitur ut illa in mari insula [Aenaria] fluctus mari-
timos ipsa accipit atque propulsat, omnemque vim
classium praedonum beluarum procellarum ipsa per-
petitur, intus autem in lacu aliam insulam protegit
ab omnibus periculis ac difficultatibus tutam, omnium
vero deliciarum voluptatumque participem—namque
illa intus in lacu insula aeque undis alluitur, auras
salubres aeque recipit, habitatur aeque, mare aeque

---

[1] Kluss. for Cod. *illa.* It is impossible that Fronto should
not have known where Aenaria was.

---

[1] Referring to a letter not preserved.
[2] Off Naples. It is mentioned in connection with Marius
by Plutarch.

arm.[1] I, too, have done something to-day since one
o'clock on my couch, for I have been successful with
nearly all the ten similes; in the ninth I call you
in as my ally and adjutant, for it did not respond so
readily to my efforts in dealing with it. It is the
one of the inland lake in the island Aenaria;[2] in
that lake there is another island, it, too, inhabited.
From this we draw a certain simile. Farewell,
sweetest of souls. My Lady[3] greets you.

FRONTO TO MARCUS AURELIUS AS CAESAR

To my Lord.   ? 139 A.D.

1. As to the simile, which you say you are
puzzling over and for which you call me in as your
ally and adjutant in finding the clue, you will not
take it amiss, will you, if I look for the clue
to that fancy within your breast and your father's[4]
breast? Just as the island lies in the Ionian or
Tyrrhenian sea, or, maybe, rather in the Adriatic, or,
if it be some other sea, give it its right name—as
then that sea-girt island (Aenaria) itself receives and
repels the ocean waves, and itself bears the whole
brunt of attack from fleets, pirates, sea-monsters
and storms, yet in a lake within protects another
island safely from all dangers and difficulties, while
that other nevertheless shares in all its delights
and pleasures (for that island in the inland lake is,
like the other, washed by the waters, like it catches
the health-giving breezes, like it is inhabited, like it

---

[3] Probably the mother of Marcus, to whom Fronto sends a
greeting in the next letter.

[4] His adopted father, the emperor Antoninus Pius.

prospectat—item pater tuus imperii Romani molestias ac difficultates ipse perpetitur, te tutum[1] intus in tranquillo sinu suo socium dignitatis gloriae bonorumque[2] omnium participem tutatur. Igitur hac imagine Vat. 122 multimodis uti potes ubi patri | tuo gratias ages, in qua oratione locupletissimus et copiosissimus te esse oportet. Nihil est enim quod tu aut honestius aut verius aut libentius in omni vita tua dicas quam quod ad ornandas patris tui laudes pertinebit. Postea ego quamcumque εἰκόνα huic[3] addidero, non aeque placebit tibi, ut haec quae ad patrem tuum pertinet: tam hoc scio quam tu novisti. Quam ob rem ipse aliam εἰκόνα nullam adiciam, sed rationem qua tute quaeras ostendam. Tu quas εἰκόνας in eandem rem demonstrata ratione quaesiveris et inveneris, mittito mihi ut, si fuerint scitae atque concinnae, gaudeam et amem te.[4]

2. Iam primum illud scis εἰκόνα ei rei adsumi ut aut ornet quid aut deturpet aut aequiparet aut deminuat aut ampliet aut ex minus credibili credibile efficiat. Ubi nihil eorum usus erit, locus εἰκόνος non erit. Postea ubi re⟨i⟩ propositae imaginem scribes, ut, si pingeres, insignia animadverteres eius rei cuius imaginem pingeres, item in scribendo facies. Insignia autem cuiusque rei multis modis eliges, τὰ

---

[1] *tutum . . . tutatur* : query *totum* or *autem*.

[2] Another reading given in the margin of Cod. is *honorum*.

[3] Cod. has *huc*.

[4] These three words occur as an interlinear correction in the Codex after *ostendam*. Ehrenthal suggested their transposition.

looks out on the sea), so your father bears on his own shoulders the troubles and difficulties of the Roman empire while you he safeguards safely in his own tranquil breast, the partner in his rank and glory and in all that is his. Accordingly you can use this simile in a variety of ways, when you return thanks to your father,[1] on which occasion you should be most full and copious. For there is nothing that you can say in all your life with more honour or more truth or more liking than that which concerns the setting forth of your father's praises.[2] Whatever simile I may subsequently suggest will not please you so much as this one which concerns your father. I know this as well as you feel it. Consequently I will not myself give you any other simile, but will shew you the method of finding them out for yourself. You must send me any similes you search out and find by the method shewn you for that purpose, that if they prove neat and apt I may rejoice and love you.

2. Now, in the first place, you are aware that a simile is used for the purpose of setting off a thing or discrediting it, or comparing, or depreciating, or amplifying it, or of making credible what is scarcely credible. Where nothing of the kind is required, there will be no room for a simile. Hereafter when you compose a simile for a subject in hand, just as, if you were a painter, you would notice the characteristics of the object you were painting, so must you do in writing. Now, the characteristics of a thing you will pick out from many points of view,

[1] For the honour of being made "Caesar" in 139. It could no doubt refer to the Consulship in 145, or the *Tribunicia Potestas* in 147; but these dates are too late.

[2] Marcus painted this portrait with a loving hand in his *Thoughts*, i. 6, vi. 30.

Vat. 121

ὁμογενῆ, τὰ ὁμοειδῆ, τὰ ὅλα, τὰ μέρη, τὰ ἴδια, τὰ διάφορα, τὰ ἀντικείμενα, τὰ ἑπόμενα καὶ | παρακολουθοῦντα, τὰ ὀνόματα, τὰ συμβεβηκότα, τὰ στοιχεῖα, et fere omnia ex quibus argumenta sumuntur : de quibus plerumque audisti, quom Θεοδώρου locos ἐπιχειρημάτων tractaremus.   Eorum si quid memoriae tuae elapsum est, non inutile erit eadem nos retractare, ubi[1] tempus aderit.   In hac εἰκόνε,[2] quam de patre tuo teque depinxi, ἔν τι τῶν συμβεβηκότων ἔλαβον, τὸ ὁμοῖον τῆς ἀσφαλείας καὶ τῆς ἀπολαύσεως.   Nunc tu per hasce vias ac semitas, quas supra ostendi, quaeres quonam modo Aenariam commodissime venias.

3. Mihi dolor cubiti haud multum sedatus est. Vale, Domine, cum eximio ingenio.   Dominae meae matri tuae dic salutem.   Τὴν δὲ ὅλην τῶν εἰκόνων τέχνην alias diligentius et subtilius persequemur : nunc capita rerum adtigi.[3]

(Naber, p. 211.)

LAUDES FUMI ET PULVERIS

Ambr. 240,
middle of
col. 2

| CAESARI suo FRONTO.

1. Plerique legentium forsan rem de titulo contemnant, nihil <enim> serium potuisse fieri de fumo et pulvere : tu pro tuo excellenti ingenio profecto existimabis lusa sit opera[4] ista an locata.

---

[1] Schopen for Cod. *detractare tibi*.   [2] So Cod.
[3] This is followed in the Cod. Vat. by the letter, given above, which is found in Cod. Ambr. 136 as *Epist. Graec.* 6.
[4] Plautine.

the likenesses of kind, the likenesses of form, the whole, the parts, the individual traits, the differences, the contraries, the consequences and the resultants, the names, the accidents, the elements, and generally everything from which arguments are drawn, the point in fact so often dwelt upon when we were dealing with the commonplaces of the arguments of Theodorus.[1] If any of them have slipped your memory, it will not be amiss for us to go over them afresh when time serves. In this simile, which I have sketched out about your father and you, I have taken one of the accidentals of the subject, the identity of the safety and the enjoyment. Now it remains for you, by those ways and paths which I have pointed out above, to discover how you may most conveniently come at your Aenaria.

3. The pain in my elbow is not much better. Farewell, my Lord, with your rare abilities. Give my greeting to my Lady your mother. On another occasion we will follow out,[2] with more care and exactness, the whole art of simile-making; now I have only touched upon the heads of it.

Eulogy of Smoke and Dust

Fronto to his own Caesar.   ? 139 A.D.

1. The majority of readers may perhaps from the heading despise the subject, on the ground that nothing serious could be made of smoke and dust. You, with your excellent abilities, will soon see whether my labour is lost or well laid out.

---

[1] There were two rhetoricians of this name, one of Byzantium, the other of Gadara. The latter is probably meant.

[2] We have more on the subject in a letter to Marcus's mother (*Epist. Graec.* 1).

2. Sed res poscere videtur de ratione scribendi
pauca praefari, quod nullum huiuscemodi scriptum
Romana lingua extat satis nobile, nisi quod poetae in
comoediis vel atellanis adtigerunt. Qui se eiusmodi
rebus scribendis exercebit, crebras sententias conquiret, easque dense conlocabit et subtiliter coniung-
et, neque verba multa geminata supervacanea | in-
ferciet; tum omnem sententiam breviter et scite
concludet. Aliter in orationibus iudiciariis, ubi sedulo
curamus ut pleraeque sententiae durius interdum et
incautius [1] finiantur. Sed contra istic laborandum
est, ne quid inconcinnum et hiulcum relinquatur,
quin omnia ut in tenui veste oris detexta et revi-
mentis sint cincta. Postremo, ut novissimos in epi-
grammatis versus habere oportet aliquid luminis,
sententia clavo aliquo [2] vel fibula terminanda est.

3. In primis autem sectanda est suavitas. Namque hoc genus orationis non capitis defendendi nec
suadendae legis nec exercitus hortandi nec inflam-
mandae contionis scribitur, sed facetiarum et voluptatis.[3] Ubique vero ut de re ampla et magnifica
loquendum, parvaeque res magnis adsimilandae com-
parandaeque. Summa denique in hoc genere orationis virtus est adseveratio. Fabulae deum vel
heroum tempestive inserendae; item versus congru-

Ambr. 248

---

[1] For this *incomtius* and *incultius* have been suggested.
For the sense *cp.* Seneca, *Ep.* 114, *ad med.*

[2] Fröhner for Cod. *clavi aliqua.*

[3] Novák supplies *causa* with these genitives.

---

[1] The best of such *nugalia* that we possess is Lucian's on
the Fly. Dio wrote one on the Gnat, and even Plato on

2. But the subject seems to require a little to be said first on the method of composition, for no writing of this kind of sufficient note exists in the Roman tongue,[1] except some attempts by poets in comedies or Atellane farces. Anyone who practises this kind of composition will choose out an abundance of thoughts and pack them closely and cleverly interweave them, but will not stuff in superfluously many duplicate words, nor forget to round off every sentence concisely and skilfully. It is different with forensic speeches, where we take especial care that many sentences shall end now and again somewhat roughly and clumsily. But here, on the contrary, pains must be taken that there should be nothing left uncouth and disconnected, but that everything, as in a fine robe, should be woven with borders and trimmed with edgings. Finally, as the last lines in an epigram ought to have some sparkle, so the sentence should be closed with some sort of fastening or brooch.

3. But the chief thing to be aimed at is to please. For this kind of discourse is not meant as a speech for the defence in a criminal trial, nor to carry a law, nor to hearten an army, nor to impassion the multitude, but for pleasantry and amusement. The topic, however, must everywhere be treated as if it were an important and splendid one, and trifling things must be likened and compared to great ones. Finally, the highest merit in this kind of discourse is an attitude of seriousness. Tales of Gods or men must be brought in where appropriate; so, too, per-

Fever. There were others on Gout, Blindness, Deafness, and Baldness. *cp.* also Augustine, *De Vera Relig.* lxxvii., who says that some had written the praises of ashes and dung *verissime atque uberrime.*

entes et proverbia accommodata et non inficete con-
ficta mendacia, dum id mendacium argumento aliquo
lepido iuvetur.

4. Cum primis autem difficile est argumenta ita
disponere ut sit ordo eorum rite connexus. Quod

Ambr. 247 ille | Plato Lysiam culpat in Phaedro, sententiarum
ordinem ab eo ita temere permixtum, ut sine ullo
detrimento prima in novissimum locum transferantur,
et novissima in primum, eam culpam ita devitabimus,
si divisa generatim argumenta nectemus, non sparsa
nec sine discrimine aggerata, ut ea quae per saturam
feruntur, sed ut praecedens sententia in sequentem
laciniam aliquam porrigat et oram praetendat; ubi
prior sit finita sententia, inde ut sequens ordiatur;
ita enim transgredi potius videmur quam transilire.

5. Verum hi non . . . . Variatio vel cum detrimento aliquo gratior est in oratione quam recta
continuatio[1] . . . . Iocularia austere, fortia h<ilari>-

Ambr. 254 ter dicenda[2] . . . . . . | . . modo dulce illud in-
corruptum sit et pudicum, Tusculanum et Ionicum,
id est Catonis et Herodoti.[3] . . . . In omni re
facilius est rationem dicendi nosse quam vim agendi

Ambr. 253 obtinere[4] . . . . re sic est qui | sicuti bene velle et
bene precari, quae res voce animoque sine opibus
perpetrantur.[5]

6. Igitur ut quisque se benignissimum praestabit,
ita is plurimos laudabit, nec tantum eos, quos alii
quoque laudibus ante decoraverint, verum conquiret

---

[1] From the margin of the Codex. [2] *Ibid.* [3] *Ibid.* [4] *Ibid.*
[5] This sentence is repeated in the margin of the Codex,
but with *opere* for *opibus.* Should not *sicut* be *sciat?*

tinent verses and proverbs that are applicable, and ingenious fictions, provided that the fiction is helped out by some witty reasoning.

4. One of the chief difficulties, however, is so to marshal our materials that their order may rest on logical connexion. The fault for which Plato blames Lysias in the Phaedrus, that he has mingled his thoughts in such careless confusion that the first could change places with the last and the last with the first without any loss, is one which we can only escape if we arrange our arguments in classes, and so concatenate them, not in a scattered way and indiscriminately piled together like a dish of mixed ingredients, but so that the preceding thought in some sort overlaps the subsequent one and dovetails into it; that the second thought may begin where the first left off; for so we seem to step rather than jump from one to the other.

5. But these do not . . . . Variety even with some sacrifice is more welcome in the discourse than a correct continuity . . . . Merry things must be severely said, brave things with a smile . . . . only let that sweetness be untainted and chaste, of Tusculan and Ionian strain, that is in the style of Cato or Herodotus . . . . In every case it is easier to master the method of speaking than to possess the power of performing . . . . to wish (others) well and to pray for their welfare, things which are compassed by voice and mind without aid.

6. Accordingly the more generously disposed a man shews himself, the more persons will he praise, nor those only whom others before him decked with praises ; but he will choose out Gods and men that

deos et homines a ceterorum laudibus relictissimos, ibique signum benignitatis expromet ; ut agricola agrum intactum si conserat, laboriosus est ; sacerdos si apud fanum desertum et avium sacrificet, religiosus est.

7. Laudabo igitur deos infrequentes quidem a laudibus, verum in usu cultuque humano frequentissimos, *Fumum* et *Pulverem*, sine quis neque asae [1] neque foci nec viae, quod volgo aiunt, nec semitae usurpantur. Quodsi quis hoc ambigit, habendusne sit Fumus in numero deorum, cogitet Ventos quoque in deum numero haberi, quaeque sunt fumo simillimae, Nebulas Nubesque putari deas et in caelo conspici et, ut poetae ferunt, amiciri deos nubibus, et Iovi Iunonique cubantibus nubem ab arbitris obstitisse, quod<que> unice [2] divinae naturae proprium est, nec fumum manu prehendere nec solem queas, neque vincire neque verberare neque detinere neque, vel minimum rimae si dehiscat,[3] excludere [4]

End of Quaternion (xxxvii. or xxxviii.) . . . .

(Naber, p. 214.)

| LAUDES NEGLEGENTIAE

<CAESARI suo Fronto>.

1. . . . .
Nam qui nimis anxie munia conficiunt parum amic-
Ambr. 242 itiae confidunt [5] . . . . | . . Agitavi laudes

---

[1] An Umbrian form for *ara*.
[2] Alan for Cod. *nunc* ; query *sane*.
[3] Heind. for Cod. *deposcat*. [4] There is a large gap here.
[5] From the margin of the Codex.

44

have been most passed by in the praises of others, and there give proofs of his generous disposition, just as a farmer shews his industry, if he sows a field never before ploughed, and a priest his devotion, if he sacrifices at a desolate and inaccessible shrine.

7. I will therefore praise gods who are indeed not much in evidence in the matter of praises, but are very much in evidence in the experience and life of men, *Smoke* and *Dust*, without whom neither altars, nor hearths, nor highways, as people say, nor paths can be used. But if any cavil at this, whether Smoke can be counted among gods, let him consider that Winds too are held to be gods and though they can scarcely be distinguished from Smoke, Clouds and Mists, are reckoned goddesses and are seen in the sky, and according to the poets gods " are clad in clouds," [1] and a cloud shielded from onlookers Jove and Juno as they couched.[2] Again, and this is a property peculiar to the divine nature, you cannot grasp smoke in the hand any more than sunlight, nor bind nor beat nor keep it in nor, if there be the slightest chink open, shut it out . . . .

EULOGY OF NEGLIGENCE

FRONTO to his own Caesar.   ? 139 A.D.

1. . . . .
For those, who are too anxious in the performance of their duties, rely too little on friendship . . . . . .
. . . . I have taken upon myself to indite the

---

[1] Horace, *Od.* i. 2, 31
[2] Homer, *Il.* xiv. 350.

Neglegentiae conscribere, quas cur nondum etiam
[etiam id] conscripserim, ut res est, id quoque

Ambr.
238, 237

neglego[1] . . . . | . . . . | . . . .
temperantia coercetur. Volgo etiam laudata indulgentia promptam peccatis hominum veniam dare : nisi
delicta facile neglegas,[2] parum clementer indulgeas.

2. Quod autem quis intutam et expositam periculis
neglegentiam putet, mihi omne contra videtur, multo
multoque diligentiam magis periculis obnoxiam esse.
Namque neglegentiae haud quisquam magno opere
insidias locat, existimans etiam sine insidiis semper
et ubique et uti libeat neglegentem hominem in
proclivi fore fallere: adversus diligentes vero et
circumspectos et excubantes[3] opibus fraudes et
captiones et insidiae parantur. Ita ferme neglegentia
contemptu tutatur, diligentia astu oppugnatur. Et
erratis neglegentia venia paratior datur et benefactis
gratior[4] gratia habetur. Nam praeter opinionem
gratum est ceterarum rerum indiligentem bene
facere in tempore haud neglexisse.

3. Iam illud a poetis saeculum aureum memoratum,
si cum animo reputes, intellegas neglegentiae sae-

Ambr.
229

culum fuisse, quom ager neg|lectus fructus uberes
ferret, omniaque utensilia neglegentibus nullo negotio suppeditaret. Hisce argumentis neglegentia
bono genere nata, dis accepta, sapientibus probata,

---

[1] Two pages are lost. [2] Mai for Cod. *intellegas*.
[3] Schopen for Cod. *exultantes*.
[4] Heind. for Cod. *gratiis*.

praises of *Negligence,* and the reason why I have never to this day indited them, that too, as the subject demands, I neglect to give . . . .
. . . . is checked by self-control. Generally too is the mildness praised, which readily pardons the sins of men, but unless you good-naturedly neglect offences, you are not likely to deal over mildly with them.

2. A man may think negligence to be unsafe and exposed to dangers, but my view is clean contrary, that it is diligence which is much much more liable to perils. For there is not one who takes the trouble to lay traps for negligence, judging that even without a trap it would be easy work to take in a negligent man always and everywhere and at pleasure: against the diligent, however, and the wide-awake and those who watch over their wealth, wiles and deceptions and traps are made ready. So general is it for negligence to be safeguarded by contempt, diligence to be assailed by craft. Mistakes too, committed through negligence are more readily pardoned and for kindnesses so done a more gracious gratitude is felt. For that a man in all other respects neglectful should not have neglected to do a kindness in season is from its unexpectedness grateful.

3. Now the famous golden age celebrated by the poets, if you think over it, you will find to have been the age of negligence, when the earth neglected bore rich crops and, without trouble taken, provided all the requisites of life to those who neglected it. These arguments shew that negligence comes of good lineage, is pleasing to the Gods, commended by

virtutum particeps, indulgentiae magistra, tuta ab insidiis grataque benefactis, excusata in erratis, et ad postremum aurea declarata. Multa[1] de Favorini nostri pigmentis fuci quisnam appingere <pro>hibet? Ut quaeque mulier magis facie freta est, ita facilius cutem et capillum neglegere; plerisque autem, ut sese magno opere exornent, diffidentia formae diligentiae illecebras creari.

4. Myrtum buxumque ceteraque tonsilia arbusta atque virgulta summa diligentia et studio radi rigari comi solita, humi reptare aut ibidem haud procul a solo cacumina erigere: at illas intonsas abietes neglectasque piceas caput aemulum nubibus abdere.[2]

5. Non aeque diligentes ad quaerendum victum et comparandum cibum leones ut formicas esse, texendi vero araneas diligentiores esse quam Penelopam ullam vel Andromacham. Et omnino tenuibus in-

Ambr.
230 geniis et . . . . | . . . . et voluntariis quod
Ambr.
243, 244 vel praecipuum . . . . | . . . . | . . . .
. . . .[3] statuit quem admodum . . . . Quota, oro te, portio Lucullanae . . . . caesam aureo . . . .
. . . .

---

[1] Mai read the Codex, but doubtfully, as *multa certe*, and after *appingere* [*vide*]*licet*.

[2] From the margin for *addere*, which is in the text of Cod.

[3] The gap to *statuit* is half a column, from there to *aureo* about thirteen lines, and eleven lines are lost after *aureo*.

the wise, has her share of virtues, is the teacher of
mildness, shielded from traps, welcomed in well-
doing, pardoned in faults, and, finally, pronounced
golden. Who pray prevents us from painting-in
much colour from the paint-box of our friend
Favorinus[1]? The more a woman relies on her
looks, the more easily does she neglect her com-
plexion and her coiffure; but with most women
it is because they distrust their beauty that all
the alluring devices which care can discover are
brought into being that they may particularly adorn
themselves.

4. The myrtle and the box and all the other
shrubs and bushes that submit to the shears, accus-
tomed as they are to being most diligently and
carefully pruned, watered, and trimmed, creep on
the ground, or raise their tops but little over the
soil where they stand; but those unshorn firs and
neglected pines hide their aspiring heads amid the
clouds.

5. Lions are not so diligent in seeking their food
and procuring their prey as ants, while spiders are
more diligent in weaving than any Penelope or
Andromache. And altogether insignificant abilities
. . . .
. . . . How small
a part, I ask you, of the Lucullan . . . .
. . . .

[1] A philosopher and rhetorician of Arles, a friend of the
emperor Hadrian and of Herodes Atticus and Fronto.

Ad M. Caes. iii. 9 (Naber, p. 47).

Vat. 119

| HAVE mi magister optime.

1. Scio natali die quoiusque pro eo, quoius is dies natalis est, amicos vota suscipere ; ego tamen, quia te iuxta ac[1] memet ipsum amo, volo hoc die tuo natali mihi bene precari. Deos igitur omnes, qui usquam gentium vim suam praesentem promptamque hominibus praebent, qui vel somniis vel mysteriis vel medicina vel oraculis usquam iuvant atque pollent, eorum deorum unumquemque mihi votis advoco, meque pro genere cuiusque voti in eo loco constituo, de quo deus ei rei praeditus facilius exaudiat.

2. Igitur iam primum Pergami arcem ascendo et Aesculapio supplico, uti valetudinem magistri mei bene temperet vehementerque tueatur. Inde Athenas degredior, Minervam genibus nixus obsecro et oro, si quid ego umquam litterarum sciam, ut id potissimum ex Frontonis ore in pectus meum commigret. Nunc redeo Romam deosque viales et permarinos[2] votis imploro, uti mihi omne iter tua praesentia comitatum sit, neque ego tam saepe tam saevo desiderio fatiger. Postremo omnes omnium | populorum praesides deos, atque ipsum lucum, qui Capitolium montem strepit,†[3] quaeso tribuat hoc nobis, ut istum diem quo mihi natus es tecum firmato[4] laetoque concelebrem. Vale mi dulcissime et carissime magister. Rogo, corpus cura, ut quom venero videam te. Domina mea te salutat.

Vat. 114

---

[1] Cod. *aut.*   [2] Klussmann for Cod. *promarinos.*
[3] Haupt suggests *sacpit.*   [4] Cod. *firmo te.*

---

[1] Especially worshipped by Pius and Marcus.
[2] These words point to an early letter.

M. CORNELIUS FRONTO

? 140–143 A.D.

HAIL, my best of masters.

1. I know that on everyone's birthday his friends undertake vows for him whose birthday it is. I, however, since I love you as myself, wish to offer up on this day, which is your birthday, hearty prayers for myself. I call, therefore, with my vows to hear me each one of all the Gods, who anywhere in the world provide present and prompt help for men; who anywhere give their aid and shew their power in dreams or mysteries, or healing, or oracles; and I place myself according to the nature of each vow in that spot where the God who is invested with that power may the more readily hear.

2. Therefore I now first climb the citadel of the God of Pergamum and beseech Aesculapius[1] to bless my master's health and mightily protect it. Thence I pass on to Athens and, clasping Minerva by her knees, I entreat and pray that, if ever I know aught of letters, this knowledge may find its way into my breast from the lips of none other than Fronto.[2] Now I return to Rome and implore with vows the Gods that guard the roads and patrol the seas that in every journey of mine you may be with me, and I be not worn out with so constant, so consuming a desire for you. Lastly, I ask all the tutelary deities of all the nations, and the very grove, whose rustling fills the Capitoline Hill, to grant us this, that I may keep with you this day, on which you were born for me, with you in good health and spirits. Farewell, my sweetest and dearest of masters. I beseech you, take care of yourself, that when I come I may see you. My Lady greets you.

Ad M. Caes. iii. 10 (Naber, p. 48).

DOMINO meo.

Omnia nobis prospera sunt, quom tu pro nobis optas, neque enim quisquam dignior alius te, qui a dis quae petiit impetret; nisi quod, ego quom pro te precor, nemo alius te dignior est pro quo impetretur. Vale, domine dulcissime. Dominam saluta.

Ad M. Caes. iii. 1 (Naber, p. 40).

<CAESARI suo Fronto.>

.... <oratio nisi gravitate>[1] | verborum honest-atur, fit plane impudens atque impudica. Denique idem tu, quom in senatu vel in contione populi dicendum fuit, nullo verbo remotiore usus es,[2] nulla figura obscura aut insolenti: ut qui scias eloquentiam Caesaris tubae similem esse debere, non tibiarum, in quibus minus est soni, plus difficultatis.

Vat. 126: Quat. vii. begins

Ad M. Caes. v. 59 (Naber, p. 92).

Vat. 109, col. 2

| HAVE mi magister optime.

Egone ut studeam quom tu doleas, praesertim quom mea causa doleas? Non me omnibus incommodis sponte ipse adflictem? Merito hercule. Quis

---

[1] Added by Mai.
[2] This possibly points to a later date than 140–143.

M. CORNELIUS FRONTO

FRONTO TO MARCUS AURELIUS AS CAESAR

To my Lord.   ? 140–143 A.D.

All is well with us since your wishes are for us,
for there is no one who deserves more than you to
win from the Gods fulfilment of his prayers, unless I
should rather say that, when I pray for you, there is
no one who deserves more than you the fulfilment of
prayers offered on your behalf.   Farewell, most sweet
Lord.   Greet my Lady.

FRONTO to his own Caesar.   ? 140–143 A.D.

. . . . unless speech is graced by dignity of language, it becomes downright impudent and indecent.
In fine you too, when you have had to speak in the
Senate or harangue the people, have never used a
far-fetched word,[1] never an unintelligible or unusual
figure, as knowing that a Caesar's eloquence should
be like the clarion not like the clarionet, in which
there is less resonance and more difficulty.

MARCUS AURELIUS TO FRONTO

HAIL, my best of masters.[2]   ? 140–143 A.D.

What, am I to study while you are in pain,
above all in pain on my account? Shall I not of
my own accord punish myself with every kind of
penance? It were only right, by heaven. For

---

[1] cp. Thoughts, viii. 30, and below, Ad Ant. i. 1.
[2] This would seem to be an early letter, in spite of its
position in the Codex.

enim tibi alius dolorem genus, quem scribis nocte
proxima auctum, quis alius eum suscitavit, nisi Centumcellae, ne me dicam? Quid igitur faciam, qui
nec te video et tanto angore | discrucior? Adde eo
quod etiamsi libeat studere, iudicia prohibent, quae,
ut dicunt qui sciunt, dies totos eximent.[1] Misi tamen
hodiernum γνώμην et nudiustertianum locum com-
munem. Heri totum diem in itinere adtrivimus.
Hodie difficile est ut praeter vespertinam γνώμην
quicquam agi possit. Nocte, inquis, tam longa dormis?
Et dormire quidem possum, nam sum multi somni;
sed tantum frigoris est in cubiculo meo, ut manus
vix exseri possit. Sed re vera illa res maxime mih-
animum a studiis depulit, quod, dum nimium litteras
amo, tibi incommodus apud Portum[2] fui, ut res
ostendit. Itaque valeant omnes Porcii et Tullii et
Crispi, dum tu valeas, et te vel sine libris firmum
tamen videam. Vale, praecipuum meum gaudium,
magister dulcissime. Domina mea te salutat. Γνώμας
tres et locos communes mitte.

(Naber, p. 237.)

| M. FRONTONIS ARION

1. ARION Lesbius, proinde quod Graecorum me-
moria est, cithara et dithyrambo primus, Corintho,

---

[1] The reading of the margin of Cod. for text *exhibent*.
[2] So m¹ of Cod., but corrected to *Porcium*, says Mai.

---

[1] On the coast of Etruria (now Civita Vecchia), 47 miles
from Rome. Pius inherited the magnificent villa built there
by Trajan. [2] *i.e.* for the purpose of writing or study.

who else brought on that pain in the knee, which you write was worse last night, who else if not Centumcellae,[1] not to mention myself? What then shall I do, who cannot see you and am racked with such anxiety? Besides, however much I might be minded to study, the courts forbid it, which, as those say who know, will take up whole days. Still I send you to-day's maxim and the day-before-yesterday's commonplace. The whole day yesterday we spent on the road. To-day it is hard to find time for anything but the evening maxim. *Do you sleep,* say you, *the livelong night?* Aye, I can sleep, for I am a great sleeper; but it is so cold in my room that I can scarcely put my hand outside the bed-clothes.[2] But in good sooth what most of all put my mind off study was the thought that by my undue fondness for literature[3] I did you an ill turn at the Harbour,[4] as the event shewed. And so farewell to all Catos and Ciceros and Sallusts, as long as you fare well and I see you, though with never a book, established in health. Farewell, my chief joy, sweetest of masters. My Lady greets you. Send me three maxims and commonplaces.

Marcus Fronto's Arion [5]

? 140–143 A.D.

1. Arion of Lesbos, according to Greek tradition foremost as player on the lyre and as dithyrambist,

---

[3] Possibly Fronto had brought Marcus some books from Rome.   [4] Centumcellae.

[5] Fronto follows Herodotus, as Gellius also professes to do. Fronto probably intended this piece to be a model of narrative for his pupil. It seems to be of the matter-of-fact style (*siccum genus*) for which Fronto was celebrated.

ubi frequens incolebat, secundum quaestum profectus, magnis divitiis per oram Siciliae atque Italiae
paratis [1] Corinthum Tarento regredi parabat. Socios
navales Corinthios potissimum delegit ; eorum navem
audacter re bona maxima [2] onerat. Nave in altum
provecta cognovit socios, quae [3] veherent cupidos
potiri, necem sibi machinari. Eos precibus fatigat
aurum omne ipsi [4] haberent, unam sibi animam sin-

erent. Postquam id frustra | orat, aliam tamen ve-
niam impetravit, in exitu vitae quantum possit [5] can-
taret. Id praedones in lucro duxere, praeter spolia
summum artificem audire, cuius vocem praeterea
nemo umquam post illa auscultaret. Ille vestem
induit auro intextam itemque citharam insignem.
Tum pro puppi aperto maxime atque edito loco
constitit, sociis inde consulto per navem ceteram
dispersis. Ibi Arion studio impenso cantare orditur
scilicet mari et caelo artis suae supremum com-
memoramentum. Carminis fine cum verbo in mare
desilit : delphinus excipit, sublimem avehit, navi
praevortit, Taenaro exponit, quantum delphino fas
erat, in extimo litore.

2. Arion inde Corinthum proficiscitur : et homo
et vestis et cithara et vox incolumes. Periandrum
regem Corinthium, cui per artem cognitus acceptus-
que diu fuerat, accedit ; ordine memorat rem gestam
in navi et postea in mari. Rex homini credere,
miraculo addubitare, navem et socios navales dum

---

[1] Novák *partis.*

[2] Heind. for Cod. *maxime* (*cp.* Aul. Gell. xvi. 19, also of
Arion, *re bona multa*).

[3] Eussner for Cod. *qui.* But Mai says *potiri* may be *auri*
in the Cod.

[4] For Cod. *sibi.*   [5] Cod. *possiet.*

setting out from Corinth, where he constantly sojourned, in pursuit of gain, after amassing great riches in the coast-towns of Sicily and Italy, prepared to make his way home from Tarentum to Corinth. For his ship's crew he chose Corinthians by preference, and boldly freighted their ship with his immense gains. When the ship was well out at sea, he realized that the crew, coveting the wealth which they carried, were plotting his death. He wearied them with prayers to take all his gold for themselves, but leave him his life alone. When that boon was denied him, he was yet granted another grace, in taking farewell of life to sing as much as he would. The pirates put it down as so much to the good that over and above their booty they should hear a consummate artist sing, to whose voice moreover no one should ever thereafter listen. He donned his robe embroidered with gold, and withal his famous lyre. Then he took his stand before the prow in the most open and elevated place, the crew being afterwards intentionally scattered over the rest of the ship. There Arion, exerting all his powers, began to sing, for sea and sky, look you, the last reminder of his skill. His song ended, with a word on his lips he sprang into the sea: a dolphin received him, carried him on his back, outstripped the ship, landed him at Taenarus as near the shore as a dolphin might.

2. Thence Arion made his way to Corinth, man and robe and lyre and voice all safe; presented himself before Periander, the king of Corinth, who had long known him and esteemed him for his skill; recounted in order what had happened on the ship and subsequently in the sea. The king believed the man but did not know what to think of the miracle, and

reciperent opperiri. Postquam cognovit portum in-
vectos, sine tumultu acciri[1] iubet; voltu comi verbis
lenibus percontatur, num quidnam super Arione
Lesbio comperissent. Illi facile respondent Tarenti
| vidisse fortunatissimum mortalem secundo rumore
aur<um> quaerere, <artemque> esse <cithara>[2] cantare ; quo diutius amore et lucro et laudibus retineri.
Quom haec ita dicerent, Arion inrupit <salvos illaes-
usque[3] ita ut in puppi> steterat cum veste auro
intexta et cithara insigni. Praedones inopina<to
visu> consternati sunt,[4] neque quicquam post illa ne-
gare aut non credere aut deprecari ausi sunt. Del-
phini facinus <ad Taenarum testatur[5]> delphino
residens homo parva figura atque ut argumento
magis quam simulacro composita.

Ad M. Caes. iii. 2 (Naber, p. 40).

| AURELIUS CAESAR Frontoni suo salutem.

    Saepe te mihi dixisse scio[6] quaerere te quid
maxime faceres gratum mihi. Id tempus nunc adest:

Ambr. 165 *(margin)*

Vat. 126, toward end of col. 1 *(margin)*

---

[1] Naber for Cod. *accipi* (*cp.* Herod. κληθέντας).
[2] Mai. He reads *pretioque* for *artemque.* Brakman prefers *famaque.*
[3] I have added these words, which just fill the gap ; or *sospes incolumisque* would stand equally well.
[4] For Cod. *cum,* Naber *tum.*
[5] Cod. *visitur* (Mai).   [6] Query *scis.*

---

[1] Or possibly "love of his art."
[2] This and the next four letters refer to a trial at Rome, in which the famous Greek rhetorician, Herodes Atticus, one

waited for the return of ship and crew. When he
learnt that they had put into harbour, he gave orders
for their being summoned without any excitement;
questioned them with a pleasant countenance and
gentle words as to whether they had any news of
Arion the Lesbian. They answered glibly that they
had seen that most fortunate of men at Tarentum
making golden profits and applauded by all, his profession being to sing to the lyre; and that his stay
was prolonged by reason of his popularity,[1] his profits,
and his praises. As they were saying this, Arion
sprang in safe and sound, just as he had stood on the
ship's stern with his gold-embroidered robe and his
famous lyre. The pirates were dumbfounded at the
unexpected sight, nor did they thereafter attempt
any denial or disbelief or exculpation. The dolphin's
exploit is recorded by a statue set up at Taenarus
of a man seated on a dolphin, small in size
and executed as a subject-piece rather than as a
likeness.

? 140-143 A.D.

Aurelius Caesar to his own Fronto greeting.[2]

It is a fact that you have often said to me, *What
can I do to give you the greatest pleasure?* Now is the

of Marcus's teachers and his friend, was accused by the
Athenians of various crimes. Their principal spokesman was
Demostratus, who is mentioned, II. 220 n., 221, 235. Of
the circumstances we only know what the Letters tell us.
But a very similar accusation was brought against him nearly
thirty years later (see Philostratus, *Vit. Soph.* p. 242,
Kayser). Herodes must have been honourably acquitted on
the present occasion, as he was made consul in 143. The
trial, one must suppose, preceded the consulship, as he could
hardly have been elected to it with such accusations hanging
over him.

nunc amorem erga te meum augere potes, si augeri
potest. Adpropinquat cognitio, in qua homines non
modo orationem tuam benigne audituri, sed indign-
ationem maligne spectaturi videntur. Neque ullum
video qui te in hac re monere audeat. Nam qui
minus amici sunt malunt te inspectare inconstantius
agentem; qui autem magis amici sunt, metuunt ne
adversario tuo amiciores esse videantur, si te ab accusatione eius propria tua abducant. Tum autem, si
quod tu in eam rem dictum elegantius meditatus es,
per silentium dictionem auferre tibi non sustinent.

Vat. 125   Ideo,[1] sive | tu me temerarium consultorem sive
audacem puerulum sive adversario tuo benivolen-
tiorem esse existimabis, non propterea quod rectius
esse arbitrabor, pedetemptius tibi consulam. Sed
quid dixi *consulam?* qui id a te postulo et magno
opere postulo et me, si impetro, obligari tibi repro-
mitto. Sed[2] dices *Quid! si lacessitus fuero, non eum
simili dicto remunerabo?* At ex eo tibi maiorem
laudem quaeres, si nec lacessitus quicquam res-
ponderis. Verum si prior fecerit, respondenti tibi
utcumque poterit ignosci: ut autem non inciperet,
postulavi ab eo et impetrasse me credo. Utrumque
enim vestrum pro suis quemque meritis diligo, et
scio illum quidem in avi mei P. Calvisii domo edu-
catum,[3] me autem apud te eruditum. Propterea
maximam curam in animo meo habeo, uti quam

---

[1] Ehrenthal for Cod. adeo.   [2] Müller for Cod. et.
[3] Naber for Cod. eruditum.

opportunity. If my love for you admits of any increase, you can increase it now. The trial approaches in which men, it seems, will not only give a generous ear to your eloquence, but turn a grudging eye upon your angry animosity. And I see no one else who can venture to advise you in this matter. For those who are less friendly to you prefer to see you acting unlike yourself, while those who are truer friends are afraid of seeming too friendly to your opponent if they divert you from accusing him as you are entitled to do. Then again, if you have conned some especially choice phrase for the occasion, they cannot bear to rob you of its due delivery by an enforced silence. And so, even if you think me an ill-advised counsellor or a forward boy, or too partial to your opponent, I will not, for all that, shew any the more hesitation in pressing upon you what I think the best counsel. But why have I said *counsel*, whereas it is a favour I claim, urgently claim, from you and, if it is granted, promise to be bound to you in return ? But you will say, *What ! if assailed, shall I not requite in like terms ?* Nay, you will win by this means greater glory for yourself if, even when assailed, you make no reply.[1] Still, if he is the first to attack, it will be excusable in you to answer as you can; however, I have begged of him not to begin, and I think I have got my way. For I love both of you, each one for his own merits, and I do not forget that he was brought up in the house of my grandfather,[2] P. Calvisius, and I educated under you. Wherefore I am most anxious that this very disagreeable business

[1] Marcus practised what he preached in the second trial of Herodes, mentioned above.

[2] His maternal grandfather. It seems as if Herodes was not yet a teacher of Marcus.

honestissime negotium istud odiosissimum trans-
igatur. Opto ut consilium comprobes, nam voluntatem probabis. Ego certe minus sapienter magis
scripsero, quam minus amice tacuero. Vale mi
Fronto carissime et amicissime.

Ad M. Caes. iii. 3 (Naber, p. 41).

| Domino meo Caesari Fronto.

Merito ego me devovi tibi, merito fructus vitae
meae omnes in te ac tuo parente constitui. Quid
fieri amicius, quid iucundius, quid verius potest?
Aufer ista, obsecro, *puerulum audacem* aut *temerarium*[1]
consultorem. Periculum est plane ne tu quicquam
pueriliter aut inconsulte suadeas! Mihi crede, si
tu vis—si minus, egomet mihi credam—seniorum a
te prudentiam exsuperari. Denique in isto negotio
tuum consilium canum et grave, meum vero puerile
deprendo. Quid enim opus est aequis et iniquis
spectaculum praebere? Sive sit iste Herodes vir
frugi et pudicus, protelari conviciis talem a me
virum non est verum ; sive nequam et improbus est,
non aequa mihi cum eo certatio, neque idem detri-
menti[2] capitur. Omnis enim cum polluto com-

---

[1] These two adjectives are distinguished in the *De Differentiis Vocabulorum*, attributed to Fronto, and possibly
written by him for his pupils : see Mai's *Fronto*, ed. 1823,
p. 349.

[2] Mai reads the Codex as *detrimentum*, Brakman as here
given.

should be handled as honourably as possible. I trust my advice will commend itself to you, for my goodwill you must commend. At any rate, I would rather fail in judgment by writing than fail in friendship by keeping silence. Farewell, my Fronto, most beloved and most loving of friends.

? 140-143 A.D.

FRONTO to my Lord Caesar.

Rightly have I devoted myself to you, rightly invested in you and your father all the gains of my life. What could be more friendly, what more delightful, what more true[1]? But I beseech you, away with your *forward boys* and *rash counsellors!* There is danger, forsooth, of anything you suggest being childishly conceived or ill-advised! Believe me, if you will—if not, I will for my part believe myself—that in good sense you leave your elders far behind. In fact, in this affair, I realise that your counsel is weighty and worthy of a greybeard, while mine is childish. For what is the good of providing a spectacle for friends and foes? If your Herodes be an honourable and moral man, it is not right that such a man[2] should be assailed[3] with invectives by me; if he is wicked and worthless, my fight with him is not on equal terms, nor do we stand to lose the same. For any contact with what is unclean

---

[1] Fronto is probably punning on Marcus's name *Verus*. Hadrian gave him the pet name of *Verissimus*, which Justin Martyr also uses, and it appears on the coins of Tyras on the Euxine.

[2] We can scarcely keep the assonance : " It is not right that such a wight."

[3] Lit. "keep at a distance with darts."

plexus, tametsi superes, commaculat. Sed illud
verius est, probum virum esse, quem tu dignum
tutela tua iudicas. Quod si umquam scissem, tum
me di omnes male adflixint, si ego verbo laedere
ausus fuissem quemquam amicum tibi. Nunc me
velim pro tuo erga me amore, quo sum | beatissimus,
in hac etiam parte consilio iuves. Qui<n>[1] nihil
extra causam dicere debeam, quod Herodem laedat,
non dubito. Sed ea quae in causa sunt—<sunt>
autem <sane>[2] atrocissima—quemadmodum tractem,
id ipsum est quod addubito, et consilium posco.
Dicendum est de hominibus liberis crudeliter ver-
beratis et spoliatis, uno vero etiam occiso ; dicendum
est de filio impio et precum paternarum immemore ;
saevitia et avaritia exprobranda ; carnifex quidam
[Herodes][3] in hac causa est constituendus. Quodsi
in istis criminibus, quibus causa nititur, putas debere
me ex summis opibus adversarium urgere et premere,
fac me, Domine optime et mihi dulcissime, consilii
tui certiorem. Si vero in his quoque remittendum
aliquid putes, quod tu suaseris, id optimum factu[4]
ducam. Illud quidem, ut dixi, firmum et ratum
habeto, nihil extra causam de moribus et cetera eius
vita me dicturum.[5] Quodsi tibi videbitur servire me

---

[1] Naber for Cod. *qui*.   [2] For Cod. *sunt*.
[3] *Herodes* appears to be a gloss.
[4] Schopen for Cod. *factum*.   [5] m[1] of Cod. has *edicturum*.

---

[1] It is curious that Fronto did not know of this friendship and, indeed, more about such a man as Herodes.
[2] Herodes himself is meant, not his son, as generally
supposed. His father left by his will a yearly sum of
money to every Athenian citizen. But Herodes compounded

contaminates a man, even though he come off best.
But the former supposition is the truer, that he,
whom you count worthy of your patronage, is a
virtuous man. Had I had an inkling of the fact,
may all the gods plague me if I should ever have
ventured to say a word against any friend of yours.[1]
As it is I should wish you for the great love you
bear me, wherein I am most blest, to help me with
your advice on this point also. I quite admit that I
ought not to say anything, which does not bear on
the case, to damage Herodes, but those facts which
do bear on it—and they are undoubtedly of a
most shocking character—how am I to deal with
them? that is the very thing I am in doubt about,
and I ask your advice. I shall have to tell of freemen cruelly beaten and robbed, of one even slain;
I shall have to tell of a son unfilial[2] and deaf to
his father's prayers, cruelty and avarice will have
to be denounced; there is one who must in this
trial be made out a murderer. But if on those
counts, on which the indictment is based, you think
I ought to press and assail my opponent with might
and main, assure me, best of Lords and sweetest to
me, that such is your opinion. If, however, you
think that I ought to let him off lightly in these
also, I shall consider what you advise to be the best
course. You may, indeed, as I said, rest assured of
this, that I shall not go outside the case itself to
speak of his character and the rest of his life. But
if you think I must do the best for my case, I

with the Athenians for a single payment of 5 minae. However, by deducting from this sum moneys owed by them to
his father, he exasperated the citizens against himself, and
this may have caused the high-handed proceedings described
here. See Philost. *Vit. Soph.* 236, Kays.

causae debere, iam nunc admoneo ne me immoderate usurum quidem causae occasione, atrocia enim sunt crimina et atrocia dicenda. Illa ipsa de laesis et spoliatis hominibus ita | a me dicentur ut fel et bilem sapiant : sicubi graeculum et indoctum dixero, non erit internecivum.

Vale, Caesar, et me ut facis ama plurimum. Ego vero etiam literulas tuas disamo[1] : quare cupiam, ubi quid ad me scribes, tua manu scribas.

Ad M. Caes. iii. 4 (Naber, p. 43).

Have Domine.

Clausa iam et obsignata epistula priore, venit mihi in mentem fore uti et qui causam hanc agunt— acturi autem complures videntur—dicant aliquid in Herodem inclementius : cui rei, quemadmodum me unum putes,[2] prospice. Vale Domine et vive, ut ego sim beatus. Acturi videntur Capreolus, qui nunc abest, et Marcianus noster ; videtur etiam Villianus.

Ad M. Caes. iii. 5 (Naber, p. 43).

Have mi Fronto carissime.

Iam hinc tibi, Fronto carissime, gratias ago habeoque, quom consilium non tantum non repudi-

---

[1] The Codex has room for a letter between *dis* and *amo.* Possibly Fronto uses *disamo* (cp. *disperco*) for *deamo.*

[2] For Cod. *putas.*

warn you herewith that I shall not even use in a
disproportionate manner the opportunity my case
gives me, for shocking charges are made and must
be spoken of as shocking. Those in particular which
concern the robbing and injuring of freemen shall
be so told by me as to smack of gall and spleen:
if I chance to call him a greekling and unlearned,
it need not mean war to the knife.[1]

Farewell, Caesar, and love me, as you do, to the
utmost. I, indeed, dote on the very characters of
your writing: wherefore, whenever you write to me,
I would have you write with your own hand.

Fronto to Marcus Aurelius as Caesar

? 140–143 A.D.

Hail, my Lord.

After I had already closed and sealed the preceding letter, it occurred to me that those who plead
in this case—and many seem likely to plead in it—
may speak against Herodes in less measured terms.
Take care how you think that I alone am concerned in
this affair. Farewell, my Lord, and live, that I may
be happy. Capreolus, who is now away, and our
friend Marcianus[2] seem likely to plead; Villianus too,
it seems.

Marcus Aurelius to Fronto

? 140–143 A.D.

Hail, my dearest Fronto.

I must acknowledge and tender you at once,
my dearest Fronto, my thanks, that, so far from

---

[1] In spite of Fronto's speech they became great friends.
See below, *Ad. Ant.* ii. 8.

[2] Probably not the jurist, mentioned in the *Digest*, who
was later. Nothing is known of the persons named.

asti, sed etiam comprobasti. De iis autem, quae per litteras amicissimas tuas consulis, ita existimo. Omnia quae ad causam quam tueris adtinent plane proferenda; quae ad tuas proprias adfectiones adtinent, licet iusta | et provocata sint, tamen reticenda. Itaque neque fidem in negotio pannychio[1]† neque modestiam in existimatione tua laeseris . . . .[2] et dicant quae <velint, quom> una haec cura maxime me exercet, ne quid tu tale dicas, quod tuis moribus indignum, negotio inutile,[3] circumstantibus reprehensibile videatur esse. Vale mi Fronto carissime et iucundissime mihi.

Ad M. Caes. iii. 6 (Naber, p. 44).

Domino meo.

Ita faciam, quod ad haec nomina, quod ad vitam, ut te velle intellexero faciam; teque oro et quaeso ne umquam quod a me fieri volueris <taceas>. Sed ut nunc <bene> suades, ita <suade, si tal>e umquam adversus voluntatem tuam quicquam incipiam. Malim etiam <omnia nomina . . . , quae in>[4] causa sunt, singillatim sint; ut Ciceronis modum proferamus. Nam quom in tantulum id[5] consultum cogunt, versu† cupio,[6] praesertim qu<om> . . . .

---

[1] This word is certainly corrupt. We seem to want a word like *odiosissimum* of Marcus's previous letter.

[2] A gap of about thirty-four letters, but the word *ceteri* can be read.

rejecting my advice, you have approved it. As to the points on which you consult me in your very friendly letter, my opinion is this. Whatever has relation to the case, which you safeguard, should obviously be put forward; whatever to your own private feelings, although legitimate and provoked by the facts, must, nevertheless, be left unsaid. So will you not wound your honour in an all-night business, nor your own standard of self respect. (Let the others conduct the case as they will) and say what they please, since the one thing that greatly concerns me is, that you should say nothing that shall seem unworthy of your character, useless to your case, and to your audience deserving of blame. Farewell, my dearest, and to me most delightful Fronto.

Fronto to Marcus Aurelius as Caesar

? 140–143 A.D.

To my Lord.

I will act, my Lord, as to these counts and as to my whole life in the way I see you wish me to act; and I pray and beseech you never to forbear mentioning what you wish done by me, but dissuade me, as you are now rightly doing, if I ever undertake any such thing against your wishes. I should prefer (all the counts . . . . in the) case to be taken separately, that we may apply the method of Cicero. For when they compress that decision into so little, I desire . . . . but a fight

---

³ Schopen for Cod. *invite.*

⁴ About forty letters are lost here.

⁵ m¹ of Cod. has *rel.*

⁶ J. W. E. Pearce suggests *valde cupio . . . quod petis ipse pugna milius,* etc.

sed pugna mi\<nime> hoc modo transigi possit.
Quodsi agemus perpetuis orationibus, licet extra
causam nihil progrediar, tamen | et oculis acrioribus
et voce vehementi et verbis gravibus utendum,
\<hinc>[1] autem \<nutu> hinc digito irato, quod
\<modeste> hominem tuum ferre decet. Sed difficile
est ut istud ab eo impetrari possit, dicitur enim
cupidine agendi flagrare. Nec reprehendo tamen
ne hoc quidem, se\<d vide> ne tibi ipsa illa \<quae>
in causa sunt infestius pro\<ferre> videatur. Verum
et ipse suades inprimis fidei parendum : et si armis
vel palaestrica lu\<das>, ne has quidem ludicras
exercitationes sine contentione confici posse . . . .
facundior . . . . laudavi beatius *opicum* tuum.

Ad M. Caes. iv. 1 (Naber, p. 58).

\<DOMINO meo Fronto>.

Quoniam scio quanto opere sis anxius[2] . . . .
\<oves> | et columbae cum lupis et aquilis cantantem
sequebantur, immemores insidiarum et unguium et
dentium. Quae fabula recte interpretantibus illud
profecto significat, fuisse egregio ingenio eximiaque
eloquentia virum, qui plurimos virtutum suarum
facundiaeque admiratione devinxerit ; eumque amicos
et sectatores ita instituisse, ut quamquam diversis

---

[1] The words in brackets that follow are added by Eussner.

[2] These words are from the Index in the Codex. They
are followed by a gap of two pages, containing the first half
of the letter, the purport of which can be partly gathered
from Marcus's answer.

could never be conducted in this way. But if we proceed with unbroken speeches, though I go no step outside the case, my glance must needs be somewhat keen, and my voice vehement, and my words stern, and I must shew anger with a gesture here and a finger there; and this your man[1] ought to bear with composure. But it is no easy matter to get that concession from him, for he is said to be inflamed with a passion for pleading. Nor yet do I find fault with even this; but take heed that he seem not to you to put forward what actually belongs to his case too bitterly. But it is your own plea that honour should be the first consideration: and if one practises arms or wrestling, not even these mimic exercises can be carried through without strife . . . . I have praised more happily your "country bumpkin."[2]

Fronto to Marcus Aurelius as Caesar

Fronto to my Lord.   ? 140–143 A.D.

Since I know how anxious you are . . . . sheep and doves with wolves and eagles followed the singer, regardless of ambushes and talons and teeth. This legend rightly interpreted surely signifies this, that Orpheus[3] was a man of matchless genius and surpassing eloquence, who attached to himself numerous followers, from admiration of his virtues and his power of speech, and that he so trained his friends and followers, that, though met

---

[1] Herodes appears to be meant.

[2] *Opicus*, another form for *Oscan* = a rude, unlettered person.

[3] Orpheus appears on the Alexandrine coins of Marcus.

nationibus convenae, variis moribus imbuti, concord-
arent tamen et consuescerent et congregarentur,
mites cum ferocibus, placidi cum violentis, cum super-
bis moderati, cum crudelibus timidi : omnes deinde
paulatim vitia insita exuerent, virtutem sectarentur,
probitatem condiscerent, pudore impudentiam, obsequio contumaciam,[1] benignitate malivolentiam
commutarent. Quodsi[2] quis umquam ingenio tantum valuit ut amicos ac sectatores suos amore inter
se mutuo copularet, tu hoc profecto perficies multo
facilius, qui ad omnes virtutes natus es prius quam
institutus. Nam prius quam tibi aetas institutioni
sufficiens adolesceret, iam tu perfectus atque omni-
bus bonis artibus |[3] absolutus : ante pubertatem vir
bonus, ante togam virilem dicendi peritus. Verum
ex omnibus virtutibus tuis hoc vel praecipue admir-
andum, quod omnes amicos tuos concordia copulas.
Nec tamen dissimulaverim multo hoc esse difficilius
quam ut ferae ac leones cithara mitigentur : quod tu
facilius obtinebis, si unum illud vitium funditus ex-
tirpandum eruendumque curaveris, ne liveant neve
invideant invicem amici tui sibi,[4] neve quod tu alii
tribueris aut benefeceris, sibi quisque illud deperire
ac detrahi putet. Invidia perniciosum inter homines
malum maximeque internecivom, sibi aliisque pariter
obnoxium ; sed si procul a cohorte tua prohibueris,

Vat. 227

---

[1] Schopen for Cod. *contumeliam.*

[2] Naber for Cod. *quo si.*

[3] In this page are traces of a third writing, which like the
second refers to the *Acta Concilii.*

[4] Added by Brakman from the margin of Cod.

together from different nations and endowed with
diverse characteristics, they, nevertheless, lived
sociably together in unity and concord, the gentle
with the fierce, the quiet with the violent, the meek
with the proud, the sensitive with the cruel. Then
all of them gradually put off their ingrained faults,
went after virtue and learned righteousness, ex-
changed shamelessness for a sense of shame, self-
will for deference, ill-feeling for kindliness. But if
ever anyone by his character had so much influence
as to unite his friends and followers in mutual love
for one another, you assuredly will accomplish this
with far greater ease, for you were formed by nature
before you were fitted by training for the exercise of
all virtues.[1] For before you were old enough to be
trained, you were already perfect and complete in all
noble accomplishments, before adolescence a good
man, before manhood[2] a practised speaker. But of
all your virtues this even more than the others is
worthy of admiration, that you unite all your friends
in harmony. And I cannot conceal my opinion that
this is a far harder task than to charm with the lyre
the fierceness of lions and wild beasts: and you will
achieve this the more easily, if you set yourself to
uproot and utterly to stamp out this one vice of
mutual envy and jealousy among your friends, that
they may not, when you have shewn attention or
done a favour to another, think that this is so much
taken from or lost to themselves. Envy among men
is a deadly evil and more fatal than any, a curse to
enviers and envied alike. Banish it from your circle
of friends, and you will keep them, as they now are,

[1] So Dio, lxxi. 35, § 6, and Zonaras, ii: ἦν γὰρ καὶ φύσει
ἀγαθὸς ἀνήρ, πλεῖστα δὲ καὶ ἀπὸ παιδείας βελτίων ἐγένετο.
[2] Marcus would have assumed the *toga virilis* about 135 A.D.

uteris amicis concordibus et benignis, ut nunc uteris. Sin aliqua pervaserit, magna molestia magnoque labore erit restinguendum.

Sed meliora quaeso fabulemur. Amo Iulianum— inde enim hic sermo defluxit— ; amo omnes qui te diligunt ; amo deos qui te tutantur, amo vitam propter te ; amo litteras tecum ; <cum amicis>[1] tuis mihi amorem tui ingurgito.

Ad M. Caes. iv. 2 (Naber, p. 60).

<Have mi magister> | carissime.[2]

1. Quamquam ad te cras venio, tamen tam amicis tamque iucundis litteris tuis, tam denique elegantibus nihil, ne hoc quidem tantulum, rescribere non sustineo, mi Fronto carissime. Sed quid ego prius amem? pro quo prius habeam gratiam? Idne primum commemorem, quod in tantis domesticis studiis tantisque extrariis negotiis occupatus, tamen ad Iulianum nostrum visendum mea maxime gratia—nam sim ingratus nisi id intellegam—ire conisus es? *Sed non magnum est.* Tamen ita[3] est, si cetera addas, tanto temporis spatio ibi te demorari, tantum sermocinari, idque de me sermocinari, aut quod ad valetudinem eius consolandam esset; aegrum commodiorem sibi, amicum amiciorem mihi facere ; tum autem de iis singillatim ad me perscribere ; inibi

---

[1] Mai to fill an equivalent gap. But query *< ex epistulis >* ?
[2] Naber adds the words in brackets. Mai begins the letter with *Carissime* and gives a different heading.
[3] For Cod. *ut.*

harmonious and kindly; but let it in any way spread among them, and it can only be stamped out with immense toil and immense trouble.

But prithee let us talk of better things. I love Julianus—for this discussion originated with him—; I love all who are fond of you; I love the Gods who watch over you; I love life for your sake; with you I love letters; like all your friends I take in deep draughts of love for you.

MARCUS AURELIUS TO FRONTO

HAIL, my dearest of masters.   ? 140–143 A.D.

1. Although I am coming to you to-morrow, yet I cannot refrain, my dearest Fronto, from writing some answer, however trifling, to a letter so friendly, so delightful, so felicitous as yours. But what am I to love first? feel grateful first for what? Shall I not mention this first, that, occupied though you are with such important pursuits at home and business no less important outside, you nevertheless made a point of going to see our friend Julianus[1] chiefly—for I were ungrateful if I did not realize this—on my account. *But,* you will say, *there is not much in that.* Yet it does amount to much, if you count in all the rest, your staying there so long, having so protracted a talk, a talk, too, about me, or something to cheer him up in his illness, your making a sick man more comfortable in himself, a friend more friendly to me; then again, your writing out for me a detailed account of all this, giving in your letter most welcome

---

[1] Probably Salvius Julianus, the great jurist, who is mentioned in the *Digest,* xxxvii. 14, 17 Pr. by Marcus as *amicus noster.*

scribere nuntium de ipso Iuliano optatissimum, verba
suavissima, consilia saluberrima. Quid illud, quod
dissimulare nullo modo possum, apud te sum [1] dissi-
mulaturus? Utique illud ipsum quod tanta ad me
scripsisti, quom cras venturus essem: id vero mihi

Vat. 177 longe fuit gratissimum ; | in eo Ego [2] me beatissimum
supra omnes homines arbitratus sum, nam quanti me
faceres quantamque amicitiae meae haberes fiduciam,
in eo maxime atque dulcissime ostendisti. Quid ego
addam, nisi *te merito amo?* Sed quid dico *merito?*
Nam utinam pro tuo merito te amare possem ! Atque
id est quod saepe absenti atque insonti tibi irascor
atque succenseo, quod facis ne te ut volo amare
possim, id est ne meus animus amorem tuum usque
ad summum columen eius persequi posset.

2. De Herode quod dicis perge, oro te ; ut Quintus
noster ait, *pervince pertinaci pervicacia.* Et Herodes te
amat et ego istic hoc ago et, qui te non amat, profecto neque ille animo intellegit, neque oculis videt ;
nam de auribus nihil dico, nam omnium aures tuae
voculae [3] subserviunt sub iugum subactae. Mihi et
hodiernus dies verno die longior et nox veniens
hiberna nocte prolixior videtur atque videbitur. Nam
cum maximo opere Frontonem meum consalutare,
tum harum recentium litterarum scriptorem praecipue cupio complecti.

3. Haec cursim ad te scripsi, quia Maecianus

---

[1] Naber for Cod. *alium,*

[2] In the Cod. this word has a capital and is spaced.

[3] The margin of Cod. has *tuis voculis.* The singular has a
depreciatory sense in Cicero, *Ad Att.* ii. 23, and Propert.
i. 16. 7.

news of Julianus himself, the kindest of words, the most wholesome of counsels! Why should I try to dissemble before you what, do what I will, I can never dissemble? At any rate, the very fact of your writing me so long a letter, when I was to come to you to-morrow—that, I confess, was to me the most gratifying thing of all; in that did I think myself above all men most blest, for by it you have shewn me in the most marked and the sweetest way how much you make of me, and how great is the confidence you have in my friendship. What shall I say more except *I love you deservedly?* But why do I say *deservedly?* Would that I could love you as you deserve! Aye, and that is why I am often full of wrath and indignation against you when away and guiltless, because you make it impossible for me to love you as I wish, that is, for my soul to follow your love up to its supreme height.

2. With respect to Herodes proceed with what you say, I beseech you: as our Quintus[1] has it, *prevail with persevering persistence.* Herodes loves you, and I am doing my best in that quarter, and assuredly he who does not love you neither sees with his eyes nor understands with his heart: of ears I say nothing, for the ears of all hearers have passed under the yoke and are slaves of your voice. To me this day seems, and will seem, longer than a spring day, and the coming night more tedious than a night in winter. For as I desire intensely to greet my Fronto, so I long above all to embrace the writer of this last letter.

3. I have written this to you hurriedly because

---

[1] Ennius probably.

ur|gebat, et fratrem tuum maturius ad te reverti aequom erat. Quaeso igitur, si quod verbum absurd_ius aut inconsultior sensus aut infirmior littera istic erit, id tempori apponas. Nam quom te ut amicum vehementissime diligam, tum <me> meminisse oportet, quantum amorem amico, tantum reverentiae magistro praestare debere. Vale mi Fronto carissime et supra omnes res dulcissime.

4. Sota Ennianus remissus a te et in charta puriore et volumine gratiore et littera festiviore quam antea fuerat videtur. Gracchus cum cado musti maneat, dum venimus, neque enim metus est Gracchum interea cum musto defervere posse. Valeas[1] semper anima suavissima.

Ad M. Caes. iii. 18 (Naber, p. 56).

| Magistro suo Caesar suus.

In quantum me iuverit lectio orationum istarum
Gracchi, non opus est | me dicere, quom tu scias optime, qui me ut eas legerem doctissimo ingenio ac benignissimo animo tuo hortatus es. Ne autem sine comite solus ad te liber tuus referretur, libellum istum addidi. Vale mi magister suavissime, amice amicissime, cui sum debiturus quidquid litterarum sciero.

[1] Mai for Cod. *valeat.*

---

[1] Called *amicus noster* by Marcus and Verus in *Digest*, xxxvii. 14, 17 Pr. He was one of Marcus's teachers, and wrote a book for him *De Asse ac Ponderibus*, which is still extant.

M. CORNELIUS FRONTO

Maecianus[1] was pressing, and it was right that your brother should return to you in good time. I beseech you, therefore, if you find any solecism or confusion of thought or shaky letter herein, put it down to haste. For though I am desperately fond of you as a friend, at the same time I must not forget that I ought to shew no less respect to my master than love to my friend. Farewell, my Fronto, dearest and beyond all things sweetest to me.

4. The *Sota*[2] of Ennius, which you have returned, seems to be on clearer paper, in a more handsome volume and a prettier hand than before. Let Gracchus[3] bide with the cask of new wine until we come. There is no risk of Gracchus fermenting out[4] meanwhile along with the wine. Fare ever well, my sweetest soul.

? 140–143 A.D.

His own Caesar to his Master.

I need not say how pleased I was at reading those speeches of Gracchus, for you will know well enough, since it was you who, with your experienced judgment and kind thoughtfulness, recommended them for my reading. That your book might not be returned to you alone and unaccompanied, I have added this letter. Farewell, my sweetest of masters and friendliest of friends, to whom I am likely to be indebted for all the literature I shall ever know.

[2] According to Teuffel's *Latin Literature*, *Sota* (Σωτᾶς) = *Sotades*. There was a metre called Sotadean, but probably named from a licentious Greek poet mentioned by Martial (*Epigr.* ii. 86).

[3] See next letter.

[4] Possibly the word means "to cool down" (*cp. defervescere*) and refers to the vehemence of Gracchus's style, see II. 49.

Non sum tam ingratus ut non intellegam quid mihi
praestiteris, quom excerpta tua mihi ostendisti et
quom cotidie non desinis in viam me veram inducere
et "oculos" mihi "aperire," ut vulgo dicitur. Merito
amo.

Ad M. Caes. i. 1 (Naber, p. 3).

<Caesari suo Fronto>

. . . .[1] | mittam igitur tibi quantum pote librum
hunc descriptum. Vale, Caesar, et ride et omnem
vitam laetare et parentibus optimis et eximio ingenio
tuo fruere.

Ad M. Caes. i. 2 (Naber, p. 3).

M. Caesar [Iⲧp.] Frontoni magistro meo I.

1. Quid ego <de>ista mea fortuna satis[2] dixerim,
vel quomodo istam necessitatem meam durissimam
condigne incusavero, quae me istic ita animo anxio
tantaque sollicitudine praepedito adligatum adtinet,
neque me sinit ad meum Frontonem, ad meam pul-
cherrimam animam confestim percurrere, praesertim
in huiusmodi eius valetudine prope accedere, manus
tenere, ipsum denique illum pedem, quantum sine
incommodo fieri possit, adtrectare sensim, in balneo
fovere, ingredienti manum subicere? Et tu me
amicum vocas, qui non abruptis omnibus cursu con-

---

[1] Two pages are lost.
[2] Heind. adds <*digne*> to give a construction to *fortuna.*

---

[1] Excerpts from Terence, Vergil, Cicero, and Sallust, entitled *Exempla Elocutionum*, attributed by some to Fronto,
have come down to us. Marcus followed this habit of
making extracts. See *Thoughts*, iii. 14, and below, *Ad Caes.*
ii. 10.

M. CORNELIUS FRONTO

I am not so ungrateful as not to recognize what a
favour you have done me by letting me see your
extracts,[1] and by ceasing not to lead me daily in the
right way and, as the saying goes, "to open my
eyes." Deservedly do I love you.

143 A.D.

FRONTO to his own Caesar.

. . . . I will send you, therefore, as far as I can,
this book copied out. Farewell, Caesar, and smile
and be happy all your life long and enjoy the best
of parents and your own excellent abilities.

Baiae, 143 A.D.

MARCUS CAESAR Imperator[2] to my master Fronto.

1. What shall I say, that is adequate, as to my
ill-fortune, or how inveigh as it deserves against this
most hard necessity which keeps me a prisoner
here with a heart so anxious and fettered with such
great apprehension and does not let me run at once
to my Fronto, to my most beautiful of souls, above
all to be with him at a time when he is so unwell,
to clasp his hands and in fine, as far as may be
without pain, to massage the poor foot itself, foment
it in the bath, and support him as he steps in? And
do you call me a friend, who do not throw aside all

---

[2] Marcus did not receive the Imperium till 147 (with the
Trib. Pot.), nor was he styled Imperator till 161. There
must be some error in the word. The number (I.) that
follows the heading may mean the first letter by Marcus in
the Codex, in which case the whole first quaternion, which
is lost, must have contained letters of Fronto.

cito <ad te>[1] pervolo? Ego vero magis sum claudus
cum ista[2] mea verecundia, immo pigritia. O me—
quid dicam! metuo quicquam dicere quod tu audire
nolis; nam tu quidem me omni modo conisus es
iocularibus istis tuis ac lepidissimis verbis a cura

movere, atque te omnia ista aequo animo | perpeti
posse ostendere. At ego ubi animus meus sit nescio:
nisi hoc scio, illo nescio quo ad te profectum eum
esse. Cura, miserere, omni temperantia abstinentia
omni[3] istam tibi pro tua virtute tolerandam, mihi
vero asperrimam nequissimamque, valetudinem de-
pellere.

2. Ad <quas>[4] aquas proficisceris et quando, et
nunc ut commode agas, cito, oro, perscribe mihi et
mentem in pectus meum repone. Ego interim vel
tales tuas litteras mecum gestabo. Vale mihi Fronto
iucundissime: quamquam ita me dispositius[5] dicere
oportet—nam tu quidem semper aves†—: o qui ubique estis di boni, valeat oro meus Fronto iucundis-
simus atque carissimus mihi: valeat semper integro
inlibato incolumi corpore: valeat et mecum esse
possit. Homo suavissime, vale.

Ad M. Caes. i. 3 (Naber, p. 5).

Caesari suo Fronto.

1. Tu, Caesar, Frontonem istum tuum sine fine
amas, vix ut tibi homini facundissimo verba sufficiant

---

[1] Novák.　　[2] For Cod. *icita.*　　[3] For Cod. *omnem.*
[4] Added by Naber. Studemund says the Codex seems to
have *proficiscens.*

hindrances and fly in hot haste to you? I, indeed,
am more lame than you with that diffidence or, rather,
laziness of mine. Oh, as to myself—what shall I say?
I am afraid of saying something you would not like
to hear, for you indeed have always striven in every
way, with your humorous sallies and your wittiest of
words, to divert my mind, and to shew me that *you*
can put up with all your ills with unruffled fortitude.
But where my fortitude has gone to I know not, if it
be not yonder in some mysterious way to you. For
mercy's sake endeavour with all self-denial and all
abstinence to shake off this attack which you, indeed,
can endure with your usual courage, but to me it is
the worst and sorest of trials.

2. Write and tell me quickly, I beseech you, to
what waters you are going and when, and how well you
now are, and set my mind going in my breast again.
Meanwhile I will carry about your letter in spite
of its sad tenor. Farewell, my most delightful
Fronto: and yet I ought to put it more correctly
thus—for to fare well is, of course, always your
wish—: O ye kind Gods, that are everywhere, grant,
I beseech you, health to my Fronto, dearest to me
and most delightful: let him ever be well with a
hardy, hale, healthy body: let him be well and able
to be with me. Most charming of men, farewell.

143 A.D.

Fronto to his own Caesar.

1. So without end, Caesar, is your love for this
Fronto of yours, that for all your eloquence words

---

⁵ Klussm. for Cod. *dispositus.* Heind. preferred *dis potius.*

ad expromendum amorem tuum et benivolentiam
declarandam. Quid, oro te, | fortunatius, quid me
uno beatius esse potest, ad quem tu tam flagrantes [1]
litteras mittis? Quin etiam, quod est amatorum
proprium, currere ad me vis et volare.

2. Solet mea Domina parens tua interdum ioco [2]
dicere, se mihi quod a te tanto opere diligar invidere.
Quid, si istas litteras tuas legerit, quibus tu deos
etiam .pro salute mea votis advocas et precaris? O
me beatum! ore tuo me dis commendatum! Putasne
ullus dolor penetrare sciat corpus aut animum meum
prae tanto gaudio? Proced . . . . [3] babae! Neque
doleo iam quicquam nec aegre fero: vigeo, valeo,
exulto: quo vis, veniam; quo vis, curram. Crede
istud mihi, tanta me laetitia perfusum, ut rescribere
tibi ilico non potuerim; sed eas quidem litteras, quas
ad priorem epistulam tuam iam rescripseram, dimisi
ad te: sequentem autem tabellarium retinui, quo ex
gaudio resipiscerem. Ecce nox praeteriit, dies hic
est alter, qui <iam> [4] prope exactus est, necdum quid
aut quemadmodum tibi rescribam reperio. Quid enim
ego possim iucundius, quid blandius, quid amantius,
quam tu scripsisti mihi pro<ponere? Unde> [5] gaudeo
quod ingratum me | et referundae gratiae imparem
facias, quoniam, ut res est, ita me diligis ut ego te
magis amare vix possim.

3. Igitur ut argumentum aliquod prolixiori epistulae reperiam, quod, oro te, ob meritum sic me

---

[1] Cod. *fraglantes*, as almost always (not = *fragrantes*).
[2] Naber *iocose* for Cod. *loci* (m² *loco*) *dis.cere*.
[3] Naber *prosiluerim* for Cod. *proced* . . .
[4] Hauler.   [5] Brakman.

are scarcely forthcoming fully to express your love and set forth your goodwill. What, I ask you, can be more fortunate, what more happy than I alone am, to whom you send such glowing letters? Nay, more, and this is peculiar to lovers, you wish to run, aye, to fly, to me.

2. My Lady, your mother, is wont at times to say in fun that she envies me for being loved so much by you. What if she read this letter of yours, in which you even beseech the Gods and invoke them with vows for my health? O, happy that I am! commended by your lips to the Gods! Can any pain, think you, find its way into body or mind of mine to count against delight so great? . . . . hurrah! No longer do I feel any pain, nor any distress: I am whole, I am well, I leap for joy; whither you wish, I will come; whither you wish, I will run. Believe me when I say that I was so steeped in delight as not to be able to answer your letter at once; but the letter indeed, which I had already written in answer to your previous one, I have sent off to you. However, I have kept back the second messenger that I might recover from my joy. And lo, the night has passed, a second day is already here, which is already almost spent, and still what and how to write back to you I find not. For what professions of mine could be more sweetly, what more winningly, what more lovingly expressed than yours for me? And so I rejoice that you make me ungrateful and put a due requital beyond my powers, since, as the matter stands, your affection for me is so great that I can scarcely exceed your love.

3. Therefore, to provide some matter for a longer letter, let me ask you for what desert of mine

amas? Quid iste Fronto tantum boni fecit ut eum
tanto opere tu diligas? Caput suum pro te aut
parentibus tuis devovit? Succidaneum se pro vestris
periculis subdidit? Provinciam aliquam fideliter ad-
ministravit? Exercitum duxit? Nihil eorum. Ne
cotidianis quidem istis officiis circa te praeter ceteros
fungitur; est[1] immo, s<i> verum velis, satis infre-
quens. Nam neque domum vestram diluculo ventitat,
neque cotidie <te> salutat, neque ubique comitatur,
nec semper spectat. Vide igitur ut, si quis inter-
roget cur Frontonem ames, habeas in promptu quod
facile respondeas.

4. At ego nihil quidem malo quam amoris erga me
tui nullam extare rationem. Nec omnino mihi amor
videtur qui ratione oritur[2] et iustis certisque de causis
copulatur: amorem ego illum intellego fortuitum et
liberum et nullis causis servientem, impetu potius
quam ratione conceptum, qui non officiis, uti lignis,[3]
sed sponte ortis vaporibus caleat. Baiarum ego | calid-
os specus malo quam istas fornaculas balnearum,
in quibus ignis cum sumptu atque fumo accenditur
brevique extinguitur. At illi ingenui vapores puri
perpetuique sunt, grati pariter et gratuiti. Ad eundem prorsus modum amicitiae istae officiis calentes[4]
fumum interdum et lacrimas habent: ubi primum
cessaveris, extinguuntur: amor autem fortuitus et
iugis est et iucundus.[5]

5. Quid, quod neque adolescit proinde nec corrob-
oratur amicitia meritis parta ut ille amor subitus et

Ambr. 76

---

[1] Hauler for Cod. *et*. He has given his revision of this
letter in *Zei/sch. f. d. öst. Gymn.* 54 (1907), pp. 32–37.
[2] m² of Cod. has *munitur*.
[3] Query *lignis <ignis>*.   [4] m² of Cod. gives *calent*.
[5] m² of Cod. gives *iugis est fortuitus amor et iucundus*.

you love me so. What benefit has your Fronto bestowed upon you so great that you should shew him such affection? Has he given up his life for you and your parents? Has he braved perils vicariously in your stead? Has he been the faithful governor of some province? Has he commanded an army? Nothing of the kind. Not even those everyday duties about your person does he discharge more than others; nay, he is, if you wish the truth, remiss enough. For neither does he haunt your house at daybreak, nor pay his respects to you daily, nor attend you everywhere, nor keep you always in sight. See to it then that, if anyone ask you why you love Fronto, you have an easy answer ready.

4. And yet there is nothing I like better than that there should be no reason for your love of me. For that seems to me no love at all which springs from reason and depends on actual and definite causes: by love I understand such as is fortuitous and free and subject to no cause, conceived by impulse rather than by reason, that needs no services, as a fire logs, for its kindling, but glows with self-engendered heat. To me the steaming grottoes of Baiae are better than your bath-furnaces, in which the fire is kindled with cost and smoke, and anon goes out. But the natural heat of the former is at once pure and perpetual, as grateful as it is gratuitous. Just in the same way your rational friendship, kept alight with services, not unfrequently means smoke and watery eyes: relax your efforts for an instant and out they go: but love fortuitous is eternal and enchanting.

5. Again, friendship that is won by desert has no such growth or firm texture as the love that is

repentinus? Ut non aeque adolescunt in pomariis hortulisque arbusculae manu cultae rigataeque ut ille in montibus aesculus et abies et alnus et cedrus et piceae, quae sponte natae, sine ratione ac sine ordine sitae, nullis cultorum laboribus neque officiis sed ventis atque imbribus educantur.[1]

6. Tuus igitur iste amor incultus et sine ratione exortus, spero, cum cedris porro adolescet et aesculis: qui si officiorum ratione coleretur, non ultra myrtos laurusque procresceret, quibus satis odoris, parum roboris. Et omnino quantum fortuna rationi, tantum amor fortuitus officioso amori antistat.

Ambr. 75 7. Quis autem ignorat rationem humani consilii | vocabulum esse, Fortunam autem deam dearumque praecipuam? templa fana delubra passim Fortunae dicata, Rationi nec simulacrum neque aram usquam consecratam? Non fallor igitur quin[2] malim amorem erga me tuum fortuna potius quam ratione genitum.

8. Neque vero umquam ratio fortunam aequiparat, neque maiestate neque usu neque dignitate. Nam neque aggeres manu ac ratione constructos montibus comparabis neque aquaeductus amnibus neque receptacula fontibus. Tum ratio consiliorum prudentia appellatur, vatum impetus divinatio nuncupatur. Nec quisquam prudentissimae feminae consiliis potius

[1] The margin of Cod. has *evocantur* as a variant.
[2] So Cod.

[1] The alder seems out of place among upland and forest trees.

sudden and at first sight. So in orchards and gardens the growth of shrubs, reared and watered by hand, is not like that of the oak and the fir and the alder[1] and the cedar and the pine on their native hills which, springing up self-sown and set without plan and without order, owe nothing to the toil or services of a planter, but are fostered by the wind and the rain.

6. That love of yours, therefore, unplanted and sprung up without reason, will, I trust, grow steadily on with the cedars and the oaks; whereas if it were cherished by reason of services done, it would not outgrow the myrtles and the bays, which have scent enough but too little strength. In a word, love spontaneous is as superior to love earned by service as fortune is to reason.

7. But who is there knows not that reason is a term for human judgment, while Fortuna is a Goddess and the chief of Goddesses? that temples, fanes, and shrines have been dedicated to Fortuna[2] all the world over, while to Reason has been consecrated neither image nor altar anywhere? I cannot be wrong then in preferring that your love for me should be born rather of fortune than of reason.

8. Indeed reason can never compare with fortune either in grandeur or utility or worth. For neither can you match your pyramids, raised by hand and reason, against the hills, nor your aqueducts against the rivers, nor your cisterns against the fountains. Again, reason that guides our actions is called wisdom, the intuition of the seer is named divination. Nor is there anyone who would rather put faith in

[2] See Plutarch, *On the Fortune of the Romans*, ch. x. ; and for the various Fortunes *cp. De Orat., ad init.*

accrederet[1] quam vaticinationibus Sibyllae. Quae
omnia quorsum tendunt? Ut ego recte malim impetu et forte potius quam ratione ac merito meo
diligi. Quam ob rem etiam si qua iusta ratio est
amoris erga me tui, quaeso, Caesar, sedulo demus
operam ut ignoretur et lateat. Sine homines am-
bigant disserant disputent coniectent requirant, ut
Nili caput, ita nostri amoris originem.

9. Sed iam hora decimam tangit, et tabellarius |
tuus mussat. Finis igitur sit epistulae. Valeo[2]
revera multo quam opinabar commodius. De aquis
nihildum cogito. Te, Dominum meum, decus morum, solacium <maximu>m, multum amo. Dices
num amplius quam ego te? Non sum tam ingratus ut
hoc audeam dicere. Vale, Caesar, cum tuis parentibus, et ingenium tuum excole.

Ad M. Caes. i. 4 (Naber, p. 9).

M. Caesar Frontoni magistro salutem.

1. Accipe nunc perpaucula contra somnum pro
insomnia: quamquam, puto, praevaricor, qui adsidue
diei ac noctis somno adsum, neque eum desero neque
is[3] me deserat, adeo sumus familiares. Sed cupio
hac sua accusatione offensus paulisper a me abscedat
et lucubratiunculae aliquam tandem facultatem trib·
uat. Igitur ἐπιχειρήματα <ποι>κίλα[4]: e quibus illo

---

[1] Ehrenthal for Cod. *accederet.*
[2] Added by m[2] in the Codex over the line. Du Rieu and
Brakman read *ego* in the Codex after *valeo.*
[3] Mai has *ille,* for which there is not enough space in the
Codex. Klussm. would read *sino.*
[4] Hauler reads the Codex ... σκιλα *eiusdem*; Mai has *et
quidem* for *e quibus.*

the wisest of women than in the oracles of the Sibyl. What is the drift of all this? To shew that I do right in preferring to be loved by intuition and chance rather than by reason and my desert. Wherefore, even if there is any adequate reason for your love for me, I beseech you, Caesar, let us take diligent pains to conceal and ignore it. Let men doubt, discuss, dispute, guess, puzzle over the origin of our love as over the fountains of the Nile.

9. It is now close on four o'clock and your messenger is muttering. So my letter must end. I am really much better than I expected; I have given up all idea of waters. Dearly do I love you, my Lord, the glory of our age, my chiefest solace. You will say, *Not surely more than I love you?* I am not so ungrateful as to dare say that. Farewell, Caesar, and your parents too, and cultivate your abilities to the full.

Baiae, 143 A.D.

M. CAESAR to his master Fronto, greeting.

1. Hear now a very few points in favour of wakefulness against sleep[1]: and yet methinks I am guilty of collusion, in that I side with sleep night and day without ceasing: I desert him not, nor is he likely to desert me, such cronies are we. But my hope is that he may be huffed at my indictment of him and leave me for a little space, and give me a chance at last of burning some midnight oil. Now for subtle arguments: of which[2] my first indeed

---

[1] This letter is evidently an answer to a *Pro Somno* of Fronto's. By " collusion " he means being really in favour of sleep while pretending to plead against it.

[2] If we keep Hauler's reading of the Codex *eiusdem*, the pronoun would seem to refer to Theodorus (see p. 38), for we can hardly assent to Hauler's view that σκιλα refers to Squilla Gallicanus, to whom there is a letter below, *Ad Am.* i. 25.

primo utar epichiremate, quodsi [1] tu dices faciliorem me materiam mihi adsumpsisse accusandi somni, quam te qui laudaveris somnum—quis enim, inquis, non facile somnum accusaverit?—ego t<ibi[2]: cui>us facilis accusatio, <eius>dem difficilis laudatio; cuius difficilis laudatio, eius non utilis usur|patio.

2. Sed hoc transeo. Nunc, quando apud Baias agimus in hoc diuturno Ulixi labyrintho, ab Ulixe mihi paucula quae ad hanc rem adtinent sumam. Non enim ille profecto εἰκοστῷ demum ἔτει venisset εἰς πατρίδα γαῖαν, neque in isto lacu tam diu oberasset, neque alia omnia quae Ὀδυσσείαν faciunt perpessus esset, nisi tum γλυκὺς ὕπνος ἐπῆλθε κεκμηῶτα. Quamquam τῇ δεκάτῃ ἀνεφαίνετο πάτρις ἄρουρα—sed quid somnus fecit?

> βουλῇ δὲ κακῇ νίκησεν ἑταίρων·
> ἀσκὸν μὲν λῦσαν, ἄνεμοι δ' ἐκ πάντες ὄρουσαν,
> τοὺς δ' αἶψ' ἁρπάξασα φέρεν πόντονδε θύελλα
> κλαίοντας γαίης ἀπὸ πατρίδος.

Quid rursum apud insulam Trinacriam?

> οὐδ' ἄνεμοι[3] γλυκὺν ὕπνον ἐπὶ βλεφάροισιν ἔχευαν.
> Εὐρύλοχος δ' ἑτάροισι κακῆς ἐξήρχετο βουλῆς.

Postea, ubi Ἠελίοιο βόας καὶ ἴφια μῆλα—ἔσφαξαν καὶ ἔδειραν—καὶ μῆρ' ἐκάη καὶ σπλάγχν' ἐπάσαντο, quid tum expergitus Ulixes?

> οἰμώξας δὲ θεοῖσι μετ' ἀθανάτοισι γεγώνευν·
> ἦ με μάλ' εἰς ἄτην κοιμήσατε νηλέϊ ὕπνῳ.

---

[1] Buttmann *quo.* [2] Cod. *igit<ur cui>us.*
[3] Quom iam Ehr. = just when. [4] So Cod. for οἱ δ' ἄρα μοι.

---

[1] Marcus seems to refer to Ulysses being driven backwards and forwards along the coast (*Odyss.* xii.).

shall be this, in regard to which, if you say that I have taken up an easier theme in accusing sleep than you who have praised it—for who, say you, cannot easily bring an indictment against sleep?—I will counter thus : what is easy to indict is hard to praise ; what is hard to praise can serve no useful purpose.

2. But I let that pass. For the nonce, as we are staying at Baiae in this interminable labyrinth[1] of Ulysses, I will take from Ulysses a few things which bear on my subject. For he surely would not have taken *twenty years his fatherland to reach*,[2] nor have wandered so long about that pool, nor gone through all the other adventures which make up the *Odyssey*, had not then *sweet sleep seized his weary limbs*.[3] Yet *on the tenth day his native soil appeared*[4]— but what did sleep do ?

> *The evil counsel of my crew prevailed :*
> *The bag they opened, and forth rushed the winds ;*
> *The fierce gale caught and swept them to the sea,*
> *Weeping with sorrow, from their native shore.*[5]

What again took place at the island of Trinacria?[6]

> *Nor winds sweet sleep upon mine eyelids shed :*
> *Eurylochus his crew ill counsel gave.*[7]

Afterwards, when the *Sungod's oxen and fat flocks . . they slew and flayed . . and burnt the thighs and ate the flesh*,[8] what then Ulysses when awaked ?

> *Wailing I cried to all the Gods on high,*
> *Who ruthless to my ruin made me sleep.*[9]

[2] *Odyss.* iii. 117.   [3] *Ibid.* x. 31.   [4] *Ibid.* 29.
[5] *Ibid.* 46.   [6] Sicily.   [7] *Odyss.* xii. 338.
[8] *Ibid.* xi. 108 ; xii. 359, 364.   [9] *Ibid.* xii. 370, 372.

Somnus autem Ulixen ne patriam quidem suam
diu agnosceret sivit, cuius καὶ καπνὸν | ἀποθρώσκοντα
νοῆσαι [1] ἱμείρετο.

3. Nunc a Laertio ad Atridam transeo. Nam illud
πασσυδίῃ, quod eum decepit, cuius causa tot legiones
funduntur fugantur, ex somno et ex somnio profecto
oritur.

Quod,[2] quom ὁ ποιητὴς Agamemnona laudat, quid
ait ?

ἔνθ' οὐκ ἂν βρίζοντα ἴδοις Ἀγαμέμνονα δῖον·

quid cum reprehendit ?—

οὐ χρὴ παννύχιον εὕδειν βουληφόρον ἄνδρα,

quos quidem versus orator egregius mire quondam
evertit.

4. Transeo nunc ad Q. Ennium nostrum, quem tu
ais ex somno et somnio initium sibi <scribendi> [3]
fecisse. Sed profecto nisi ex somno suscitatus esset,
numquam somnium suum narrasset.

5. Hinc ad Hesiodum pastorem, quem dormientem
poetam ais factum. At enim ego meminisse olim
apud magistrum me legere :

ποιμένι μῆλα νέμοντι παρ' ἴχνιον ὀξέος ἵππου
Ἡσιόδῳ Μουσέων ἑσμὸς ὅτ' ἠντίασεν·

τὸ "ὅτ' ἠντίασεν" vides quale sit, scilicet ambulanti
obviam venisse Musas.

---

[1] m[2] of the Codex adds ἧς γαίης θανέειν.
[2] Naber *quid*.   [3] Schopen.

---

[1] *Odyss.* i. 58.   [2] *Iliad*, iv. 223.   [3] *Ibid.* ii. 24.

Sleep, however, did not allow Ulysses a long recognition of his native land, from which he *yearned to see even the smoke leap upwards.*[1]

3. Now I leave the son of Laertes for the son of Atreus. For that *with all haste,* which beguiled the latter, and led to the defeat and rout of so many legions, surely sprang from sleep and a dream.

Again, when the poet would praise Agamemnon, what says he?—

Then none might see the godlike Agamemnon sleeping—[2]

what, when he is finding fault?—

No councillor should sleep the whole night long,[3]

verses indeed, which an illustrious orator [4] once wrested in a strange fashion.

4. I now pass on to our friend Q. Ennius, who, you say, drew from sleep and a dream [5] his first inspiration to write. But, marry, had he never waked from sleep, he had never told his dream.

5. From him let us to Hesiod the shepherd, who became a poet, you say, in slumber. But, indeed, I remember reading once upon a time at school:

When on the swift steed's track he was leading his sheep to the pasture,
Hesiod once was met in the way by a bevy of Muses.[6]

That *was met,* you see what it implies? Why, that he was walking when the Muses met him.

---

[4] Fronto. Jerome calls certain translations of the Scriptures *non versiones sed eversiones.*

[5] Cicero (*Acad.* ii. 16) quotes the beginning of Ennius's own account of the dream : *Visus Homerus adesse poeta.*

[6] *cp.* Hesiod, *Theog.* 22 f.

Quid autem tu de eo existimas, quem qui pulcherrime laudat quid ait ?—

Ambr. 98

νήδυμος ἥδιστος θανάτῳ | ἄγχιστα ἐοικώς.

6. Haec satis tui amore \<potius\> quam meae fiduciae[1] luserim. Nunc bene accusato somno dormitum eo : nam vespera haec ad te detexui. Opto ne mihi somnus gratiam referat.

Ad M. Caes. i. 5 (Naber, p. 11).

M. Caesari Domino suo Fronto.

1. Domum reverso mihi epistula reddita est, quam tu videlicet Romam mihi scripseras, et erat lata Romam ; deinde hodie relata et paulo ante mihi est reddita ; in qua pauca quae ego pro somno dixeram tu multis et elegantibus argumentis refutasti ita scite, ita subtiliter et apte, ut si vigilia tibi hoc acuminis et leporis adfert, ego prorsus vigilare te mallem. Sed enim vespera scripsisse te ais, quom paulo post dormiturus esses. Igitur adpropinquans et imminens tibi somnus tam elegantem hanc epistulam fecit. Namque ut crocus, ita somnus, priusquam prope adsit, longe praeolet, longeque delectat.

2. Ut a principio igitur epistulae tuae incipiam, elegantissime *praevaricari* te ais, quod[2] . . . . \<verbum[3] adeo proprium\> | est ut eo sublato aliud subdi

Ambr. 85

---

[1] This word has no proper construction. Query *meae fide causae*.   [2] Two pages are lost here.
[3] Possibly the word *labyrintho* is meant.

---

[1] *Odyss.* xiii. 80.

What, again, do you think of that, of which its most eloquent advocate says what?

Sweet dreamless sleep, death's counterfeit.[1]

6. Enough of this trifling which I have indulged in more from love of you than from my own faith in it. Now after soundly abusing sleep, I am off to sleep: for I have spun all this out for you in the evening. I hope sleep will not pay me out.

143 A.D.

Fronto to his Lord Marcus Caesar.

1. On my return home I received your letter which you had, of course, written to me at Rome, and to Rome it had gone; then it was brought back to-day and delivered to me a little while ago. In it, with many happy arguments, you confute the little I had said for sleep so cleverly, so subtly and aptly, that if wakefulness brings you such sharpness and wit,[2] I would absolutely prefer you to keep awake. But, indeed, you confess that you wrote in the evening just before going to sleep. It was the near approach, therefore, and overshadowing of sleep that produced so felicitous a letter. For, like the saffron, sleep, ere it comes close, sheds its fragrance from afar and delights at a distance.

2. To begin, then, with the opening of your letter, *collusion* with sleep, as you term it, is most happy . . . . the word[3] is so apt that, were it withdrawn,

[2] In a fragment of a letter to Marcus as emperor, Charisius, *Ars Grammatica*, ii. 223, 8, quotes from Fronto *adest etiam usque quaque tibi natura situs lepos et venustas.*

[3] This must refer to some word in the lost pages, not to *praevaricor*, which characterizes Marcus' treatment of the theme in general.

eiusdem usus et ponderis non possit. Illud vero dictum[1] elegans . . . . aut a via tua quae ais,[2] *neque alia omnia quae* Ὀδυσσείαν *faciunt.*

3. Enimvero omnia istaec inter Graecos versus Latina ita scite alternata sunt a te et interposita, ut est ille in pyrrhicha versicolorum discursus, quom amicti cocco alii, alii luteo et ostro et purpura, alii aliisque[3] cohaerentes concursant.

4. Iam a Laertio ad Atridam eleganter transistı. Ecce autem circa Q. Ennium malitiosam pilam dedisti, quom ais, *nisi ex somno exsuscitatus esset, numquam somnium suum narrasset.* <Eruat>[4] aliquid Marcus meus Caesar, si pote, argutius. Praestigiae nullae tam versutae, nulla, ut ait Laevius, *decipula tam insidiosa.* Qui<d>, si ego id postulo, ne expergiscare? Quin postulo ut dormias. Aliud[5] scurrarum proverbium : *en cum quo in tenebris mices.* Sed sumne ego beatus qui haec intellego et perspicio et insuper agnomine[6] *magister* appellor? Quo pacto ego magister? qui unum hoc quod te docere cupio, ut dormias, non impetro. Perge uti libet, dummodo di te mihi, sive prodormias sive pervigiles,[7] | protegant. Vale, meum gaudium, vale.

Ambr. 86

---

[1] Fronto may be referring to the word *lacus.* A page is lost here. A marginal note in the Codex gives *Baiae, Lucrinus,* and *Avernus,* as mentioned in the lost part.

[2] The six preceding words are very uncertain.

[3] Novák for Cod. *aliique.* For dance see Gayet, *Pius,* p. 27.

[4] Studemund reads the Codex, doubtfully, as *Oderit me.*

[5] Query *audı id.*

[6] Cod. has *acnomine* above *magister*; Naber reads *magno nomine.*

nothing of equal currency and force could be put in its place. That, again, is a happy expression . . . . or that turn of yours beside the mark where you say *nor all the other things which make up the Odyssey.*

3. Indeed all that Latin context is interwoven by you and alternates as skilfully with the Greek verses as the movements of the gaily-drest performers in the Pyrrhic reel when they run together, coalescing now with these, now with those, dressed some in scarlet, others in damask,[1] and crimson, and purple.

4. Again, your transition from Laertius to Atrides was neatly done. But come, that was a nasty return you gave Q. Ennius when you said that, *had he not awaked from sleep he could not have recounted his dream.* See if my Marcus Caesar can evolve anything more dexterous than that. No sleight of word so clever, no *snare,* as Laevius says, *so cunningly set.* What if I beseech you never to wake up? Nay, I beseech you to sleep. Another jester's[2] proverb: *Marry, one with whom you can play odd and even in the dark!* But am I not blest in seeing and realizing this, and above all in being called by the title master? How I master? who cannot get my way in this one thing I would have you learn—to sleep. Go your own way, provided that, whether you wake early or sleep long, the Gods keep you for me. Farewell, my joy, farewell.

---

[1] For the meaning of *luteus* see Fronto *apud* Gell. ii. 26, § 8.

[2] Cicero, *De Off.* iii. 19, calls it *rusticorum proverbium.* To "flash with the fingers" was to raise some of them sharply for another to rap out the number, a game still played in Italy and called *mora.*

---

[7] Naber says there is a gap of one line <*incolumem te servent et* Mähly>, which Studemund denies.

Ad M. Caes. iii. 14 (Naber, p. 52).

Vat. 241 *ad fin.* | Magistro meo.

Epistula Ciceronis mirifice adfecit animum meum. Miserat Brutus Ciceroni librum suum corrigendum . . . .[1]

Ad M. Caes. iii. 15 (Naber, p. 52).

<Domino meo>.

Vat. 190 1. . . . . | molliantur atque ita efficacius sine ulla ad animos offensione audientium penetrent. Haec sunt profecto quae tu putes *obliqua et insincera et anxia et verae amicitiae minime accommodata.* At ego sine istis omnem orationem absurdam et agrestem et inconditam,[2] denique inertem atque inutilem puto. Neque magis oratoribus arbitror necessaria eiusmodi artificia quam philosophis. In ea re non oratorum domesticis, quod dicitur, testimoniis utar, sed philosophorum eminentissimis, poetarum vetustissimis excellentissimisque, vitae denique cotidiano usu atque cultu artiumque omnium experimentis.

2. Quidnam igitur tibi videtur princeps ille sapientiae simul atque eloquentiae Socrates? Huic enim primo ac potissimo testimonium apud te denuntiavi: eone usus genere dicendi, in quo nihil est obliquum,

---

[1] Two pages are lost, to *molliantur.*

[2] Mai for Cod. *incognitam.* Frontó seems here to have in mind Quintil. vi. 3. 107: *illa est urbanitas, in qua nihil absonum, nihil agreste, nihil inconditum.*

---

[1] Possibly the book *De Virtute*; see Cicero, *Tusc.* v. 1. For his other philosophical works see Cicero, *Acad. Part.* i. 12.

M. CORNELIUS FRONTO

M. Aurelius as Caesar to Fronto

To my master.   143 A.D.
   Cicero's letter interested me wonderfully. Brutus
had sent his book[1] to Cicero for corrections . . . .

Fronto to M. Aurelius as Caesar

To my Lord.   143 A.D.
   1. . . . . be softened and so more effectually
without any friction enter into the minds of hearers.
And these are actually the things which *you* think
crooked and *insincere* and *laboured*[2] *and by no means
reconcilable with true friendship!* But *I* think all
speech without these conventions rude and rustic
and incongruous, in a word, inartistic and inept.[3]
Nor, in my opinion, can philosophers dispense with
such artifices any more than orators. In support of
my contention I will adduce not "family" evidence,
as the phrase is, from oratory, but I will call upon
the most outstanding philosophers, the most ancient
and excellent poets, in fact, the everyday practice
and usage of life and the experience of all the arts.
   2. What, then, have you to say about that master
of eloquence no less than of wisdom, Socrates?—for
him, first and foremost, I have subpoenaed as witness
before you—did he cultivate a style of speech in
which there was nothing crooked, nothing at times

[2] As in Aul. Gell. xv. 7 and Tac. *Ann.* i. 8 ; Hildebrand
on Apul. *Met.* iv. 27, takes it as = *ambigua.*
[3] Fronto is nettled at something Marcus had said against
conventional insincerities of language. It was not for nothing
that he was called *Verissimus.*

nihil interdum dissimulatum? Quibus ille modis
Protagoram et Polum et Thrasymachum et sophistas
ceteros versare et inretire solitus? Quando autem
aperta arte congressus est? Quando non ex insidiis
adortus? Quo ex homine nata inversa oratio vid-
etur, quam Graeci εἰρωνείαν | appellant? Alcibiaden
vero ceterosque adulescentes genere aut forma aut
opibus feroces quo pacto appellare atque adfari sol-
ebat? Per iurgium an per πολιτίαν? Exprobrando
acriter quae delinquerent an leniter arguendo? Neque deerat Socrati profecto gravitas aut vis, quantum[1] cynicus Diogenes vulgo saeviebat; sed vidit
profecto ingenia partim hominum ac praecipue adulescentium facilius comi atque adfabili oratione leniri
quam acri violentaque superari. Itaque non vineis
neque arietibus errores adulescentium expugnabat,
sed cuniculis subruebat, neque umquam ab eo audit-
ores discessere lacerati sed nonnumquam lacessiti.
Est enim genus hominum natura insectantibus in-
domitum, blandientibus conciliatum. Quam ob rem
facilius precariis decedimus quam violentis deterr-
emur, plusque ad corrigendum promovent consilia
quam iurgia. Ita comitati monentium obsequimur,
inclementiae obiurgantium obnitimur.

---

[1] The margin of the Codex gives *quantam* from another MS.

---

[1] As when he pretended ignorance (*dissimulatio*) to elicit
a definition from others.

dissembled? By what methods was he wont to disconcert and entrap Protagoras and Polus and Thrasymachus and the other Sophists? When did he meet them without masking his batteries? When not attack them from an ambush? From whom, if not from him, can we say that the inverted[1] form of speech, which the Greeks call εἰρωνεία, took its rise? In what fashion, again, used he to accost and address Alcibiades and the other young men who prided themselves on birth or beauty or riches? In terms of censure or in terms of suavity?[2] With bitter reproof when they went wrong, or by gently calling attention to their faults? And yet Socrates assuredly had as much seriousness or force as the cynic Diogenes shewed in his habitual brutality. But he saw, in fact, that the dispositions of men in a measure, and of young men in particular, are more easily won over by courteous and sympathetic than by bitter and unrestrained language. And so he did not attack the errors of youths with mantlets and battering rams, but sapped them with mines, and his hearers never parted from him torn, though sometimes teased. For the race of mankind is by nature stiff-necked against the high-handed, but responds readily to coaxing. Therefore we give way more willingly to entreaties than are frightened into submission by violence, and advice rather than denunciation leads us to improve. So we listen to admonition courteously conveyed, but severity of correction makes us contumacious.[3]

[2] The Greek word = *civiliter*. *cp. urbanitas* in the quotation from Quintilian in note on p. 100.

[3] Fronto imitates Sallust in the conclusion of this letter. The last words are a good specimen of a Frontonian *sententia* or γνώμη.

Ad M. Caes. iii. 16 (Naber, p. 53).

Domino meo.

1. Quod tu me putes somnum cepisse, totam paene noctem pervigilavi, mecum ipse reputans num forte nimio | amore tui remissius et clementius delictum aliquod tuum aestimarem; num tu ordinatior perfectior iam in eloquentia esse debueris, sed ingenium tuum vel desidia vel indiligentia claudat.[1] Haec mecum anxie volutans inveniebam te multum supra aetatem, quanta[2] est, multum supra tempus quo operam his studiis dedisti, multum etiam supra opinionem meam, quamquam de te sperem immodica, in eloquentia promovisse. Sed, quo<d> mihi tum venit nocte media in mentem, qualem hypothesim scribis! nimirum ἐπιδεικτικήν, qua nihil est difficilius. Cur? Quia, quom sint tria ferme genera ὑποθέσεων <ἐπιδεικτικῶν συμβουλευτικῶν> δικανικῶν, cetera illa multo sunt proniora, multifaria<m> procliva vel campestria, τὸ ἐπιδεικτικὸν in arduo situm. Denique quom aeque tres quasi formulae sint orationis, ἰσχνὸν μέσον ἁδρόν, prope nullus in epidicticis τῷ ἰσχνῷ locus, qui est in di<canic>is[3] multum necessarius.

Vat. 148

---

[1] For the more usual *claudico*, as elsewhere in Fronto. The Codex for *ingenium tuum* has *ingenio tuo*, which would require some such word as *obstet*.

[2] For Cod. *quantus* (m¹) or *quantam* (m²).

[3] For Cod. *dicia*: Crossley suggests *dicis* = δίκαις.

---

[1] The epideictic kind (*genus demonstrativum* of Quintilian) was for show speech, such as panegyrics, speeches of thanks

M. CORNELIUS FRONTO

Fronto to Marcus Aurelius as Caesar

To my Lord.   143 A.D.

1. As for your thinking that I slept soundly, I lay awake nearly all night considering with myself whether, maybe from too great partiality for you, I did not think too lightly and indulgently of some shortcoming of yours; whether you should not by now be more trained, more advanced in eloquence, were not your abilities hampered either by sloth or carelessness. Turning these things over anxiously in my mind, I found that you had made much greater progress in eloquence than could be expected from your age, youthful as it is; much greater than the time that you have devoted to these studies would warrant, much greater than the hopes, and those no mean ones, which I had formed of you. But as it came to me only in the dead of night, what a subject you are writing on! actually one of the epideictic kind,[1] the most difficult of all. Why? Because of all the three generally received kinds of subject, the epideictic, the deliberative, the forensic, the first is set on a steep hill, the others are much less of a climb, being in many respects on sloping or level ground. In short, while there are similarly three types, as it were, of oratory, the plain, the medium, the luxuriant, in epideictic speeches there is practically no place for the plain style, which in forensic

---

to the Emperor, and μελέται, like the set declamations of the Greek rhetoricians. Quintilian (xii. 58) distinguishes three styles in oratory as (1) *subtile*, (2) *floridum* (*namque id ἀνθηρὸν appellant*) or *medium*, (3) *grande ac robustum* ; but Gellius (vii. 14) as *gracilis*, *mediocris*, *uber*. The subject here referred to as occupying Marcus may be the speech mentioned in the next letter.

Omnia ἐν τῷ ἐπιδεικτικῷ ἁδρῶς dicenda, ubique or-
nandum, ubique phaleris utendum; pauca τῷ μέσῳ
χαρακτῆρι.

2. Meministi autem tu plurimas lectiones, quibus

usque adhuc versatus | es, comoedias, atellanas, orat
ores veteres, quorum aut pauci aut praeter Catonem
et Gracchum nemo tubam inflat; omnes autem mu-
giunt vel stridunt potius. Quid igitur Ennius egit
quem legisti? Quid tragoediae ad versum sublim-
iter faciendum te iuverunt? Plerumque enim ad
orationem faciendam versus, ad versificandum oratio
magis adiuvat. Nunc nuper coepisti legere ornatas
et pompaticas orationes. Noli postulare statim eas
imitari posse. Verum, ut dixi, incumbamus, conit-
amur. Me vade me praede me sponsore celeriter
te in cacumine eloquentiae sistam. Di facient,
di favebunt. Vale, Domine, καὶ ἔλπιζε καὶ εὐθύμει
καὶ χρόνῳ καὶ ἐμπειρίᾳ πείθου. Matrem Dominam
saluta.

Quom Persarum disciplinam memorares, bene
bat![1]<u>unt ais.

Ad M. Caes. iii. 17 (Naber, p. 55).

HAVE mi Fronto merito carissime.

Intellego istam tuam argutissimam strofam,
quam tu quidem benignissime repperisti; ut, quia

[1] Query battuunt, of fencing. See Suet. Cal. 32; 54.

---

[1] Fronto, according to Cl. Mamertus, excelled in pompa
(the epideictic speech); according to Macrobius, in the siccum
genus (forensic).

ones is quite essential. In the epideictic speech everything must be said in luxuriant style, everywhere
there must be ornament, everywhere trappings must
be used. The medium style admits but sparingly of
these.

2. But you remember the numbers of books, of
which you have up to the present made the acquaintance, comedies, farces, old-time orators, few of whom,
perhaps none save Cato and Gracchus, blow a trum-
pet, but all bellow or, rather, shriek. What, then,
has Ennius done for you now you have read him?
What help have tragedies been to you in composing
verse in the grand style? For generally it is verse
that gives the best assistance to composing speeches
and speeches to writing verse. You have but lately
begun to read florid and showy[1] speeches. Do not
expect to be able to imitate them all at once. But,
as I said, let us bend to the oars, let us make a great
effort. Quickly shall I set you upon the very pin-
nacle of eloquence: I will be your surety for it, your
bondsman, your bail. The Gods will assist in it, the
Gods will accomplish it. Farewell, my Lord, be
sanguine and stout-hearted and trust to time and
practice. Greet your Lady mother.

When you spoke of[2] the Persian training,
batt⟨u⟩unt was a happy word of yours.

M. AURELIUS TO FRONTO

143 A.D.

HAIL, my deservedly dear Fronto.

I see through that most subtle ruse of yours,
which you indeed hit upon in pure kindness of heart.

[2] Either in a letter or perhaps in the speech. If the former,
it may have been in connexion with their being taught to
speak the truth.

laudando me fidem propter egregium erga me amorem tuum non habebas, vituperando laudi fidem quaereres. | Sed o me beatum, qui a Marco Cornelio meo, oratore maximo, homine optimo, et laudari et reprehendi dignus esse videor! Quid ego de tuis litteris dicam benignissimis verissimis amicissimis? verissimis tamen usque ad primam partem libelli tui, nam cetera, ubi me comprobas, ut ait nescio quis Graecus, puto Theophrastus,[1] τυφλοῦται γὰρ τὸ φιλοῦν περὶ τὸ φιλούμενον, item tu partim meorum prope caeco amore interpretatus es. Sed—tanti est me non recte scribere et te nullo meo merito sed solo tuo erga me amore laudare, de quo tu plurima et elegantissima ad me proxime scripsisti—ego, si tu volueris, ero aliquid. Ceterum litterae tuae id effecerunt, ut quam vehementer me amares sentirem. Sed quod ad ἀθυμίαν meam adtinet, nihilo minus adhuc animus meus pavet et tristiculus est, ne quid hodie in senatu dixerim, propter quod te magistrum habere non merear. Vale mi Fronto—quid dicam nisi—amice optime.

Ad M. Caes. ii. 1 (Naber, p. 25).

<Domino meo.>[2]

1. | Posterioribus litteris tuis, cur orationem in senatu non recitaverim, requisisti. At ego et edicto

Vat. 154

Vat. 160

---

[1] For Cod. *Thucydides*. Jerome quotes the words as from Theoph., but they occur also in Plato, *Legg.* v. 731 E.

[2] The title is left blank. This letter follows in the Codex the first Greek letter (*Epist. Graec.* 1) which is contained in Vat. 166, 165, and again in Ambr. 157 among the Greek letters.

For not being able to win credit for your praise of me by reason of your signal partiality in my case you sought to make it credible by throwing in some abuse.[1] But happy am I that I am thought worthy of blame no less than of praise by my Marcus Cornelius, greatest of orators and best of men! What shall I say of your letter so kind, so true, so loving?—true, that is, as far as the first part of its contents goes, but for the rest, where you express approval of me, as some Greek, Theophrastus I think, says, *the lover is blind to the faults of his loved one,* so have you been almost blinded by love in your judgment of some of my work. But so greatly do I value the fact that, though I do not write well, I should yet be praised by you for no desert of mine, but only because of your love for me, of which you have lately sent me such numerous and such happily-worded assurances that, since you wish it, I *will* be something. At all events, your letter had the effect of making me feel how much you loved me. But as to my despondency, nevertheless, I am still nervous in mind and a little depressed, lest I shall have said something in the Senate to-day, such that I should not deserve to have you as my master. Farewell, my Fronto, my—what shall I say but—best of friends.

Fronto to Marcus Aurelius as Caesar

To my Lord.   *July,* 143 A.D.

1. In your last letter you ask me why I have not delivered my speech in the Senate. Well, I

---

[1] Droz (*De Frontonis Instit. Orat.* p. 47) thinks Fronto had been reading an epideictic speech of Marcus's and been disappointed by it.

gratias agere Domino meo patri tuo debeo, sed edictum quidem circensibus nostris proponam, cuius principium id ipsum erit: *Quo die primum beneficio maximi Principis ederem spectaculum gratissimum populo maximeque populare, tempestivom <me>[1] duxisse gratias agere, ut idem dies*—hic aliqua sequatur tulliana conclusio. Orationem autem in senatu recitabo Augustis idibus. Quaeras fortasse cur <tam>[2] tarde? Quoniam ego numquam <quam>[3] primum officio sollenni quoquo modo fungi propero. Sed ut tecum agere debeo sine fuco et sine ambagibus, dicam quid cum animo meo reputem. Divum Hadrianum avum tuum laudavi in senatu saepenumero studio impenso et propenso quoque; et sunt orationes istae frequenter in omnium manibus. Hadrianum autem ego, quod bona venia pietatis tuae dictum sit, ut Martem Gradivom, ut Ditem Patrem, propitium et placatum magis volui

Vat. 159 quam amavi. Quare? Quia ad aman|dum fiducia aliqua opus est et familiaritate: quia fiducia mihi defuit, eo quem tanto opere venerabar non sum ausus diligere. Antoninum vero ut solem ut diem ut vitam ut spiritum amo, diligo, amari me ab eo sentio. Hunc nisi ita laudo, ut laudatio mea non in *Actis Senatus* abstrusa lateat, sed in manibus hominum oculisque versetur, ingratus sum etiam adversus te. Tum, quod cursorem fugitivom ferunt dixisse, *domino sexagena currebam, mihi centena, ut fugiam, curram,*[4] ego

---

[1] Or query *duxi me.*   [2] Orelli.   [3] Haupt.
[4] The margin of Cod. has *cur non* before *curram.*

have to return thanks to my Lord your Father by proclamation also, and that I shall issue at my Games in the Circus; it will begin with these very words: *On the day on which, by the kindness of our great Emperor, I am exhibiting a spectacle most attractive to the people and popular in the highest degree, I have thought it a good opportunity to return thanks to him, that the same day*—to be followed by some Ciceronian conclusion. My speech I shall deliver on August 13th. You will ask, perhaps, *Why so late?* Because I am never in a hurry to discharge a solemn duty at the first possible moment, and anyhow. But, as I ought to deal with you without disguise and without circumlocution, I will tell you what is in my mind. I often praised your grandfather, the deified Hadrian, in the Senate, with a steady zeal, aye, and a ready, and those speeches are constantly in everyone's hands. Yet, if your filial feeling towards him will allow me to say so, I wished to appease and propitiate Hadrian, as I might Mars Gradivus or Father Dis, rather than loved him. Why? Because love requires some confidence and intimacy. Since, in my case, confidence was lacking, therefore I dared not love one whom I so greatly revered. Antoninus, however, I love, I cherish like the light, like day, like life, like breath, and feel that I am loved by him. Him I must so praise that my praise be not hidden away in the *Journals of the Senate*,[1] but come into the hands and under the eyes of men, else am I ungrateful also towards you. Again, as the runaway syce is reported to have said, *I have run sixty miles for my master, I will run a hundred for myself, to escape;*[2] so I, too,

[1] The official record, like our "Hansard." Julius Caesar introduced the custom of keeping this record.
[2] Cp. Plut., *Banquet of Seven Wise Men,* § 16.

quoque quom Hadrianum laudabam, domino curre-
bam ; hodie autem mihi curro, mihi inquam, meoque
ingenio hanc orationem conscribo. Ad meum igitur
commodum faciam lente otiose clementer.

2. Tu si et valde properas, aliter te interim ob-
lecta ; basia patrem tuum, amplectere, postremo ipse
eum lauda. Ceterum quidem in idus Augustas tibi
expectandum est ut quod vis[1] quale vis audias. Vale,
Caesar, et patrem promerere ; et si quid scribere vis,
lente scribe.

Ad M. Caes. ii. 2 (Naber, p. 26).

| Mɪ Fronto consul amplissime.[2]

1. Manus do, vicisti : tu plane omnes, qui umquam amatores fuerunt, vicisti amando. Cape coro-
nam : atque etiam praeco pronuntiet palam pro tuo
tribunali victoriam istam tuam—M. Κορνήλιος Φρόντων
ὕπατος νικᾷ, στεφανοῦται τὸν ἀγῶνα τῶν μεγάλων φιλο-
τησίων. Ἀt ego, quamquam superatus, tamen nihil
de mea prothymia decessero aut defecero. Igitur tu
quidem me, <mi> magister,[3] magis amabis quam
ullus hominum ullum hominem amat ; ego vero te,
qui minorem vim in amando possideo, magis amabo
quam ullus hominum te amat, magis denique, quam
tu temet ipsum amas. Iam mihi cum Gratia certa-
men erit, quam timeo ut superare possim. Nam
illius quidem, ut Plautus ait, "amoris imber grandi-
bus guttis non vestem modo permanavit, sed in
medullam ultro pluit." [4]

---

[1] Orelli for Cod. *quidvis.*
[2] *Mi* is added by m² of the Codex, and *consul* is Naber's
reading.   [3] Added by m² over *magis.*
[4] From the margin of Cod. for *fluit* in the text.

when I praised Hadrian, ran for my master, but to-day I run for myself; for myself, I say, and write this speech to please myself. I shall compose it, therefore, at my ease, slowly, leisurely, placidly.

2. If you are very impatient for it, amuse yourself the while in other ways; kiss your father, embrace him, lastly, praise him yourself. But you may certainly look forward to hearing on August 13th what you would wish and expressed as you would wish. Farewell, Caesar, and prove worthy of your father, and if you wish to write anything, write slowly.

MARCUS AURELIUS TO FRONTO

My most honourable consul, Fronto. 143 A.D.

1. I give in, you have won: beyond question you have conquered in loving all lovers that have ever lived. Take the wreath and let the herald, too, proclaim in the ears of all before your tribunal this your victory—*M. Cornelius Fronto, consul, is the winner. He is crowned in the contest of the Great Friendship-Games.* Yet, though vanquished, will I not falter or fail in my devotion. Therefore shall you indeed my master, love me more than anyone of men loves any man, while I, who have less energy in loving, will love you more than anyone else loves you, more, in fact, than you love yourself. I see I shall have a competitor in Gratia,[1] and I fear that I may not be able to surpass her. For, as Plautus says, in her case, "not only has the rain of love drenched her dress with its thunder-drops, but soaked into her very marrow." [2]

[1] Fronto's wife.

[2] The nearest passage to this in our extant Pl. is *Most.* i. ii. 62 : *pro imbre amor advenit in cor meum. Is usque in pectus permanavit.*

2. Quas tu litteras te ad me existimas scripsisse!
Ausim dicere, quae me genuit atque aluit, nihil umquam tam iucundum tamque mellitum eam ad me
scripsisse. Nec hoc fit facundia aut eloquentia tua:

alioqui non modo mater mea sed omnes qui | spirant,
quod faciunt, confestim tibi cesserint: sed istae
litterae ad me tuae neque disertae neque doctae,
<at> tanta benignitate scatentes, tanta adfectione
abundantes, tanto amore lucentes, non satis proloqui
possum ut animum meum gaudio in altum sustu-
lerint, desiderio flagrantissimo[1] incitaverint,[2] postremo, quod ait Naevius, animum *amore capitali* com-
pleverint.

3. Illa alia epistula tua, qua indicabas cur tardius
orationem, qua laudaturus es Dominum meum, in
senatu prolaturus esses, tanta <me> voluptate adfecit, ut temperare non potuerim—et videris tu an
temere feceris—quin eam ipsi patri meo recitarem.
Quanto opere autem eum iuverit, nihil me oportet
persequi, quom tu et illius summam benivolentiam et
tuarum litterarum egregiam elegantiam noris. Sed
ex ea re longus sermo nobis super te exortus est,
multo multoque longior quam tibi et quaestori tuo
de me. Itaque nec tibi dubito ibidem in foro diu
tinnisse auriculas. Comprobat igitur Dominus et
amat causas propter quas recitationem tuam in longi-
orem diem protulisti . . . .[3]

---

[1] For Cod. *fraglantissimo*.
[2] The margin of Cod. gives *incenderint* as the reading of
another copy. [3] Four pages are lost here.

2. If you only knew what a letter you have written me![1] I could venture to say that she who bore me and nursed me, even she never wrote me anything so delightful, so honeyed. Nor is this due to your word-mastery or eloquence, for apply that test and not my mother only but all that breathe would, as they do, yield the palm at once to you. But I cannot express in words how that letter of yours to me, not for its eloquence or learning, but bubbling up as it does with so much kindness, brimful of such affection, sparkling with so much love, has lifted my heart up to the heavens, inspired it with the most glowing fondness, in a word, as Naevius says, filled it *with a love transcendent.*

3. That other letter of yours, in which you pointed out why you were going to put off the delivery of the speech in the Senate in which you intend to eulogize my Lord, delighted me so much that—forgive me if I was too hasty—I could not refrain from reading it aloud to my father himself. I need not dwell on the pleasure it gave him, for you know his entire good-will towards you and the matchless felicity of your letter. But from this occasion arose a long talk between us about you, much, much longer than yours and your quaestor's[2] about me. So your ears too must have been tingling about that time in the forum. My Lord, then, quite approves and sympathizes with your reasons for putting off the delivery of your speech till later . . . .

---

[1] Not the letter (*Ad M. Caes.* i. 3) given on p. 83, as Brakman thinks.

[2] Possibly Victorinus, or Fronto's brother Quadratus.

Ad M. Caes. ii. 4 (Naber, p. 29).

Vat. 167,
col. 2

| Magistro meo.

Ego ab hora quarta et dimidia in hanc horam
scripsi et Catonis multa legi et haec ad te eodem
calamo scribo et te saluto et quam commode agas
sciscitor. O quam diu te non vidi | . . . .

Quat. iv.
ends

Ad M. Caes. ii. 5 (Naber, p. 29).

Ambr. 110

<M. Caesar consuli amplissimo magistro suo.>

. . . .[1] vi|deatur.   Polemona ante hoc triduum
declamantem audivimus, ἵνα τι καὶ περὶ ἀνθρώπων
λαλήσωμεν. Si quaeris quid visus sit mihi, accipe.
Videtur mihi agricola strenuus, summa sollertia praeditus, latum fundum in sola segete frumenti et vit-
ibus occupasse, ubi sane et fructus pulcherrimus et
reditus uberrimus. Sed enim nusquam in eo rure ficus
Pompeiana vel holus Aricinum vel rosa Tarentina
vel nemus amoenum vel densus lucus vel platanus
umbrosa: omnia ad usum magis quam ad voluptatem,
quaeque [magis] laudare oporteat, amare non libeat.
Satisne ego audaci consilio et iudicio temerario[2]
videar, quom de tantae gloriae viro existimo? Sed
quom me recordor tibi scribere, minus me audere

---

[1] Six pages are lost from *vidi* in *Ad Caes.* ii. 4 above.
[2] Orelli adds <*uti*>.

---

[1] See Pliny, *N.H.* xv. 19.
[2] *ibid.* xix. 41. The cabbage of Aricia (*brassica oleracea*) is
said by Pliny to be the most useful of all, but the argument
requires that it should be only for pleasure.

M. CORNELIUS FRONTO

Marcus Aurelius to Fronto

To my Master.
143 A.D.

From half-past ten till now I have been writing and have also read a good deal of Cato, and I am writing this to you with the same pen, and I greet you and ask you how well you are. Oh, how long it is since I saw you! . . . .

August, 143 A.D.

M. Caesar to the most honourable consul his master.

. . . . Three days ago we heard Polemo declaim—that we may have some talk about men also. If you would like to know what I think of him, listen. He seems to me like a hard-working farmer endowed with the utmost shrewdness, who has laid out a large holding with corn-crops only and vines, wherein beyond question the yield is the fairest and the return the richest. But, indeed, nowhere in all that estate is there a fig tree of Pompeii,[1] or a vegetable of Aricia,[2] or a rose or Tarentum, nowhere a pleasant coppice or a thick-set grove, or a shady plane-tree; all for profit rather than for pleasure, such as one would be bound to praise but not disposed to love. In judging a man of such reputation,[3] am I, think you, bold enough in my purpose and rash enough in my judgment? But when I remember that I am writing to you, I feel that I

---

[3] From an interesting anecdote in Philost. (*Vit. Soph.* p. 231, Kays.) we find that Marcus formed a higher estimate of Polemo in later life.

quam tu velis arbitror.   Nos istic vehementer aestu-
amus—habes et hendecasyllabum ingenuum.   Igitur
priusquam poetari incipio, pausam tecum facio.
<Vale>, desiderantissime homo et tuo Vero caris-
sime, consul amplissime, magister dulcissime.   Vale
mi semper anima dulcissima.

Ad M. Caes. i. 8 [should be ii. 1] (Naber, p. 20).

Ambr. 60

|Caesari Aurelio Domino meo consul tuus Fronto.[1]

1. Quae sunt[2] aures hominum hoc tempore!
Quanta in spectandis orationibus elegantia!   Ex
Aufidio nostro scire poteris quantos in oratione mea
clamores concitarit, quantoque concentu laudantium
sit exceptum *omnis tunc imago patriciis pingebatur in-
signibus.*   At ubi genus nobile cum ignobili comparans
dixi *ut si quis ignem de rogo et ara accensum similem
putet, quod aeque luceat,* ad hoc pauci[3] admurmurati
sunt.

2. Quorsum hoc retuli?   Uti te, Domine, ita compares, ubi quid in coetu hominum recitabis, ut scias
auribus serviendum: plane nec ubique nec omni
modo, attamen nonnumquam et aliquantum.[4]   Quod
ubi facies, simile facere te reputato atque illud facitis
ubi eos, qui bestias strenue interfecerunt, populo
postulante ornatis aut manumittitis, nocentes etiam

---

[1] This letter is preceded in the Codex by the mutilated
letter to Herodes (Ambr. 59), which is also given again
among the *Epist. Graecae.*
[2] Schopen for Cod. *sint.*   [3] m[1] in Cod. *pauculi.*
[4] Schopen for Cod. *aliquando.*

am not bold enough for your taste. On that point
I am desperately doubtful—there's a home-grown
hendecasyllable for you! So I must call a halt with
you before I fall into the poetic vein. Farewell,
most missed of men and dearest to your Verus,[1]
most honourable consul, master most sweet. Farewell, my sweetest soul.

After August 13, 143 A.D.

To my Lord Aurelius Caesar your consul Fronto.

1. What nice ears men have nowadays! What
taste in judging of speeches! You can learn from
our Aufidius[2] what shouts of applause were evoked
in my speech, and with what a chorus of approval
were greeted the words *in those days every bust was
decorated with patrician insignia;* but when, comparing
a noble with a plebeian race, I said, *As if one were to
think the flame kindled on a pyre and on an altar to be
the same because both alike give light,*[3] at this a few
murmurs were heard.

2. Why have I told you this? That you, my
Lord, may be prepared, when you speak before an
assembly of men, to study their taste, not, of course,
everywhere and by every means, yet occasionally
and to some extent. And when you do so, remind
yourself that you are but doing the same as you do
when, at the people's request, you honour or enfran-
chise those who have slain beasts manfully in the

---

[1] His name at this time was Marcus Aurelius Verus.

[2] *i.e.* Victorinus, afterwards the son-in-law of Fronto.
He was one of Marcus's school friends. Lucian, writing a
little later, speaks similarly of the critical audiences (*Quom.
Hist. Scrib.* 10). The passage here quoted may have appealed
to patrician pride ; or its cadence with its repetition of the
letter *i* may have pleased the hearers.

[3] Cp. Tertull. *Apol.* 48.

homines aut scelere damnatos, sed populo postul-
ante | conceditis. Ubique igitur populus dominatur
et praepollet. Igitur ut populo gratum erit, ita facies
atque ita dices.

3. Hic summa illa virtus oratoris atque ardua est,
ut non magno detrimento rectae eloquentiae [1] aud-
itores oblectet; eaque delenimenta, quae mulcendis
volgi auribus comparat, ne cum [2] multo ac magno
dedecore fucata sint: potius ut in compositionis
structuraeque mollitia sit delictum quam in sententia
impudenti.[3] Vestem quoque lanarum <malo> mollitia delicatam esse quam colore muliebri, filo tenui
aut serico, purpuream ipsam, non luteam nec croc-
atam. Vobis praeterea, quibus purpura et cocco uti
necessarium est, eodem cultu nonnumquam oratio
quoque est amicienda. Facies istud, et temperabis
et moderaberis modo temperamentoque optimo. Sic
enim auguror: quicquid umquam in eloquentia factum sit, te id perfecturum, tanto ingenio es praeditus
tantoque te studio exerces et labore, quom in aliis
vel sine ingenio studium vel sine studio solum ingenium egregiam gloriam pepererit. Certum habeo te,
Domine, aliquantum temporis etiam prosae orationi |
conscribendae [4] impendere. Nam etsi aeque pernic-

---

[1] Heindorf for Cod. *recta eloquentia*.
[2] m² in the Codex strikes out these two words.
[3] m¹ has *impudentia*.   [4] For Cod. *inscribendae*.

---

[1] Marcus himself refused to do this; see Dio, lxxi. 29.
It was subsequently forbidden by law (Cod. ix. xlvii. 12).
[2] For *luteus* see Aul. Gell. ii. 26, § 8, = "flame-coloured,"
used of a bride's veil. For Fronto's thought *cp.* Seneca,
Ep. 114 and 100 §§ 5 ff., *quorundam non est compositio,*

arena ;[1] criminals even they may be or felons, yet you
release them at the people's request. Everywhere,
then, the people prevail and get their way. Therefore must you so act and so speak as shall please
the people.

3. Herein lies that supreme excellence of an orator,
and one not easily attainable, that he should please
his hearers without any great sacrifice of right eloquence, and should let his blandishments, meant to
tickle the ears of the people, be coloured indeed, but
not along with any great or wholesale sacrifice of
dignity : rather that in its composition and fabric
there should be a lapse into a certain softness but
no wantonness of thought. So too in a garment,
I should prefer it to be of the softness that belongs
to wool rather than to an effeminate colour ; it should
be of finely woven or silken thread, and itself purple
not flame-red[2] or saffron. You and your father,
moreover, who are bound to wear purple and crimson,
must on occasion clothe your words too in the same
dress. You will do this and be restrained and
moderate with the best moderation and restraint.
For this is what I prophesy, that what has ever been
done in eloquence will be done to the full by you, so
great is your natural capacity, and with such zeal
and application do you devote yourself to learning ;[3]
although, in others, either application without
capacity, or capacity alone without application, has
won outstanding glory. I feel sure, my Lord, that
you spend no little time in writing prose also. For

modulatio est ; adeo blanditur et molliter labitur ; and *lege
Ciceronem ; compositio una est ; pedem servat lenta et sine
infamia mollis.*

[3] Capit. *Vit. Mar.* iii. 7, says of Marcus : *tantum operis et
laboris studiis impendit, ut corpus adficeret.*

itas equorum exercetur sive quadrupede <cursu>[1] currant atque exerceantur seu tolutim, attamen ea quae magis necessaria, frequentius sunt experiunda.

4. Iam enim non ita tecum ago ut te duos et viginti annos natum cogitem. Qua aetate vixdum quicquam veterum lectionum adtigeram[2] deorum et tua virtute profectum tantum in eloquentia adsecutus es, quantum senioribus ad gloriam sufficiat et, quod est difficillimum, in omni genere dicendi. Nam epistulae tuae, quas adsidue scripsisti, mihi satis ostendunt quid etiam in remissioribus et tullianis facere possis.

5. Pro Polemone rhetore, quem mihi tu in epistula tua proxime exhibuisti tullianum, ego in oratione, quam in senatu recitavi,[3] philosophum reddidi, nisi me opinio fallit, perantiquom.[4] An quid tu dicas,[5] Marce, quemadmodum tibi videtur fabula Polemonis a me descripta? Plane multum mihi facetiarum contulit istic Horatius Flaccus, memorabilis poeta mihique propter Maecenatem ac Maecenatianos hortos Ambr. 55 meos non | alienus. Is namque Horatius sermonum libro secundo[6] fabulam istam Polemonis inseruit, si recte memini, hisce versibus :—

> *Mutatus Polemon ponas insignia morbi,*
> *Fasciolas, cubital, focalia, potus ut ille*
> *Dicitur ex collo furtim carpsisse coronas,*
> *Postquam et inpransi correptus voce magistri.*

[1] Niebuhr.   [2] Heind. for Cod. *adegeram*.
[3] On Aug. 13, 143.   [4] Cod. *perāticum*.
[5] Buttmann would read *iudicas*.   [6] *Satires*, ii. 3, 254.

---

[1] Marcus was born April 26, 121 A.D.

[2] Polemo, a tipsy gallant, bursting into the lecture room of Xenocrates, was converted by what he heard to better ways, and succeeded him as head of the Academy.

[3] Augustus gave the site of the cemetery on the Esquiline

though the swiftness of steeds is equally well exercised whether they run and practise at a gallop or a trot, yet the more serviceable qualities must be the more frequently put into requisition.

4. For by now I do not treat you as if I thought you were twenty-two [1] years old. At an age when I had scarcely touched any of the ancient authors you, by the grace of the gods and your own merit, have made such progress in eloquence as would bring fame to greybeards, and that, too—a far from easy task—in every branch of the art. For your letters, which you write so regularly, are enough to shew me what you can further do in that more familiar and Ciceronian vein.

5. Instead of Polemo the rhetorician, whom you lately presented to me in your letter as a Ciceronian, I have given back to you in my speech, which I delivered in the Senate, a philosopher,[2] if I am not mistaken, of the hoariest antiquity. Come, what say you, Marcus, how does my version of the story of Polemo strike you? Of course, Horatius Flaccus, a famous poet, and one with whom I have a connexion through Maecenas and my "gardens of Maecenas,"[3] supplied me with plenty of smart things on that subject. For this Horatius, in his second book of *Satires*, brings in the story of Polemo, if I remember rightly, in the following lines :—

Would you the marks of mental ill forswear,
The scarf, spats, lappet, that the rake declare?
Be changed, like Polemo, who, in drunken rage,
Scoffed at the teaching of the sober sage;
But cut to the heart by what he heard, 'tis said,
Plucked off by stealth the garlands from his head.

to Maecenas, who covered it with 25 feet of earth and there laid out his "gardens," of which Fronto was now the owner. See Lanciani, *Ancient Rome*, p. 67 (1889).

6. Versus, quos mihi miseras, remisi tibi per Victorinum nostrum atque ita remisi: chartam diligenter
lino transui, et ita linum obsignavi ne musculus iste
aliquid aliqua rimari possit. Nam mihi ipse de tuis
hexametris numquam quicquam impertivit, ita est
malus ac malitiosus. Sed ait te de industria cito et
cursim hexametros tuos recitare: eo se memoriae
mandare non posse. Remuneratus est igitur a me
mutuo. Paria habet, ne ullum hinc versum audiret.
Memini etiam te frequenter, ne cuiquam versus tuos
ostenderem, admonuisse.

7. Quid est, Domine? Certe hilaris es, certe bene
vales, omnium rerum certe sanus es. Male dum
similiter ne umquam nos perturbes ut natali tuo per-
turbasti, cetera | minus laboro. Εἴ τί σοι κακόν, εἰς
Πυρραίων κεφαλήν. Vale meum gaudium, mea secur-
itas hilaritas gloria. Vale et me, obsecro, omni
modo ames qua ioco qua serio.

Epistulam matri tuae scripsi, quae mea impudentia
est, Graece, eamque epistulae ad te scriptae implicui.
Tu prior lege et, si quis inerit barbarismus, tu qui a
Graecis litteris recentior es corrige, atque ita matri
redde. Nolo enim me mater tua ut opicum contem-
nat. Vale, Domine, et matri savium da, quom epistulam dabis, quo libentius legat.

6. The verses which you sent me I have sent you back by our Victorinus, and this is how I have sent them. I have carefully sewn the paper across with thread, and so sealed the thread that that little mouse should not poke his nose in anywhere. For he himself has never given me any information about your hexameters, so naughty is he and knavish. But he says that you purposely recite your hexameters so glibly and so fast that he cannot commit them to memory. So I have paid him back in his own coin: tit for tat—not to hear a line out of the packet. I remember, too, that you have often impressed upon me not to let anyone see your verses.

7. How is it with you, my Lord? Surely you are cheerful, surely you are well, surely sound in all respects. Other things are of little consequence, so you never give us the bad fright you did on your birthday.[1] If any evil threatens you, " may it fall on the Pyrrhaeans' heads." [2] Farewell, my joy, my refuge, happiness, glory. Farewell, and love me, I beseech you, every way in jest as in earnest.

I have written your mother a letter, such is my assurance, in Greek, and enclose it in my letter to you. Please read it first, and if you detect any barbarism in it, for you are fresher from your Greek than I am, correct it and so hand it over to your mother. I should not like her to look down on me as a goth. Farewell, my Lord, kiss your mother when you give her my letter, that she may read it the more gladly.

[1] April 26.
[2] See Zenob. *Prov. Cent.* iv. 2. Nothing is known of the Pyrrhaeans.

Ad Antoninum Pium, 1 (Naber, p. 163).

IMPERATORI Antonino Pio Augusto Fronto.[1]

Ambr. 342, *ad init.*

| Ut meministi, Caesar, quom tibi in senatu gratias agerem, desiderio quodam <dicendi> . . . . quae distuler<am> . . . . senatu frequentior . . . . sum. Nam litteras, quae <eo> die recitabantur . . . . librum . . . . Dominus . . . . Bene vale.[2]

Ad Antoninum Pium, 2 (Naber, p. 163).

M. FRONTONI Antoninus Caesar.

Quanta <sit erga> me tua <benivolentia iam pridem> hercule <satis scio, sed hoc plane admiror, ista nova et ingenio tuo digna . . . . orator>[3] op-

Ambr. 341

time | in tam trita et adsidua tibi materia invenire te[4] posse. Sed videlicet valde potens est, quod summe efficere possis, etiam velle. Nihil istis sensibus validius, nihil elocutione, salva sanitate tamen, civilius. Neque enim hoc <c>omittam,[5] ut te iustissima laude fraudem, dum metuo ne insolenter laudes meas laudem. Bene igitur accepisti et rectissimo opere, cui plane seposita materia omnis honor debetur. Ceterum ad ostentandum mihi animum tuum non multum egit; nam esse te benignissimum omnium factorum et dictorum meorum conciliatorem bene noveram. Vale mi Fronto carissime mihi.

---

[1] The title may have been added by Mai.

[2] The letter covered about twenty-five lines, or one column of the Codex.

[3] The mutilated passage covers about eight lines: so I understand Mai, but possibly he means that eight lines are lost between *quanta* and *me*.

[4] Ehrenthal for Cod. *et*.   [5] Mai.

M. CORNELIUS FRONTO

Fronto to the Emperor Antoninus Pius Augustus.

As you remember, Caesar, when I returned thanks[1] to you in the Senate . . . .
. . . .
. . . .
. . . . Farewell.

Antoninus Caesar to Marcus Fronto.

How great is your good-will towards myself I have long known well enough, by heaven, but what astonishes me . . . . best of orators, is that in a subject to you so hackneyed and thread-bare you can find anything to say that is new and worthy of your abilities. But no doubt the mere wish is an immense help towards what you can do so well. Nothing could be more effective than your thoughts, nothing more complimentary, yet without any sacrifice of good sense, than your expression of them. For I will not be guilty of defrauding you of your legitimate praise for fear of arrogantly praising the praise of myself. You have done your duty pleasingly and in unexceptionable fashion, for which, apart from all question of the subject, you deserve every credit. But as for shewing me your mind, it has not done much in that way, for I knew well enough that you always would put the most favourable construction on every word and act of mine. Farewell, my Fronto, my very dear friend.

---

[1] Whether this and the following letter refer to the thanks for Fronto's consulship is not clear. If so, we should have expected Pius to give Fronto his title of consul.

Illa pars orationis tuae circa Faustinae meae honorem gratissime a te adsumpta verior mihi quam disertior visa est. Nam ita se res habet: mallem mehercule Gyaris cum illa quam sine illa in Palatio vivere.

Ad M. Caes. ii. 3 (Naber, p. 28).

<Marcus Caesar Consuli suo et magistro.>

Vat. 168

1. | Sane, si quid Graeci veteres tale scripserunt, viderint qui sciunt; ego, si fas est dicere, nec M. Porcium tam bene vituperantem quam tu laudasti usquam adverti. O si Dominus meus satis laudari posset, profecto a te satis laudatus esset! Τοῦτο τὸ ἔργον οὐ γίνεται νῦν. Facilius quis Phidian, facilius Apellen, facilius denique ipsum Demosthenem imitatus fuerit aut ipsum Catonem, quam hoc tam effectum et elaboratum opus. Nihil ego umquam cultius nihil antiquius nihil conditius nihil latinius legi. O te hominem beatum hac eloquentia praeditum! O me hominem beatum huic magistro traditum. O ἐπιχειρήματα! O τάξις! O elegantia! O lepos! O venustas! O verba! O nitor! O argutiae! O kharites! O ἄσκησις! O omnia! Ne valeam nisi aliqua[1] die virga in manus tibi tradenda erat,[2] diadema circumponendum, tribunal ponendum: tum praeco omnes nos citaret—quid nos dico? omnes, inquam, philologos et disertos istos—eos tu singulos virga perduc-

---

[1] m² of the Codex above the line.
[2] Ehrenthal *erit.* For Cod. perhaps *cp.* Hor. *Od.* i. 36. 4 Possibly *aliqua* is wrong.

---

[1] Faustina the younger, daughter of Pius, seems to be meant, as Mommsen suggested.

That part of your speech, which you most kindly devoted to honouring my Faustina,[1] seemed to me as true as it was eloquent. For this is the plain fact: By heaven, I would sooner live with her in Gyara[2] than in the palace without her.

143 A.D.

MARCUS CAESAR to his own consul and master.

1. Whether the Greeks of old ever wrote anything so good,[3] verily let those see to it who know; for myself, if I may say so, nowhere have I noticed in M. Porcius an invective so perfect as your praise. Oh, if my Lord *could* be praised enough, surely he had been enough praised by you. This work is not done in these days. Easier were it for one to rival Pheidias, easier Apelles, easier, in fine, Demosthenes himself or Cato himself, than this perfect and finished work. Never have I read anything more refined, more classical, more polished, more Latin. Oh, happy you to be gifted with such eloquence! Oh, happy I to be in the hands of such a master! What reasoned thoughts! What orderly arrangement! What elegance! What wit! What beauty! What diction! What brilliance! What subtlety! What charm! What practised skill! What everything! My life on it, but some day you ought to have the wand[4] placed in your hand, the diadem round your brow, the tribunal under your feet: then the herald should summon all of us—why do I say us? I mean all your learned folk and your eloquent—one by one you should wave them along with your wand and

---

[2] An Aegean island to which banished persons were sent.

[3] Marcus is referring to Fronto's speech of thanks to Pius in the Senate.

[4] As symbol of authority. Cp. Julian to Libanius.

eres, verbis moneres.   Mihi adhuc nullus metus huius monitionis erat ; | multa supersunt ut in ludum tuum pedem introferam.

2. Haec cum summa festinatione ad te scribo, nam quom Domini mei ad te epistulam[1] mitterem tam benignam, quid meis longioribus litteris opus erat? Igitur vale, decus eloquentiae Romanae, amicorum gloria, μέγα πρᾶγμα, homo iucundissime, consul amplissime, magister dulcissime.

3. Postea cavebis de me, praesertim in senatu, tam multa mentiri.   Horribiliter scripsisti hanc orationem.   O si ad singula capita caput tuum basiare possem ! Ἰσχυρῶς πάντων καταπεφρόνηκας ! Hac oratione lecta frustra nos studemus, frustra laboramus, frustra nervos contendimus.   Vale semper, magister dulcissime.

Epist. Graecae 1 (Naber, p. 239).

| Μητρὶ Καίσαρος[2]

1. Πῶς ἂν ἀπολογησάμενος συγγνώμης παρὰ σοῦ τύχοιμι, ὅτι σοι τούτων τῶν ἡμερῶν οὐκ ἐπέστειλα; ἢ δῆλον ὅτι τὴν ἀληθῆ τῆς ἀσχολίας εἰπὼν αἰτίαν; λόγον γὰρ συνήγαγόν τινα περὶ τοῦ μεγάλου βασιλέως. ἡ δὲ τῶν Ῥωμαίων παροιμία " φίλου τρόπον μὴ μισεῖν ἀλλ' εἰδέναι " φησὶ δεῖν. οἷος δὲ οὑμὸς τρόπος φράσω καὶ οὐκ ἀποκρύψομαι. ὑπὸ τῆς πολλῆς ἀφυίας καὶ οὐθενείας

---

[1] Probably the previous letter.
[2] This letter is given twice in the Cod., viz. Ambr. 56, Vat. 155, 165, and Ambr. 157, 158, 163, 164.

---

[1] He knows his own weakness and never feared admonition, because he knows how much he needs it and such a teacher.
[2] Demosth. 928, 6.
[3] *Horribiliter* appears to be a slang use.

admonish them with the words of your lips. For myself I never had any fear of these admonitions; I have more reasons than enough for setting foot in your school.[1]

2. I am writing this to you in the utmost haste, for what need of a longer letter from me when I send you so gracious a one of my Lord's ? Farewell, then, glory of Roman eloquence, pride of your friends, a man of mark,[2] most delightful of men, most honourable consul, master most sweet.

3. In future be chary of telling so many fibs, especially in the Senate, about me. This speech of yours is "awfully"[3] well written. Oh, if I could only kiss your head for every heading of it ! You have absolutely brought everyone else to utter shame. With this speech before our eyes, vain is our study, vain our toil, vain our efforts. Fare ever well, sweetest of masters.

FRONTO TO DOMITIA LUCILLA

To the mother of Caesar.

143 A.D.

1. What excuse[4] of mine can win your pardon for my not having written to you all this time, if it be not by my stating the true cause of my want of leisure, that I had composed a speech about our great Emperor? The Roman saw bids us "not hate a friend's ways but ken them."[5] What mine are I will tell you, and not conceal them. From my great natural incapacity and worthlessness

---

[4] A marginal note in the Codex says that this letter was to excuse Fronto's silence *post integritatem redditam.* Fronto's health seems meant.

[5] "*Amici mores noveris non oderis.*" See Trench, *On Proverbs*, p. 49, note.

ὅμοιόν τι πάσχω τῇ ὑπὸ τῶν Ῥωμαίων ὑαίνῃ καλουμένῃ,
ἧς τὸν τράχηλον κατ' εὐθὺ τετάσθαι λέγουσιν, κάμπτεσθαι

Vat. 166
δὲ ἐπὶ θάτερα | τῶν πλευρῶν μὴ δύνασθαι. κἀγὼ δὴ
ἐπειδάν τι συντάττω προθυμότερον, ἀκαμπής τίς εἰμι καὶ
τῶν ἄλλων ἁπάντων ἀφέμενος, ἐπ' ἐκεῖνο μόνον ἵεμαι
ἀνεπιστρεπτεὶ κατὰ τὴν ὕαιναν. καὶ[1] τοὺς ὄφεις δέ
φασιν τὰ ἀκόντια[2] οὕτω πως ᾄττειν κατ' εὐθύ, τὰς δὲ
ἄλλας στροφὰς μὴ στρέφεσθαι· καὶ τὰ δόρατα δὲ καὶ τὰ
τόξα τότε μάλιστα τυγχάνει τοῦ σκοποῦ, ὅταν εὐθεῖαν ᾄξῃ
μήτε ὑπ' ἀνέμου παρωσθέντα, μήτε ὑπὸ χειρὸς Ἀθηνᾶς
ἢ Ἀπόλλωνος σφαλέντα, ὥσπερ τὰ ὑπὸ Τεύκρου ἢ τὰ ὑπὸ
τῶν μνηστήρωι βληθέντα.

2. Ταύτας μὲν δὴ τρεῖς εἰκόνας ἐμαυτῷ προσείκασα,
τὰς μὲν δύο ἀγρίας καὶ θηριώδεις, τὴν τῆς ὑαίνης καὶ τὴι
τῶν ὄφεων,[3] τρίτην δὲ τὴν τῶν βελῶν καὶ αὐτὴν ἀπάν-

Ambr. 158
θρωπον | οὖσαν καὶ ἄμουσον. εἰ δὲ δὴ καὶ τῶν ἀνέμων
φαίην ἐπαινεῖσθαι μάλιστα τὸν οὔριον, ὅτι δὴ ἐπ' εὐθὺ
φέροι τὴν ναῦν, ἀλλὰ μὴ εἰς τὰ πλάγια ἀπονεύειν ἐῷ, ἡ
τετάρτη ἂν εἴη αὕτη εἰκὼν καὶ αὐτὴ βιαιά. εἰ δὲ προσ-
θείην καὶ τὸ τῆς γραμμῆς, ὅτι πρεσβυτάτη τῶν γραμμῶν
ἡ εὐθεῖά ἐστιν, πέμπτην ἂν εἰκόνα λέγοιμι, μὴ μόνον
ἄψυχον ὥσπερ τὴν τῶν δοράτων, ἀλλὰ καὶ ἀσώματον
ταύτην οὖσαν.

3. Τίς ἂν οὖν εἰκὼν εὑρεθείη πιθανή; μάλιστα μὲν

Vat. 165;
ἀνθρωπίνη, ἄμεινον δὲ εἰ καὶ μουσική· εἰ | δὲ αὖ φιλίας
καὶ ἔρωτος αὐτῇ μετείη, μᾶλλον ἂν ἔτι ἡ[4] εἰκὼν ἐοίκοι.
τὸν Ὀρφέα φασιν οἰμῶξαι ὀπίσω ἐπιστραφέντα· εἰ δὲ

---

[1] Before καὶ the Vat. Cod. has ιξ, for which Naber suggests ἔτι.

[2] Buttmann reads τοὺς ἀκοντίας.

[3] Vat. Cod. ἀκοντίων.   [4] Vat. Cod. εἴη.

I labour under much the same defect as the animal called by the Romans a hyena, whose neck, they say, can be stretched out straight forward but cannot be bent to either side.[1] So I, when I am putting together anything with more than usual care, am, in a way, immovable, and, giving up all else, aim at that alone, like the hyena not turning to the right hand or to the left. Again, they say that the snakes called "darters"[2] in much the same way project themselves straight forwards, but never move sideways; and spears and arrows are then most likely to hit the mark when they are propelled straight, neither made to swerve by the wind, nor foiled by Athene's hand or Apollo's, as were the arrows shot by Teucer or the suitors.

2. These three similes, then, have I applied to myself, two of them fierce and savage, that of the hyena and that of the snake, and a third drawn from missiles, it, too, non-human and harsh. And if, indeed, I were to say that of winds the one astern was especially to be commended because it takes a ship straight forward nor lets it make lee-way, this would be a fourth simile, and that a forcible one. And if I added this also of the line, that the straight line is the chiefest of all lines, I should produce a fifth simile, not only inanimate like that of the spears, but this one also incorporeal.

3. What simile, then, can be found convincing? One above all that is human, better still if it be also cultured; and if it partake, too, of friendship and love, the simile would be all the more a similitude. They say that Orpheus rued his turning to look

[1] Pliny, *N.H.* viii. 30.

[2] The arrow-snake, Isaiah, xxxiv. 15: so *iaculi serpentes*, Lucan ix. 720, and *cp.* Hor. *Odes*, iii. 27, 6.

κατ' εὐθὺ ἔβλεπέν τε καὶ ἐβάδιζεν, οὐκ ἂν ὤμωξεν. ἅλις
εἰκόνων. καὶ γὰρ αὕτη τις ἀπίθανος ἡ τοῦ Ὀρφέως
εἰκὼν ἐξ ᾅδου ἀνιμημένη.[1]

4. Ἀπολογήσομαι δὲ τοὐντεῦθεν ἤδη ὅθεν ἂν ῥᾷστα
συγγνώμης τύχοιμι. τί δὴ τοῦτό ἐστιν; ὅτι συγγράφων
τὸ τοῦ βασιλέως ἐγκώμιον ἔπραττον <πρῶτον>[2] μὲν ὃ
μάλιστα σοί τε καὶ τῷ σῷ παιδὶ κεχαρισμένον ἐστίν·
ἔπειτα δὲ καὶ ὑμῶν ἐμεμνήμην καὶ ὠνόμαζον δὲ ὑμᾶς ἐν τῷ
συγγράμματι, ὥσπερ οἱ ἐρασταὶ τοὺς φιλτάτους ὀνομάζ-
ουσιν ἐπὶ πάσῃ κύλικι. ἀλλὰ γὰρ ἡ τέχνωσις[3] τῶν
εἰκόνων ἐπεισρεῖ καὶ ἐπιφύεται. αὕτη γοῦν παρεφάνη,
ἣν ἐπὶ πάσαις λέγω, ἥτις καὶ δικαιότατα εἰκὼν ἂν προσ-

αγορεύοιτο, οὖσα ἐκ ζωγρά|φου· τὸν Πρωτογένη τὸν
ζωγράφον φασὶν ἕνδεκα ἔτεσιν τὸν Ἰάλυσον γράψαι,
μηδὲν ἕτερον ἐν τοῖς ἕνδεκα ἔτεσιν ἢ τὸν Ἰάλυσον γρά-
φοντα. ἐμοὶ δὲ οὐχ εἷς, δύο δὲ ἅμα Ἰαλύσω ἐγραφέσθην,
οὗ δὴ τοῖν προσώποιν οὐδὲ ταῖν μορφαῖν μόναιν ἀλλὰ καὶ
τοῖν τρόποιν καὶ ταῖν ἀρεταῖν οὐ μετρίω ὄντε ἄμφω οὐδὲ
γράφεσθαι ῥᾳδίω, ἀλλ' ὁ μέν ἐστι μέγας βασιλεὺς ἄρχων

πάσης τῆς γῆς καὶ θαλάττης, ὁ δ' ἕτερος υἱὸς μεγάλου |
βασιλέως, ἐκείνου μὲν οὕτω παῖς ὥσπερ Ἀθηνᾶ τοῦ Διός,
σὸς δὲ ὢν υἱός,[4] ὡς τῆς Ἥρας ὁ Ἥφαιστος· ἀπέστω δὲ τὸ
τῶν ποδῶν ταύτης τῆς τοῦ Ἡφαίστου εἰκόνος. ἡ μὲν οὖν
ἀπολογία αὕτη ἂν εἴη πάνυ τις εἰκαστικὴ γενομένη καὶ
γραφικὴ εἰκόνων ἔκπλεως αὐτὴ μάλα.

5. Ἔτι κατὰ τοὺς γεωμέτρας αἰτήσομαι—τὸ ποῖον; εἴ
τι τῶν ὀνομάτων ἐν ταῖς ἐπιστολαῖς ταύταις εἴη ἄκυρον ἢ

---

[1] Vat. Cod. ἀνειμένη: Ambr. ἀνημειμένη.   [2] Brakman.

[3] Mai reads ἀτεχνῶς τό, but Studemund says the Codex has
τέχνωσις.

[4] Brakman for Cod. σωνιος, with correction υἱὸς by m².

back: had he looked and walked straight ahead he
had not rued. Enough of similes. For this, too, is
somewhat unconvincing, this simile of Orpheus
fetched up from Hades.

4. But I will now for the rest plead in excuse
what will most easily win me pardon. What, then,
is this? That in writing the Emperor's encomium
I was doing, in the first place, what was especially
gratifying to you and your son; in the next I re-
membered and mentioned both of you in the composition, just as lovers name their darlings over every
cup. But, indeed, the craftmanship of similes is an
insinuating thing and grows on us. This one, at any
rate, has occurred to me, which I add to all the others,
and indeed it can most fairly be called a simile (or
likeness), being taken from a painter. Protogenes the
painter is said to have taken eleven[1] years to paint
his *Ialysus*, painting nothing but the *Ialysus* all those
eleven years. But, as for me, I painted not one but
two Ialysuses at once, being no ordinary ones either
of them, nor easy to depict, not only in respect of
their faces and figures, but also of their characters
and qualities, for the one is the great Imperator of
all land and sea, and the other the great Imperator's
son, his child in the same way as Athene is of Zeus,
but thy son as Hephaestus is of Hera. But let there
be no "halting"[2] in this simile from Hephaestus.
This defence of mine, then, would seem to be wholly
verisimilous and picturesque, full as it is in itself of
similes entirely.

5. It remains that I should, after the fashion of
geometers, ask—what? If any word in this letter be

[1] Plutarch (*Demetr.* 22) says seven years. *cp.* Pliny, *N.H.*
xxxv. 36, §§ 10, 20.
[2] For the lame Hephaestus see Hom. *Il.* i. *ad fin.*

βάρβαρον ἢ ἄλλως ἀδόκιμον ἢ μὴ πάνυ ἀττικόν, μ<ὴ
τοῦτ᾽, ἀλλ>ὰ [1] τοῦ ὀνόματός σε ἀξιῶ τὴν διάνοιαν σκοπεῖν
αὐτὴν καθ᾽ αὑτήν· οἶσθα γὰρ ὅτι ἐν αὐτοῖς [2] ὀνόμασιν καὶ
αὐτῇ διαλέκτῳ διατρίβω.[3] καὶ γὰρ τὸν Σκύθην ἐκεῖνον
τὸν Ἀνάχαρσιν οὐ πάνυ τι ἀττικίσαι φασίν, ἐπαινεθῆναι
δὲ ἐκ τῆς διανοίας καὶ τῶν ἐνθυμημάτων. παραβαλῶ
δὴ ἐμαυτὸν Ἀναχάρσιδι οὐ μὰ Δία κατὰ τὴν σοφίαν

Ambr. 164 ἀλλὰ κατὰ τὸ βάρβαρος ὁμοίως εἶναι. | Ἦν γὰρ ὁ μὲν
Σκύθης τῶν νομάδων Σκυθῶν, ἐγὼ δὲ Λίβυς τῶν Λιβύων
τῶν νομάδων. κοινὸν δὴ τὸ νέμεσθαι ἐμοί τε καὶ Ἀνα-
χάρσιδι· κοινὸν οὖν ἔσται καὶ τὸ βληχᾶσθαι νεμομένοις,
ὅπως ἄν τις βληχήσηται. οὕτως μὲν δὴ καὶ τὸ βαρ-
βαρίζειν τῷ βληχᾶσθαι προσείκασα. οὐκοῦν παύσομαι
μηδὲν ἕτερον γράφων ἀλλ᾽ ἢ εἰκόνας.

Ad M. Caes. ii. 10 (Naber, p. 33).

<MARCUS CAESAR Frontoni consuli amplissimo.>

Ambr. 102 1. . . . . | adfinitate sociatum, neque tutelae
subditum, praeterea in ea fortuna constitutum, in
qua, ut Q. Ennius ait,

Omnes dant consilium vanum atque ad voluptatem omnia;

item quod Plautus egregie in *Colace* super eadem
re ait,

  Qui data fide firmata fidentem fefellerunt,
  Subdoli subsentatores, regi qui sunt proximi,
  Qui aliter regi dictis dicunt, aliter in animo habent.

[1] Brakman.
[2] Jacobs would read ἄλλοις, and ἄλλη for αὐτῇ.
[3] Heindorf would insert οὐ.

obsolete or barbarous, or in any other way unauthorized, or not entirely Attic, look not at that, but only, I beseech you, at the intrinsic meaning of the word, for you know that I do spend time on mere words or mere idiom. And, indeed, it is said that the famous Scythian Anacharsis was by no means perfect in his Attic, but was praised for his meaning and his conceptions. I will compare myself, then, with Anacharsis, not, by heaven, in wisdom, but as being like him a barbarian. For he was a Scythian of the nomad Scythians, and I am a Libyan of the Libyan nomads. I as well as Anacharsis may browse fresh pastures, bleat therefore as well as he while browsing, just as one wills to bleat. See, I have assimilated barbarism to bleating. So will I make an end of writing nothing but similes.

143 A.D.

M. CAESAR to the most honourable consul Fronto.

1. . . . . connected by marriage[1] and not subject to guardianship and stationed besides in a social position in which, as Q. Ennius says,

All give foolish counsel, and look in all to pleasing only;

and Plautus, too, in his *Colax*, says finely on the same subject,

> *Crafty cajolers, who with fast-pledged faith*
> *Take in the trustful: these stand round a king,*
> *And what they speak is far from what they think.*

---

[1] Marcus appears to be speaking of himself. At the end of the preceding letter (*Ad M. Caes.* ii. 9, p. 146) and the beginning of this one several pages are lost.

Haec enim olim incommoda regibus solis fieri solebant, at enim nunc adfatim sunt, qui et regum filiis, ut Naevius [1] ait,

Linguis faveant atque adnutent et subserviant.

Merito ergo,[2] mi magister, ita flagro;[3] merito unum meum σκοπὸν mihi constitui; merito unum hominem cogito quom stilus in manus venit.

2. Hexametros meos iucundissime petis, quos ego quoque confestim misissem, si illos mecum haberem. Nam librarius meus, quem tu nosti, Anicetum dico, quom proficiscerer, nihil meorum scriptorum mecum misit. Scit enim morbum meum et timuit ne, si venissent in potestatem, quod soleo facerem et in furnum dimitterem. Sane istis hexametris prope nullum periculum | erat. Ut enim verum magistro meo confitear, amo illos. Ego istic noctibus studeo, nam interdiu in theatro consumitur. Itaque minus ago vespera fatigatus, luce surgo [4] dormitans. Feci tamen mihi per hos dies excerpta ex libris sexaginta in quinque tomis. Sed quom leges sexaginta, inibi sunt et Novianae [et] atellaniolae et Scipionis oratiunculae—ne tu numerum nimis expavescas.

3. Polemonis tui quom [5] meministi, rogo ne Horatii

Ambr. 101

---

[1] We should possibly read Novius, who is mentioned below.

[2] Niebuhr for Cod. *ego.*

[3] For Cod. *fraglo.* The *ita* is for *ii* added by m[2] of Cod. after *magister.*

[4] Added above *luce* by m[2] of Cod. This passage is quoted by Charisius, ii. 223, ed. Keil.   [5] Rob. Ellis for Cod. *quem.*

138

These drawbacks used formerly to be confined to
kings, but now, indeed, even the sons of kings have
more than enough of men who, as Naevius [1] says,

> *Still flatter with their tongues and still assent,*
> *And fawn upon them to their heart's content.* [2]

I do right, then, my master, in being so ardent, right
in setting before me one single aim, right in thinking of one man only when I take my pen in hand.

2. You very kindly ask for my hexameters, and I
too should have sent them at once if I had had
them with me. But my secretary—you know him, I
mean Anicetus—did not pack up any of my work
when I set out. For he knows my failing and was
afraid that, if they came into my hands, I should do
as I usually do, and consign them to the flames.
But, as a matter of fact, those particular hexameters
were in next to no danger. For, to tell my master
the truth, I dote on them. I pore over them
o' nights, for the day is spent in the theatre. And
so I get through but little in the evening, being
tired, and in the morning I get up sleepy. Still I
have made for myself these last few days five note-
books full of extracts from sixty volumes. But when
you read *sixty*, don't be staggered by the number, for
included in them are the little Atellane farces of
Novius and Scipio's speechlets.

3. As you have mentioned your Polemo, please
don't mention Horace again, who, with Polio,[3] is

---

[1] Naevius was the earliest great national poet of Rome. He
wrote an epic on the First Punic War, and also tragedies.

[2] *cp.* Shaks. *Hamlet*, III. ii, 399.

[3] Probably the Augustan poet, orator and historian,
Asinius Pollio, is meant. His archaism would recommend
him to Fronto, who subsequently quotes a work of his.
II. 142.

memineris, qui mihi cum Polione est emortuus. Vale
mi amicissime, vale mi amantissime, consul amplissime, magister dulcissime, quem ego biennio iam non
vidi. Nam quod aiunt quidam duos menses inter-
fuisse, tantum dies numerant. Eritne quom te
videbo?

Ad M. Caes. ii. 11 (Naber, p. 35).

AMPLISSIMO consuli magistro suo M. Caesar salutem.

Anno abhinc tertio me commemini cum patre
meo a vindemia redeuntem in agrum Pompei Falconis
devertere; ibi me videre arborem multorum ram-
orum, quam ille suum nomen *catachannam* nominabat.
Sed illa arbor mira et nova visa est mihi in uno trunco
omnium ferme germina <arborum ferens> . . . .[1]

Ad M. Caes. ii. 6 (Naber, p. 30).

Ambr. 109   M. AURELIUS CAESAR | consuli suo et magistro
salutem.

1. Postquam ad te proxime scripsi, postea nihil
operae pretium <fuit>[2] quod ad te scriberetur aut
quod cognitum ad aliquem modum iuvaret. Nam
διὰ τῶν αὐτῶν fere dies tramisimus—idem theatrum,
idem odium,[3] idem desiderium tuum. Quid dico

---

[1] Size of lacuna is not known.

[2] Cramer; but the error seems to lie in the word *postea*.

[3] The m[2] of Cod. gives *odeum* (ὠδεῖον), and the margin also
notes from another MS. the alternative *otium*.

dead and done with as far as I am concerned. Farewell, my dearest, my most beloved friend; farewell, my most honourable consul, my most sweet master, whom I have not seen these two years; for as to what some say, that two months [1] have intervened, they only count days. Shall I ever see you?

143 A.D.

To the most honourable consul, his master, M. Caesar, greeting.

Three years ago I remember turning aside with my father to the estate of Pompeius Falco [2] when on our way home from the vintage; and that I saw there a tree with many branches, which he called by its proper name of *catachanna*.[3] But it seemed to me a new and extraordinary tree, bearing as it did upon its single stem off-shoots of almost every kind of tree . . . .

Naples, 143 A.D.

M. AURELIUS CAESAR to his own consul and master, greeting.

1. Since my last letter to you nothing has happened worth writing of, or the knowledge of which would be of the slightest interest. For we have passed whole days more or less in the same occupations: the same theatre, the same dislike of it, the same longing for you—the same, do I say?

---

[1] July and August, the two months of Fronto's consulship, during which Fronto had to be in Rome.

[2] He appears as one of Pliny's correspondents in his *Letters*.

[3] A Punic name (?). For tree *cp.* Hissey, *Tour in Phaeton*, p. 254.

idem? immo id cotidie novatur et gliscit; et quod ait Laberius de amore, suo modo καὶ ἐπὶ ἰδίᾳ μούσῃ,

> *Amor tuus tam cito crescit quam porrus, tam firme quam palma.*

Hoc igitur ad desiderium verto, quod ille de amore ait. Volo ad te plura scribere, sed nihil suppetit.

2. Ecce quod in animum venit. Encomiographos istic audiimus, Graecos scilicet sed miros mortales, ut ego, qui a Graeca litteratura tantum absum quantum a terra Graecia mons Caelius meus abest, tamen me sperem illis comparatum etiam Theopompum aequiparare posse; nam hunc audio apud Graecos disertissimum natum esse. Igitur paene me opicum animantem ad Graecam scripturam perpulerunt homines, ut Caecilius ait, *incolumi inscientia.*

Ambr. 108 3. Caelum Neapolitanum plane commodum, | sed vehementer varium. In singulis scripulis horarum frigidius aut tepidius aut horridius[1] fit. Iam primum media nox tepida, Laurentina; tum autem gallicinium frigidulum, Lanuvinum; iam conticinium atque matutinum atque diluculum usque ad solis ortum gelidum, ad Algidum maxime; exim antemeridiem apricum, Tusculanum; tum meridies fervida, Puteolana; at enim ubi sol lautum[2] ad Oceanum profectus <est>, fit demum caelum modestius, quod genus Tiburtinum; id vespera et concubia nocte,

---

[1] Some prefer to read *torridius*, " more tropical."

[2] m² of Cod. for *latum.*

nay, one that is daily renewed and increases and, as Laberius, after his own manner and in his own peculiar style, says of love,

> *Your love as fast as any onion grows, as firm as any palm.*

This then that he says of love, I apply to my longing for you. I should like to write you a longer letter, but nothing suggests itself.

2. Stay, I have just thought of something. We have been listening to panegyrists here, Greeks, of course, but wondrous creatures, so much so that I, who am as far removed from Greek literature as is my native Caelian hill[1] from the land of Greece, could nevertheless hope, matched with them, to be able to rival even Theopompus, the most eloquent, as I hear, of all the Greeks. So I, who am all but a breathing barbarian, have been impelled to write in Greek by men, as Caecilius[2] says, of *unimpaired ignorance*.

3. The climate of Naples[3] is decidedly pleasant, but violently variable. Every two minutes it gets colder or warmer or rawer. To begin with, midnight is warm, as at Laurentum; then, however, the cockcrow watch chilly, as at Lanuvium; soon the hush of night and dawn and twilight till sunrise cold, for all the world like Algidus; anon the forenoon sunny, as at Tusculum; following that a noon as fierce as at Puteoli; but, indeed, when the sun has gone to his bath in Ocean, the temperature at last becomes more moderate, such as we get at Tibur; this continues the same during the evening and first sleep of night,

---

[1] Marcus was born on Mons Caelius, where the Annii had a residence.

[2] Caecilius Statius, a comic poet contemporary with Ennius.

[3] See Pliny, *N.H.* iii. 5.

dum *se intempesta nox,* ut ait M. Porcius, *praecipitat,*[1]
eodem modo perseverat. Sed quid ego, qui me
paucula scripturum promisi, deliramenta Masuriana
congero? Igitur vale, magister benignissime, consul
amplissime, et me, quantum ames, tantum desidera.

Ad M. Caes. ii. 7 (Naber, p. 32).

Caesari suo consul.

Meum fratrem beatum, qui vos in isto biduo vide-
rit! At ego Romae haereo compedibus aureis vinc-
tus; nec aliter Kal. Sept. expecto quam superstitiosi
stellam, qua visa ieiunium polluant. Vale, Caesar,
decus patriae et Romani nominis. Vale, Domine.

Ad M. Caes. ii. 8 (Naber, p. 32).

Domino meo.

Ambr. 107 | Gratiam meam misi ad diem natalem matri
tuae celebrandum eique praecepi ut istic subsisteret
quoad ego venirem. Eodem autem momento quo
consulatum eiuravero vehiculum conscendam et ad
vos pervolabo. Interim Gratiae meae nullum a
fame periculum fore fide mea spopondi: mater enim

---

[1] From his *Carmen de Moribus*: see Dirksen, *Opusc.* i. 244.

---

[1] Masurius Sabinus was a great jurist of Tiberius's reign.
Persius (*Sat.* v. 90) mentions a work of his called *Rubrica.*
Possibly Marcus is alluding to the jargon of minute legal
distinctions.

until, as M. Porcius says, *the dead of night falls swiftly down.* But why do I string together these Masurian[1] banalities, when I started with saying I should write a few words only? So farewell, most kindly of masters, most honourable of consuls, and let your love be the measure of your longing for me.

Fronto to Marcus Aurelius

THE consul to his own Caesar.   143 A.D.

Lucky brother[2] of mine to have seen you those two days! But I stick fast in Rome bound with golden fetters, looking forward to the first of September as the superstitious to the star,[3] at sight of which to break their fast. Farewell, Caesar, glory of your country and the Roman name. My Lord, farewell.

Fronto to Marcus Aurelius as Caesar

To my Lord.   143 A.D.

I have sent my Gratia[4] to keep your mother's birthday with her, and bidden her stay there till I come. The very moment, however, that I have laid down my consulship with the customary oath[5] I shall climb into my carriage and fly off to you. Meanwhile, I have pledged my word that my Gratia shall run no risk of starvation. For your mother will

[2] Probably named Quadratus. See *Corpus Inscr. Lat.* xv. 7438.
[3] The Jews. The same may be said of the Moslems and their fast.   [4] Fronto's wife.
[5] The oath was that he had administered his office according to law. Herodian (iv. 3) says that this was done in the old forum (ἀγορά).

tua particulas a te sibi missas cum clienta communi-
cabit.   Neque est Gratia mea, ut causidicorum uxores feruntur, multi cibi.   Vel osculis solis matris tuae
contenta vixerit.   Sed enim quid me fiet?   Ne osculum quidem usquam ullum est Romae residuum.
Omnes meae fortunae, mea omnia gaudia Neapoli
sunt.

Oro te, quis iste mos est pridie magistratum eiu-
randi?   Quid, quod ego paratus sum, dum ante
plures dies eiurem, per plures deos iurare?   Quid
est autem, quod iuraturus sum me consulatu abire?
Ego vero etiam illud iuravero, me olim consulatu
abire cupere, ut M. Aurelium complectar.

Ad M. Caes. ii. 9 (Naber, p. 33).

<Consuli amplissimo et magistro> meo optimo.

Hoc sane supererat, ut super cetera quae insig-
niter erga nos facis etiam Gratiam mitteres huc
<ad diem natalem matris meae nobiscum concele-
brandum> . . . .[1]

Epist. Graec. 2 (Naber, p. 242).

Ambr. 164,
middle of
col. 1
| Μητρὶ Καίσαρος

1. Ἑκὼν ἑκὼν νὴ τοὺς θεοὺς καὶ πάνυ γε προθυμού-
μενος τὴν ἐμὴν Κραττίαν ἐξέπεμψα συνεορτάζουσάν σοι
τὰ γενέθλια καὶ αὐτὸς ἂν ἀφικόμενος εἰ ἐξῆν.   ἀλλ'

---

[1] Several pages are missing between this fragment and the
beginning of *Ad M. Caes.* ii. 10 given above, p. 136.

share with her *protégée* the tit-bits sent her by you.
Nor is my Gratia a great eater, as lawyer's wives are
said to be. She will live contentedly enough even
on nothing but your mother's kisses. But what will
become of poor me? There is not even a single kiss
left anywhere in Rome. All my fortunes, all my
joys are at Naples.

Tell me, I beseech you, what is the custom of
laying down an office under oath a day earlier.
What, am I not ready to swear by as many more
gods as I can swear myself out of office days
sooner? Again, am I to swear that I resign my
consulship? Yea, and I will swear this, too, that I
have long wished to resign it, that I may embrace
Marcus Aurelius.

Marcus Aurelius to Fronto

143 A.D.

To the most honourable consul and my best of
masters.

Verily this alone was wanting, that over and
above all the other signal marks of your affection
towards us you should also send Gratia here to join
us in keeping my mother's birthday . . . .

Fronto to Domitia Lucilla

143 A.D.

To the mother of Marcus.

1. Willingly, willingly, by heaven, aye, with the
greatest pleasure possible, have I sent my Gratia to
keep your birthday with you, and would have come
myself had it been lawful. But for myself this

147

ἐμοὶ μὲν ἐμποδών ἐστιν ἡ ἀρχὴ πρὸς[1] τῷ ποδὶ ἥδε[2] οὖσα.
ὀλίγαι γὰρ ἡμέραι λοιπαὶ τῆς ἀρχῆς περιλείπονται καὶ
μᾶλλόν τε[3] ἄσχολοι διὰ τὰς λειτουργίας· ὧν ἀπαλλαγεὶς
ἔοικα δραμεῖσθαι πρὸς ὑμᾶς τῶν τὸν στάδιον τρεχόντων
πολὺ προθυμότερον· ὡς ἐκεῖνοί γε βραχύτατον χρόνον ἐπὶ
τῆς ὕσπληγος ἐπιστάντες, ἔπειτα ἀφεῖνται τρέχειν, ἐγὼ δὲ
τοῦτον ἤδη μῆνα δεύτερον εἴργομαι τοῦ πρὸς ὑμᾶς δρόμου.

2. Ἐχρῆν δὲ ἄρα πάσας τὰς πανταχόθεν γυναῖκας ἐπὶ
ταύτην τὴν ἡμέραν ἀθροίζεσθαι καὶ ἑορτάζειν τὰ σὰ
γενέθλια, πρώτας μὲν τῶν γυναικῶν τὰς φιλάνδρους καὶ
φιλοτέκνους καὶ σώφρονας, δευτέρας δὲ ὅσαι ἄπλαστοι
καὶ ἀψευδεῖς εἰσίν, τρίτας δὲ ἑορτάζειν τὰς εὐγνώμονας
Ambr. 148 καὶ εὐπροσίτους καὶ | εὐπροσηγόρους καὶ ἀτύφους· πολλαὶ
δὲ ἂν καὶ ἄλλαι γυναικῶν τάξεις γένοιντο τῶν σοὶ μέρους
τινὸς ἐπαίνου καὶ ἀρετῆς μετεχουσῶν, σοῦ μὲν ἀπάσας τὰς
γυναικὶ πρεπούσας ἀρετὰς καὶ ἐπιστήμας κεκτημένης καὶ
ἐπισταμένης, ὥσπερ ἡ Ἀθηνᾶ τέχνας ἁπάσας κέκτηταί τε
καὶ ἐπίσταται, τῶν ἄλλων δὲ γυναικῶν ἕν τι[4] τῆς ἀρετῆς
μέρος ἑκάστης ἐπισταμένης καὶ κατὰ τοῦτο ἐπαινουμένης,
οἷος ὁ τῶν Μουσῶν ἔπαινος ἐκ μιᾶς τέχνης καθ' ἑκάστην
διῃρημένος.

3. Εἰ δὲ ἦν ἐγὼ πρὸ θύρας[5] εἰσαγωγεύς τις εἶναι λαχὼν
τῶν τῆς ἑορτῆς ἀξίων, πρώτας ἂν Ὁμήρῳ πειθόμενος
ἀπέκλεισα τὰς τὴν εὔνοιαν ψευδομένας καὶ πλαττομένας
καὶ "ἕτερον μέν τι κευθούσας ἐνὶ φρεσὶν ἄλλο δὲ λε-
γούσας," ἅπαντα δὲ τὰ ἀπὸ γέλωτος μέχρι δακρύων

---

[1] Niebuhr for Cod. γίρος.   [2] For Cod. ηδεη.
[3] Heindorf τι.   [4] Jacobs for Cod ἐπί.
[5] Cod. θύραις.   Dobson suggests προθυραῖος.

office is a clog round my feet. For there are a few days of it left, and these more than ever taken up with its duties. Once released from them, methinks I shall run to you with far more eagerness than those who run the course; for they, after a moment's delay at the starting-place, are forthwith despatched on their race, while I have already been kept from running to you these two months.

2. The right thing, it seems, would have been that all women from all quarters should have gathered for this day and celebrated your birth-feast, first, all the women that love their husbands and love their children and are virtuous, and, secondly, all that are genuine and truthful, and the third company to keep the feast should have been the kind-hearted, and the affable and the accessible and the humble-minded; and many other ranks of women would there be to share in some part of your praise and virtue, seeing that you possess and are mistress of all virtues and accomplishments befitting a woman, just as Athena possesses and is mistress of every art, whereas of other women each one is mistress of some one branch of excellence and commended for it, just as the Muses are praised individually, each one for a single art.

3. But had I been at your door, acting as a sort of introducer of those who were worthy of the festival, the first I should have shut out, on Homer's authority, would have been those who make a pretence of good-will and are insincere, who "hide one thing in their hearts while their lips speak another,"[1] with whom everything, from

---

[1] Homer, *Il*. ix. 312.

προσποιουμένας. ὅ τοι γέλως οὕτως τὸ πρὶν ἄδολος
εἶναι πεφυκὼς ὡς καὶ τοὺς ὀδόντας τῶν γελώντων ἐπι-
δεικνύειν εἰς τοσοῦτον ἤδη περιέστηκεν κακομηχανίας καὶ
ἐνέδρας, ὡς καὶ τὰ χείλη κρύπτειν τῶν ἐξ ἐπιβουλῆς
προσγελώντων. γυναικεία δή τις αὕτη θεὸς παρὰ ταῖς
πλείσταις τῶν γυναικῶν θρησκεύεται ἡ Ἀπάτη· ἥτις γοῦν
Ἀφροδίτης τόκος ἐκ πολλῶν τινων καὶ ποικίλων θηλειῶν

Here follows
Ambr. 147 κατασκευασάμενος.[1] | . . . .

Ad M. Caes. ii. 12 (Naber, p. 35).

<M. Caesar magistro suo.>

Ambr. 106 . . . .[2] | et meus me alipta faucibus urgebat.
Sed quae, inquis, fabula? Ut pater meus a vineis
domum se recepit, ego solito more equum inscendi,
et in viam profectus sum, et paulatim provectus.
Deinde ibi in via sic oves multae conglobatae adsta-
bant ut locis solet artis,[3] et canes quattuor et duo
pastores, sed nihil praeterea. Tum pastor unus ad
alterum pastorem, postquam plusculos equites vidit,
Vide tibi istos equites, inquit, *nam illi solent maximas
rapinationes facere.* Ubi id audivi, calcar equo sub-
pingo, equum in oves inigo. Oves consternatae dis-
perguntur; aliae alibi palantes balantesque oberrant.
Pastor furcam intorquet; furca in equitem, qui me
sectabatur, cadit. Nos aufugimus. Eo pacto qui
metuebatur ne oves amitteret, furcam perdidit.
Fabulam existimas? Res vera est: at etiam plura

---

[1] For Cod. κατασκευασαμένης: ἥτις is Naber's for Cod. τις.
[2] It is not known how much is lost here.
[3] Fröhner for Cod. *locus solitarius.*

laughter to tears, is make-believe. Truly laughter, that at first was naturally so without craft as to
shew the teeth of the laugher, has now changed
round to such a depth of malice and guile that those
who laugh with sinister intent hide even their lips.
This goddess, true woman that she is, who gets most
worship from women, is Deceit, offspring, of a truth,
of Aphrodite, and compact of many and various
traits of womankind . . . .

MARCUS AURELIUS TO FRONTO.

143 A.D.

M. CAESAR to his master.
   . . . . and my wrestling-master[1] had me by
the throat. But what, you say, was the story?
When my father had got home from the vineyards,
I, as usual, mounted my horse and set off along the
road, and had gone some little distance when I came
upon a number of sheep in the road huddled together, as happens when there is little room, with
four dogs and two shepherds; that was all. Then
one of the shepherds, seeing our cavalcade, said to
his mate, *Marry, keep an eye on those mounted fellows,
they be rare hands at pillaging.* Hearing that, I dug
the spurs into my horse and galloped full tilt into the
flock. Frightened out of their wits, they ran helter-
skelter bleating and fleeting in all directions. The
shepherd whirled his crook at us. It fell on my
equerry who was following me. We got clear off.
So it chanced that he, who feared to lose his sheep,
lost his crook. Do you think this a fiction? It
really took place: yes, and there is more I could

---

[1] *cp.* Capit. *Vit. Marci*, iv. 9 *amavit pugillatum, luctamina.*
The phrase *faucibus urgere* is from Sall. *Cat.* 52.

erant quae de ea re scriberem, nisi iam me nuntius in balneum arcesseret. Vale mi magister dulcissime, homo honestissime et rarissime, suavitas et caritas et voluptas mea.

Ad M. Caes. ii. 13 (Naber, p. 36).

Magistro meo.

Gratia minor effecit,[1] quod Gratia maior fecit, ut sollicitudinem nostram vel interim minuat vel iam omnino detergeat. | Ego tibi de patrono meo M. Porcio gratias ago, quod eum crebro lectitas; tu mihi de C. Crispo timeo ut umquam gratias agere possis, nam uni M. Porcio me dedicavi atque despondi atque delegavi. Hoc etiam ipsum *atque* unde putas? Ex ipso furore. Perendinus dies meus dies festus erit, si certe tu venis. Vale, amicissime et rarissime homo, dulcissime magister.

Die[2] senatus huius magis hic futuri quam illuc venturi videmur. Sed utrumque in ambiguo est. Tu modo perendie veni, et fiat quod volt. Semper mi vale, animus meus; mater me te tuosque salutat.

Ad M. Caes. ii. 14 (Naber, p. 36).

Magistro meo.

Tu, quom sine me es, Catonem legis, at ego, quom sine te sum, causidicos in undecimam horam

Ambr. 105

---

[1] Cod. *minore fecit*; cp. Shaks. *All's Well*, II. 1. 164.
[2] Mai for Cod. *de.*

write to you of that adventure, but here comes the messenger to call me to my bath. Farewell, my sweetest of masters, most honoured and most unique of men, my joy, my treasure, my delight.

Marcus Aurelius to Fronto

To my master.   143 A.D.

Gratia[1] the younger has served, as the elder Gratia did, to calm our anxiety for the while or sweep it altogether away at once. I thank you on behalf of my patron, M. Porcius, for the frequency with which you read him : you will never, I fear, be able to return me the compliment with respect to Gaius Crispus,[2] for to M. Porcius alone have I devoted, aye and engaged, aye and given myself over heart and soul. Whence, too, think you, comes this very *aye and* ?[3] . From my very enthusiasm. The day after to-morrow shall be my gala day, if you really are coming. Farewell, dearest and most unique of men, sweetest of masters.

On the day of this Senate we seem more likely to be here than go there. But nothing is decided. Do you but come the day after to-morrow, and then let what will befall. Fare ever well for me, soul of mine. My mother greets you and yours.

Marcus Aurelius to Fronto

To my master.   143 A.D.

You, when you are away from me, read Cato ; but I, when away from you, listen to lawyers till

---

[1] As Gratia, Fronto's daughter, married Victorinus about the year 160, she is not likely to have been more than two or three years old, at the most, in 143.

[2] *i.e.* Sallust ; M. Porcius is Cato.

[3] This repeated use of *atque* was a habit of Cato's.

audio. Equidem velim istam noctem, quae sequitur, quam brevissimam esse. Tanti est minus lucubrare, ut te maturius videam. Vale mi magister dulcissime. Mater mea te salutat. Spiritum vix habeo, ita sum defessus.

Ad M. Caes. ii. 15 (Naber, p. 37).

<M. Caesar Magis>tro suo salutem dicit.

Profecto ista tua benignitate magnum mihi negotium perfecisti.[1] Nam illa cotidie tua Lorium ventio, illa in serum expectatio . . . .

Ad M. Ca·s. i. 6 (Naber, p. 13).

Ambr. 86, ad init. | M. Aurelius Caesar salutem dicit Frontoni magistro suo.

1. Nae ego[2] impudens, qui umquam quicquam meorum scriptorum tanto ingenio tanto iudicio legendum committo. Patri, Domino meo, locum ex oratione tua, quem me eligere[3] voluit, αὐ<τὸ>[4] καὶ ὑπεκρινάμην commode. Plane illa suum auctorem sibi dari flagitabant: denique mihi vix succlamatum est Ἀξίως τοῦ ποιητοῦ. Sed quod tu merito omnibus praeoptas, non diu differam.[5] Ita adfectus est auditione eorum Dominus meus, ut paene moleste ferret quod alio modo[6] ad negotium opus sibi esset, quam eo quo tu orationem habiturus intraveris. Sensuum

[1] For Cod. *perperisti* (m[1]); *proficiosta* (?) m[2].
[2] For Hauler on this whole passage see *Miscellanea Ceriani*, pp. 504 f.
[3] m[2] of Cod. *sibi praelegere.* [4] m[2] adds this above the line.
[5] J. W. E. Pearce for Cod. *differas.*
[6] m[2] *mox* and, for *opus sibi esset, arcesseretur* from another MS.

five o'clock. Oh, that this coming night might be the shortest known! so fain am I to burn less midnight oil, that I may the sooner see you. Farewell, my sweetest of masters. My mother sends her greeting. I can scarcely breathe, so tired am I.

143 A.D.

M. CAESAR to his master sends greeting.
  Verily in your kindness you have done me a great service. For that daily call at Lorium,[1] that waiting till late. . . .

144–145 A.D.

M. AURELIUS CAESAR to Fronto his master sends greeting.
  1. Nay, surely it is I who am shameless[2] in ever submitting any of my writings to be read by genius so great, by judgment so great. The passage from your speech, which the Lord my father wished me to choose out, I even declaimed with appropriate action. Needless to say, the words cried aloud for their own author to deliver them : in fact, I was scarcely greeted with *Worthy of the maker!* But I will not delay telling you what you deservedly long for most. So struck was my Lord with what he heard that he was almost put out because business required his presence at the time elsewhere than in the court where you were to deliver your speech. He greatly admired

---

[1] Pius's villa, twelve miles from Rome, on the Via Aurelia, where he died.
[2] Fronto had evidently accused himself of *impudentia* for sending Marcus something of his (? his speech) to be criticised.

facultatem, elocutionis variam virtutem, inventionis argutam[1] novitatem, orationis doctam dispositionem vehementer miratus est. Nunc credo post hoc[2] quaeris quid me maxime iuverit. Accipe; hinc coepi:

2. *" In iis[3] rebus et causis quae a privatis iudicibus iudicantur, nullum est periculum, quia sententiae eorum* Ambr. 91 *intra causarum de|mum terminos valent; tuis autem decretis, imperator, exempla publice valitura in perpetuum sanciuntur. Tanto maior tibi vis et potestas quam fatis attributa est. Fata quid singulis nostrum eveniat statuunt: tu, ubi quid in singulos decernis, ibi universos exemplo adstringis.*

3. *" Quare, si hoc decretum tibi proconsulis placuerit, formam dederis omnibus omnium provinciarum magistratibus, quid in eiusmodi causis decernant. Quid igitur eveniet? Illud scilicet, ut testamenta omnia ex longinquis transmarinisque provinciis Romam ad cognitionem tuam deferantur. Filius exheredatum se suspicabitur: postulabit ne patris tabulae aperiantur. Idem filia postulabit, nepos abnepos, frater consobrinus, patruus, avunculus, amita matertera; omnia necessitudinum nomina hoc privilegium invadent, ut tabulas aperiri vetent, ipsi possessione iure sanguinis fruantur. Causa denique Romam*

---

[1] m[2] *inclutam,* and also *astutam.*
[2] Brakman reads *opes lau* for *o post ho* and Mai also read *opes.* [3] m[1] *litis.*

---

[1] This is the only considerable fragment of Fronto's speeches which we have. Nothing more is known of the case with which it deals. Fronto's legal treatment of the

the copiousness of the matter, the varied excellence of the diction, the witty originality of the thought, the skilful arrangement of the speech. And now you are asking, I imagine, what pleased me most. Listen : I begin with this passage.

2. *" In those affairs* [1] *and cases which are settled in private courts, no danger arises, since their decisions hold good only within the limits of the cases, but the precedents which you, O Emperor, establish by your decrees will hold good publicly and for all time. So much greater is your power and authority than is assigned to the Fates. They determine what shall befall us as individuals : you by your decisions* [2] *in individual cases make precedents binding upon all.*

3. *" Therefore, if this decision of the proconsul is approved by you, you will give all magistrates of all provinces a rule for deciding all cases of the same kind. What, then, will be the result ? This evidently, that all wills from distant and oversea provinces will be brought over to Rome for cognizance in your court. A son will suspect that he has been disinherited : he will demand that his father's will be not opened. The same demand will be made by a daughter, a grandson, a great grandchild, a brother, a cousin, a paternal uncle, a maternal uncle, a paternal aunt, a maternal aunt ; relations of all degrees will usurp this privilege of forbidding the will to be opened, that they may enjoy possession the while by right of consanguinity. When, finally, the case has been*

question at issue is severely condemned by Dirksen (*Opusc.* i. 243 ff.), but it is quite impossible to believe that Fronto was as ignorant of law as his critic asserts.

[2] The Emperor could legislate either directly by *edict*, or by a judicial decision (*iudicium = decretum*), or as became usual after Nerva by a *rescript*, interpreting the law, in answer to an inquiry or petition.

remissa quid eveniet?   Heredes scripti navigabunt, ex-
heredati autem in possessione remanebunt, diem de die
ducent, dilationes petentes[1] *| fora variis excusationibus*
trahent.   Hiemps est et crudum[2] *mare hibernum est:*
adesse non potuit.   Ubi hiemps praeterierit, vernae tem-
pestates incertae et dubiae moratae sunt.   Ver exactum
est ; aestas est calida et sol navigantes urit et homo nau-
seat.   Autumnus sequitur : poma culpabuntur et languor
excusabitur.

4. *" Fingo haec et comminiscor?   Quid, in hac causa*
nonne hoc ipsum evenit?   Ubi est adversarius qui iam
pridem ad agendam causam adesse debuerat?   'In itinere
est.'   Quo tandem in itinere?   'Ex Asia venit.'   Et est
adhuc in Asia?   'Magnum iter et festinatum.'   Navi-
busne an equis an diplomatibus facit haec tam velocia
stativa?   Cum interim cognitione proposita semel a te,
Caesar, petita dilatio <est> et impetrata : proposita cog-
nitione rursum, <rursum>[3] *a te duum mensuum petita*
dilatio.   Duo menses exacti sunt idibus proximis et dies
medii isti aliquot.   Venit tandem?   Si nondum venit, at
saltem adpropinquat?   Si nondum adpropinquat, <at>
saltem profectus ex Asia est?   Si nondum profectus est,
at saltem cogitat?   Quid ille cogitat aliud quam bonis
alienis incubare, fructus diripere, agros vastare, rem
omnem dilapidare|?   Non ille ita stultus est ut malit

---

[1] The last two letters are doubtful.   The Cod. as given by
Stud. ends the word at *petent'*.   The next two letters may
be *eo*.
[2] Heindorf *dudum.*   [3] Heindorf.

referred to Rome, what will result? The heirs designate will set sail, while the disinherited will remain in possession, procrastinate from day to day, look about for delays, and so put off the courts on various pretexts. It is winter time and the wintry sea is rough; he has been unable to appear. Winter over, it is the equinoctial gales, fitful and sudden, that have delayed him. The spring is past: the summer is hot and the sun scorches voyagers, and the man is seasick. The fall follows: the fruit will be in fault and debility the excuse.

4. *" I am imagining and inventing this? What, has not this actually occurred in this case? Where is the defendant who ought to have been here this long while past to plead his cause? 'He is on his way.' On what way, prithee? 'He is coming from Asia.' And so he is still in Asia? 'It is a long way and he has made haste.'* [1] *Is it on shipboard, or horseback, or by imperial post that he makes such headlong halts? Meanwhile, as soon as the trial is fixed, you are asked, O Caesar, for a first adjournment, which is granted: the trial is fixed a second time,* [2] *a second time an adjournment of two months is asked for. The two months expired on the last ides, and since then several days have gone by. Has he come at last? If not yet come, is he, at all events, near? If not yet near, has he at least set out from Asia? If he has not yet set out, does he at least think of setting out? What else does he think of but keeping in his hands* [3] *the goods of others, plundering the proceeds, stripping the estate, wasting the whole property? He is not so foolish as to prefer coming*

---

[1] It is possible to take these words as Fronto's own—*much way has he made and with speed.*

[2] Marcus, when emperor, allowed only one adjournment; see *Digest*, ii. 12, 1.

[3] The Latin = our slang "sitting tight on."

venire ad Caesarem et vinci, quam remanere in Asia et possidere.

5. " *Qui mos si fuerit inductus, ut defunctorum testamenta ex provinciis transmarinis Romam mittantur, indignius et acerbius testamentorum periculum erit, <quam> si corpora <huc mitti mos esset> eorum qui trans maria testantur. Nam <his quidem> null<um iam potest peri>culum super<esse>.*[1] *Sepultura cadaveribus in ipsis iniuriis praesto est. Sive maria naufragos devorent sive flumina praecipites trahant sive harenae obruant sive ferae lacerent sive volucres discerpant, corpus humanum satis sepelitur, ubicumque consumitur. At ubi testamentum naufragio submersum est, illa demum et res et domus et familia naufraga atque insepulta est. Olim testamenta ex deorum munitissimis aedibus proferebantur aut tabulariis aut <ar>cis aut archiis aut opisthodomis : at iam testamenta per <ma>re <procellosum> navigarint inter onera mercium et sarcinas remigum. Id etiam superest, si quando iactu opus est, ut testamenta cum leguminibus* Ambr. 66 *iactentur| ; quin <portorium>*[2] *constituendum quod pro testamentis exigatur. Ante hac* . . . .[3]

Ambr. 58 6. | " *De funere aliquid dicamus. Sciat familia quemadmodum lugeat. Aliter plangit servus manumissus, aliter cliens laude auctus,*[4] *aliter amicus legato honoratus. Quid incertas et suspensas exequias facis ? Omnium animalium statim post mortem hereditas cernitur : ovi lana*

---

[1] Heindorf suggested the additions in brackets.

[2] J. W. E. Pearce.

[3] About one page is lost. Hauler, in *Misc. Ceriani*, pp. 504–520, promises in his forthcoming edition to throw fresh light on the pages Ambr. 65, 66.

[4] For Cod. *laudaucatus.*

to Caesar and losing his case to staying in Asia and keeping possession.[1]

5. " If this custom be brought in, that the wills of the deceased should be sent to Rome from the oversea provinces, the imperilling of wills would be more discreditable and distressing than if it were the custom for the bodies of the deceased, who make their wills oversea, to be sent to Rome. For no further peril can touch them. A corpse is assured of burial in its very mishaps. For whether it be swallowed by the sea in shipwreck, or swept away in a moment by a river, or the sands cover it, whether the beasts of the field devour it, or the birds of the air pick its bones, the human body is practically buried wherever it is dissolved. But when by shipwreck a will is engulfed, the estate and home and family in question is then and there shipwrecked and lies unburied. Time was when wills used to be brought out from the securest temples of the Gods, from muniment rooms, or chests, or archives, or temple vestries : but now shall wills sail the stormy seas amid bales of merchandise and rowers' kit. The next thing will even be for them to be jettisoned[2] with a cargo of pulse, should it become necessary to lighten the ship. Moreover, also, an import duty to be levied on wills must be fixed. In time past . . . .

6. "But to say something as to the burial. The household would know how to mourn. The slave enfranchised under the will has one way of shewing sorrow, the client mentioned with praise another, another the friend honoured with a legacy. Why throw uncertainty and delay over the funeral rites? In the case of all animals the inheritance is realized at once after death : from sheep the

---

[1] Pius punished conduct of this kind (see *Digest*, xlii. 4, 7) by adjudging the inheritance to the other claimant.

[2] *cp. Acts*, xxvii. 38.

statim detrahitur,[1] *et elephanto ebur, ungues leonibus, avi-*
bus pinnae plumaeque ; hominum hereditas post mortem
iacet, differtur, praedonibus exposta diripitur." [2]

7. Puto totum descripsi. Quid ergo facerem,
quom [3] totum admir<ar>er, quom totum amarem
hominem beatum ? Vale, disertissime, doctissime,
mihi carissime, dulcissime, magister optatissime, desiderantissime.

Herodi filius natus <hodi>e mortuus est. Id Herodes non aequo animo fert. Volo ut illi aliquid quod
ad hanc rem adtineat pauculorum verborum scribas.
Semper vale.

Ad M. Caes. i. 7 (Naber, p. 17).

Domino meo.

1. Accepi, Caesar, litteras tuas, quibus quanto
opere laetatus sim facile existimaveris, si reputaveris
singula. Primum, quod caput est omnis mei | gaudii,
quom [4] te bene valere cognovi; tum quod ita aman-
tem te mei sensi, finem ut amori nullum neque
modum statuas, quin cotidie aliquid reperias quod
circa me iucundius atque amicius facias. Ego denique olim iam me puto satis amari, tibi autem nondum

Ambr. 57

---

[1] The Codex has *detrahatur,* and *cernatur* for *cernitur*
above ; a marginal note on the former word gives the alternative *calvetur* (" shaved close ").

[2] For this passage see Hauler, *Wien. Stud.* 29, pt. 1,
1907.

[3] Klussm. for Cod. *quod.* [4] Heindorf would read *quod.*

wool is stripped at once, and from the elephant his ivory, their claws from lions, from birds their feathers and plumes ; but a man dies and his inheritance lies derelict, is put aside,[1] left as a prey to robbers, it is made away with."

7. I think I have copied out the whole. What indeed could I do, when I admired the whole man, loved the whole man—blessings on him—so much? Farewell, my master, most eloquent, most learned, most dear to me, most sweet, whom I most long for, miss the most.

The son of Herodes,[2] born to-day, is dead. Herodes is overwhelmed with grief at his loss. I wish you would write him quite a short letter appropriate to the occasion. Fare ever well.

FRONTO TO MARCUS AS CAESAR

To my Lord.   ? 144–145 A.D.

1. I have received your letter, O Caesar, and the great delight it gave me you will easily gauge if you consider these separate points. First, and this is the head and front of all my joy, that I know you are well; then because I felt that you loved me so well as not to be able to set any bound or limit to your love, so as not to find something to do for me every day more kindly and more friendly than before. In fine, I have long thought myself loved enough, but you are not yet satisfied with your affection

---

[1] The new *Thes. Ling. Lat.* gives *dissipatur* as the gloss for *differtur* here.

[2] Herodes married Annia Regilla about 143, and this would be his first son by her. His passionate grief on other occasions is noted by Lucian, *Demonax*, §§ 24, 35, and Philostr. *Vit. Soph.* 242, Kays.

etiam quantum me diligas satis est; ut non mare
ullum tam profundum quam tuus adversus me amor:
sane ut illud queri possim, cur non me amas tantum
quantum plurimum est, namque in dies plus amando
efficis, ne id quod ante [diem][1] amaveris, plurimum
fuerit?

2. Consulatum mihi putas tanto gaudio fuisse,
quanto tua tot in una re summi amoris indicia? Orationis meae particulas, quas excerpseram, recitasti
patri tuo ipse, studiumque ad pronuntiandum adhi-
buisti, qua in re et oculos mihi tuos utendos et vocem
et gestum et in primis animum accommodasti. Nec
video quis veterum scriptorum quisquam[2] me beatior
fuerit, quorum scripta Aesopus ad populum pronunti-
avit, aut Roscius. Meae vero orationi M. Caesar
actor contigit et pronunciator, tuaque ego opera
et voce audientibus placui, quom audiri a te ac
tibi placere | omnibus summe sit optabile. Non
miror itaque quod placuerit oratio oris tui dignitate
exornata. Nam pleraque propria venustate carentia
gratiam sibimet alienam extrinsecus mutuantur.
Quod evenit etiam in plebeis istis edulibus: nullum
adeo vile aut volgatum est holus aut pulpamentum,
quin elegantius videatur vasis aureis adpositum.
Idem evenit floribus et coronis; alia dignitate sunt
in Portunio[3] quom a coronariis veneunt, alia quom a
sacerdotibus in templo porriguntur.

Ambr. 61

---

[1] m² in the Codex has *dies*. Could Fronto have written
antidea for *antea*?   [2] *quis quisquam* is Plautine.
[3] These two words and *in templo* below are found in the
margin of the Codex and taken from another MS. (noted as
in alio).

for me, so that deeper than ever plummet sounded is your love toward me, insomuch that I might quite well make the complaint, Why do you not yet love me with the utmost love possible, for by loving me more from day to day you prove that your love hitherto has fallen short of its utmost measure?

2. Think you that my consulship has been such a delight as the many tokens you have given me of your love in this one case? Samples of my speech, which I had picked out for you, you read to your father yourself, and took the pains to declaim them, wherein you lent me your eyes, your voice, your gestures, and, above all, your mind for my service. Nor can I see which single one of the ancient writers, whose writings were declaimed to the people by Aesopus [1] or Roscius, was more fortunate than I. *My* speech has had Marcus Caesar for its actor and declaimer, and it was by your agency and through your voice that I pleased the hearers, whereas to be heard by you and to please you would be the height of every man's ambition. No wonder, then, my speech found favour, set off, as it was, by the dignity of your utterance. For many a thing, that lacks all intrinsic charm, borrows from elsewhere a grace that is not its own, and this is the case even with our homeliest eatables. No pot-herb, no bit of flesh is so cheap or commonplace a food as not to gain piquancy if served in a golden dish. The same is true of flowers and garlands: they have one scale of worth when sold by flower-vendors in the Flower-market, another when offered in a temple by the priests.

---

[1] Aesopus in tragedy, Roscius, who taught Cicero declamation, in comedy. Marcus, probably about this time, was studying under Geminus the comedian; see Capit. iv. 2.

3. Tantoque ego fortunatior quam fuit Hercules atque Achilles, quorum arma et tela gestata sunt a Patricole et Philocteta, multo viris virtute inferioribus: mea contra oratio mediocris, ne dicam ignobilis, a doctissimo et facundissimo omnium Caesare illustrata est. Nec ulla umquam scena tantum habuit dignitatis—M. Caesar actor, Titus imperator[1] auditor! Quid amplius cuiquam contingere potest, nisi unum quod in caelo fieri poetae ferunt, quom Jove patre audiente Musae cantant? Enimvero quibus ego gaudium meum verbis exprimere possim, quod orationem istam meam tua manu descriptam misisti mihi? Verum est | profecto quod ait noster Laberius, ad amorem iniciendum *delenimenta*[2] esse *deliramenta, beneficia* autem *veneficia.* Neque poculo aut veneno quisquam tantum flammae ad amatorem incussisset, praeut tu et facto hoc stupidum et attonitum <me> ardente amore tuo reddidisti. Quot litterae istic sunt, totidem consulatus mihi, totidem laureas triumphos togas pictas arbitror contigisse.

Ambr. 62

4. Quid tale M. Porcio aut Quinto Ennio, C. Graccho aut Titio poetae, quid Scipioni aut Numidico, quid M. Tullio tale usuvenit?[3] Quorum libri pretiosiores habentur et summam gloriam retinent, si sunt Lampadionis aut Staberii, Plautii aut D. Aurelii, Autriconis aut Aelii manu scripta exempla, aut a

---

[1] Hauler, who gives the Codex as *imp.*

[2] Ribbeck for Cod. *deliberamenta.*

[3] Dr. Hauler, from his inspection of the Codex, has added much that is new to this whole passage: see *Wien. Stud* 31, pt. 1, 1909, pp. 264 ff.

3. So much more fortunate am I than was Hercules or Achilles, for their armour and weapons were borne by Philoctetes and Patroclus, men far inferior to them in manhood, while my poor, not to say sorry, speech has been rendered famous by Caesar the most learned and eloquent of all men. Never was scene so impressive—M. Caesar actor, Titus Imperator audience! What nobler fate could befall anyone save that alone, when in Heaven, as poets tell, the Muses sing, while Jove their sire is audience? Indeed, with what words could I express my delight at your sending me that speech of mine copied out with your own hand? True, surely, is what our Laberius[1] says, that in inspiring love *charms* are but *harms*[2] and the *foison* of gifts *poison*. For never with cup or philtre could anyone so have stirred the flame of passion in a lover as by this act of yours you have dazed and amazed me by the ardour of your love. For every letter of your letter I count myself to have gained a consulship, a victory, a triumph, a robe of honour.

4. What fortune like this befell M. Porcius or Quintus Ennius, Gaius Gracchus, or the poet Titius? What Scipio or Numidicus? What M. Tullius, like this? Their books are valued more highly and have the greatest credit, if they are from the hand of Lampadio or Staberius, of Plautius or D. Aurelius, Autrico or Aelius, or have been revised by Tiro or

---

[1] A writer of mimes and an *eques* of the time of Julius Caesar.

[2] For *beneficium* and *veneficium*, *cp.* Apul. *Apol.* ii. 2. The letters were constantly interchanged. Shakespeare, *Two Gentl.* III. i. 216, puns on the words *vanished* and *banished*.

Tirone emendata aut a Domitio Balbo descripta aut
ab Attico aut Nepote.[1] Mea oratio extabit M. Cæs-
aris manu scripta. Qui orationem spreverit, litteras
concupiscet; qui scripta contempserit, scriptorem
reverebitur. Ut si simiam aut volpem Apelles
pinxi<sse>t, bestiae extremae[2] pretium adderet.
Aut quod M. Cato de . . . . .[3]

Epist. Gracc. 3 (Naber, p. 243).

<Ἡρώδῃ παρὰ Φρόντωνος>

Ambr. 146,
ad med. col.
2: and also
Ambr. 59
after lacuna
at end of
prec. letter

Ambr. 145

. . . . | τερον γε . . . . ἡμᾶς· τὸ δὲ μετριάζειν ἐν
τοῖς ἥττοσιν κακοῖς οὐ δύσκολον. ἐν παντὶ μὲν γὰρ τὸ
κατὰ κακοῦ <ἀγανακτεῖν> καὶ ἀπρο<σδοκήτως> προσπε-
σόντος ἀπρεπὲς ἀνδρὶ παιδείας πεπειραμένῳ. χαίρων δὲ
ἔγωγε μᾶλλον <ἂν ἀσ>μένως μέτρα <παραβαίνοι>|μι.[4]
τὸ γὰρ πρὸς ἡδονὴν παράλογον τοῦ πρὸς ἀνίαν αἱρετώ-
τερον. Ἀλλ' οὐδὲ τὰ τῆς ἡλικίας σοι παρῴχηκεν πρὸς
παίδων ἑτέρων ἀνατροφήν. ζημία δὲ πᾶσα σὺν ἐλπίδι
μὲν ἀποκοπτομένῃ χαλεπή· ῥᾴων δὲ ὑπολειπομένης ἐς τὸ
ἀναλαβεῖν[5] ἐλπίδος· καὶ ὁ μὴ περιμείνας ταύτην ἀγεννὴς
καὶ πολὺ τῆς τύχης αὐτῷ χαλεπώτερος. ἡ μὲν γὰρ τύχη
τὸ πάρον ἀφείλετο, ὁ δὲ ἐστέρησεν αὐτὸν καὶ τῆς ἐλπίδος.
Ὅθεν δὲ ἂν ῥᾷστα παραψυχῆς τύχοις, πείρᾳ μαθὼν ἔγωγε

---

[1] In this passage (for which see Hauler in *Mélanges de
M. Emile Chatelaine*, pp. 622 ff., and *Versam. d. deutsch.
Philologen*, 50) the corrector of the Codex adds *Plautii* in
the margin from a second MS. and substitutes *aut D. Aurelii*
for m¹ *Adurschii* or *Thursellii*, and *Autriconis* for *aut Tironis*,
adding over this the note *ex Baccola*, and *Balto* for m¹
Barbi (?).
[2] J. W. E. Pearce for Cod. . . . *emae*, as in Apul. *Met.*
iv. 31.   [3] Four pages are lost.

transcribed by Domitius Balbus, or Atticus or Nepos.
My speech will be extant in the handwriting of
M. Caesar. He that thinks little of the speech will
be in love with the very letters of it; he who disdains
the thing written will reverence the writer. Just as
if Apelles painted an ape or a fox, he would add a
value to the last of creatures. Or as M. Cato (said)
of . . . .

To Herodes from Fronto.[1]

? 144–145 A.D.

. . . . But in lesser evils to act
with composure is not difficult. For, indeed, in any
case to resent an evil, even if it befall unexpectedly,
is unseemly for a man who has tasted of education.
But it is in joy that I should be more ready to
overstep the bounds, for if we are to act unreason-
ably it is preferable to do so in reference to
pleasure than to pain. But you are not even too
old[2] to rear other children. Every loss is grievous
if hope be cut off with it, but easier to bear if hope
of repairing it be left. And he that does not avail
himself of this hope is mean-spirited and his own
enemy, much more than Fortune. For Fortune takes
away the present reality, but he deprives himself of
hope as well. And I will tell you where you can
most easily get consolation, as I have learnt by ex-

[1] The heading is lost, but the letter is certainly addressed
to Herodes Atticus in response to the request of Marcus
made in a previous letter.

[2] Herodes would not have been fifty at this time.

---

[4] According to Naber, the above lacunae cover about ten
lines. Dobson gives for the last words ἂν ἀσμένως μετριάζοιμι.

[5] So Cod. p. 59. The reading on p. 145 is ἀναχακεῖν.

ἀλλ' οὐ σοφίᾳ διδάξω. ἀεί μοι συνέβη τι τῶν δεινῶν
παθεῖν ἐρῶντι. ἤρων δὲ τότε μὲν Ἀθηνοδότου τοῦ
σοφοῦ, τότε δὲ Διονυσίου τοῦ ῥήτορος. καὶ δὴ τοῦτο
ἐννοῶν ὅτι μοι σώζοιτο κεῖνος οὗ γ' ἐρῶν τύχοιμι, ἧττον ἦν
τῇ λύπῃ καὶ τοῖς προσπίπτουσιν ἁλώσιμος. εἰ <δὲ> δή
τινος ἐρᾷς καὶ σὺ νέου γενναίου ἀρετῇ καὶ παιδείᾳ καὶ
τύχῃ καὶ σωφροσύνῃ διαφέροντος, οὐκ ἂν ἁμαρτάνοις,

Ambr. 60

ὁρμῶν ἐπ' ἐκείνῳ καὶ πᾶσαν ἀγαθῶν ἀσφάλειαν ἐπ' αὐτῷ |
τιθέμενος ὡς,[1] ἐφ' ὅσον γε ἡμῖν οὗτος περίεστιν—ἀντερ-
αστὴς γὰρ εἶναί σοί φημι, καὶ οὐκ ἀποκρύπτομαι—τὰ
ἄλλα γε πάντα ἡμῖν εὐίατα καὶ τούτου μακρῷ δεύτερα.

Ad M. Caes. iii. 19 (Naber, p. 56).

Vat. 153,
col. 2

| Magistro meo.

Qualem mihi animum esse existimas, quom
cogito quam diu te non vidi, et quam ob rem non
vidi! et fortassis pauculis te adhuc diebus, quom te
necessario confirmas, non videbo.   Igitur, dum tu
iacebis, et mihi animus supinus erit; quomque tu dis
iuvantibus bene stabis, et meus animus bene con-
stabit, qui nunc torretur ardentissimo desiderio tuo.[2]
Vale, anima Caesaris tui, amici tui, discipuli tui.

[1] Niebuhr for Cod. ὅς.
[2] The margin of Cod. has *in alio* (*i.e.* in another MS.) *tui.*

perience and not by learning. Often has it been my fate to suffer in my affections. At one time it was Athenodotus the philosopher, at another Dionysius the rhetor[1] that I loved: and yet, when I reflected that he was preserved to me whom it was my fortune to love, I was less at the mercy of grief and circumstance. But if you as well as I love a noble youth,[2] distinguished for virtue and learning and fortune and modesty, you cannot go wrong if you attach yourself to him and set in him all your assurance of good fortune, since as long as he remains to us—for I confess, and make no secret of it, that I am your rival in his love—everything else is remediable and of infinitely less importance than this.

M. AURELIUS TO FRONTO

? 144–145 A.D.

To my master.

What do you suppose are my feelings when I think how long it is since I have seen you, and why I have not seen you? And perhaps for a few days yet, while you are perforce nursing yourself, I shall not see you. So while you are down in bed, my spirits will be down too; and when by God's grace you stand on your feet, my spirits also will stand fast, that are now fevered with the most burning longing for you. Fare ever well, soul of your Caesar, of your friend, of your pupil.

---

[1] These two were masters of Fronto; see Index. Marcus (*Thoughts*, i. 13) mentions Athenodotus.

[2] Marcus is meant.

Ad M. Caes. iii. 20 (Naber, p. 56).

Domino meo.

Lectulo me teneo. Si possim, ubi ad Centumcellas ibitis, itineri idoneus esse, vii idus vos Lorii
videbo deis faventibus. | Excusa me Domino nostro
patri tuo, quem—ita vos salvos habeam—magno pondere gravius amo et colo, quom tam bene in senatu
iudicatum est, quod et provinciis saluti esset et reos
clementer obiurgasset.

Ubi vivarium dedicabitis, memento quam diligen-
tissime, si feras percuties, equum admittere. Galbam
certe ad Centumcellas produces, an potes octavi
dus[1] Lorii? Vale, Domine, patri placeto, matri dic
salutem, me desiderato. Cato quid dicat de Galba
absoluto tu melius scis: ego memini propter fratris
filios eum absolutum. Τὸ δὲ ἀκριβὲς ipse inspice. Cato
igitur dissuadet neve suos neve alienos quis liberos
ad misericordiam conciliandam producat neve uxores
neve adfines vel ullas omnino feminas. Dominam
matrem saluta.

Ad M. Caes. iii. 21 (Naber, p. 57).

Magistro meo.

Mane ad te non scripsi, quia te commodiorem
esse audieram, et quia ipse in alio negotio occupatus

[1] For octavo idus.

---

[1] A splendid villa of Trajan's on the Etrurian coast, now
Civita Vecchia. Pliny, *Ep.* vi. 31, gives a good description of it.
[2] Between Rome and Centumcellae on the Via Aurelia.

M. CORNELIUS FRONTO

To my Lord.

I am keeping my bed. If I should be fit for the journey when you go to Centumcellae[1] I shall see you, please God, at Lorium on the seventh day before the Ides. Make my apologies to my Lord your father, whom—may heaven preserve you both— I love and honour all the more intensely since the excellent decision in the Senate, which, while safeguarding the interests of the provinces, at the same time gently rebuked the offenders.

When you inaugurate your game preserve, be sure that you remember, without fail, if you strike a beast, to set your horse at full gallop. Of course you will bring Galba to Centumcellae, or can you be at Lorium,[2] on the 8th before the Ides? Farewell, my Lord, please your father, greet your mother, miss me. You know better than I what Cato says of Galba's acquittal.[3] As far as I remember he was acquitted for the sake of his nephews. But see for yourself what the truth of the matter is. Cato, in consequence, is of opinion that no one should bring into court his own or others' children to excite pity, nor wives nor relations, nor any women at all. Greet my Lady your mother.

To my master.

I did not write to you in the morning, hearing that you were better, and being myself engaged in

---

[3] He was tried for massacring nearly the whole nation of the Lusitanians by means of the basest treachery. Cato, though eighty-five years old, was his accuser. Galba brought his sons and one nephew into court to excite pity.

fueram; nec sustineo ad te umquam quicquam scribere nisi remisso et soluto et libero animo. Igitur,
si recte sumus, fac me ut sciam : quid enim optem

Vat. 175

scis ; quam | merito optem scio. Vale, meus magis-
ter, qui merito apud animum meum omnes omni re
praevenis. Mi magister, ecce non dormito, et cogo
me ut dormiam, ne tu irascaris. Aestimas utique
me vespera haec scribere.[1]

Ad M. Caes. iv. 4 (Naber, p. 66).

Vat. 149,
following
150

M. Caesar M. Frontoni magistro suo | salutem.

1. Postquam vehiculum inscendi, postquam te
salutavi, iter non adeo incommodum fecimus,[2] sed
paululum pluvia [3] aspersi sumus. Sed priusquam ad
villam venimus, Anagniam devertimus, mille fere
passus a via. Deinde id oppidum antiquum vidimus,
minutulum quidem sed multas res in se antiquas
hab<ens> et aedes sanctasque caerimonias supra
modum. Nullus angulus fuit, ubi delubrum aut
fanum aut templum non sit; praeterea multi libri
lintei, quod ad sacra adtinet.[4] Deinde in porta,
quom eximus, ibi scriptum erat bifariam sic : *Flamen
sume samentum.* Rogavi aliquem ex popularibus quid
illud verbum esset? Ait lingua Hernica pelli
culam de hostia, quam in apicem suum flamen quom
in urbem introeat imponit. Multa adeo alia didi-

---

[1] After this letter at the end of *Ad M. Caes.* iii. follow
words which Mai reads as *Caecilius s<ae>pe <r>ogatus legi
emendavi.* Havet suggests *pr(aefectus) pr(aetorio) togatus.*

[2] Before this word the Codex has *non*, erased by m². *Nos*
and *confecimus* have been suggested.   [3] Cod. *pluviae.*

[4] Another MS. noted on margin of Cod. had *pertinet.*

other business; and I never care to write at all to you unless my mind is unbent and at ease and free. Therefore, if our news is correct, assure me of it. For you know what I wish, and I know how rightly I wish it. Farewell, my master, so rightly first in my thoughts before all others on all occasions. See, my master, I am not sleepy, yet force myself to sleep that you may not be angry. You realize, at any rate, that I am writing this in the evening.

Signia, ? 144–145 A.D.

M. CAESAR to his master M. Fronto, greeting.

1. After getting into the carriage, when I had said good-bye to you, we did not have such a bad journey, though we got a slight wetting from the rain. But before reaching our country house we turned aside to Anagnia, about a mile off the main road. Then we inspected that ancient township, a tiny place, indeed, but containing many antiquities and buildings, and religious ceremonies beyond number. There was not a corner without its chapel or shrine or temple; many books too, written on linen,[1] and this has a religious significance. Then on the gate, as we came out, we found an inscription twice over to this effect: *Flamen sume samentum.*[2] I asked one of the townsfolk what the last word meant. He said it was Hernican for the pelt of the victim, which the priest draws over his peaked cap on entering the city. Quite a number of other

---

[1] Probably of Etruscan origin, and a sort of " Book of the Dead " ; *cp.* Livy, iv. 7. 12. It is said that such books have recently been found. There were some in the Ulpian library, Gell. xix. 5.

[2] " Priest, don the fell " (Dr. Rouse).

cimus quae vellemus scire; verum id solum est quod
nolimus, quom tu a nobis abes: ea nobis maxima
sollicitudo est.

2. Nunc tu postquam inde profectus es, utrumne
in Aureliam an in Campaniam abiisti? Fac scribas
mihi et an vindemias inchoaveris, et an ad villam
multitudinem librorum tuleris, et illud quoque, an me
desideres—quod ego | stulte requiro, quom[1] tu per
te facis. Nunc tu si me desideras atque si me amas,
litteras tuas ad me frequenter mittes, quod mihi
"solacium atque fomentum" sit. Nam decem partibus
tuas litteras legere malim quam omnes Massicos[2] aut
Gauranos palmites: nam Signini quidem isti nimis
rancidos racemos et acidos acinos habent, quod
vinum malim quam mustum bibere. Praeterea istas
uvas multo commodius passas quam puberes mandu-
care; nam profecto malim eas pedibus calcare quam
dentibus comesse. Sed tamen propitiae placataeque
sint, et mihi pro istis iocularibus bonam veniam
duint. Vale, mihi homo amicissime, suavissime,
disertissime, magister dulcissime. Quom videbis in
dolio mustum fervere, in mentem tibi veniat mihi sic
in pectore tuum desiderium scatere et abundare et
spumas facere. Semper vale.

[1] Cod. *quod.*   [2] For Cod. *Marsicos.*

things we learnt which we were glad to know; but
the one thing we are not glad of is that it was in
your absence : that is our chief concern.

2. Now for yourself, did you, when you left us, go to
the Aurelian district [1] or into Campania? Mind you
tell me, and whether you have begun the vintage,
and whether you have brought crowds of books to
your country house, yes, and this, too, whether you
miss me ; and yet that is a foolish question, for you
need no reminder to do that. Well, then, if you do
miss me and do love me, you will write to me often
to console me and cheer me up.[2] For I would ten
times rather have the run[3] of your letters than of all
the vineyards of the Massic[4] and the Gauran Mount :
for your clusters of Signia are too nauseous and
their berries too bitter, wherefore I would prefer their
wine to their must for drinking. Besides it is much
more agreeable to masticate the grapes parched
than pulpy, for beyond question I would rather
stamp them with my feet than champ them with
my teeth. Yet may they be gracious and forgiving,
and for these pleasantries a kindly pardon grant.
Farewell, to me most affectionate, most delightful, most eloquent of men, master most sweet.
When you see the must fermenting in the cask,
let it remind you that my longing for you wells up
thus and overflows and foams in my breast. Fare
ever well.

---

[1] *i.e.* the *regio* through which ran the *Via Aurelia.*

[2] A phrase from Cicero (*Tusc.* ii. 24, 59).

[3] Fronto plays on two meanings of *legere.*

[4] A good wine is meant. Marsic wine was poor, see Mart.
xiii 121 and Athen. i. 26. The wine of Signia was astringent
and medicinal.

Ad M. Caes. iv. 5 (Naber, p. 68).

HAVE mi magister gravissime.[1]

1. Nos valemus. Ego hodie ab hora nona noctis in secundam diei bene disposito cibo studivi; a secunda in tertiam soleatus libentissime inambulavi Vat 155 ante cubiculum meum. Deinde | calceatus sagulo sumpto—nam ita adesse nobis indictum erat—abii salutatum Dominum meum.

2. Ad venationem profecti sumus, fortia facinora fecimus, apros captos esse fando audiimus, nam videndi quidem nulla facultas fuit. Clivom tamen satis arduom successimus; inde postmeridie domum recepimus. Ego me ad libellos. Igitur calceis detractis, vestimentis positis, in lectulo ad duas horas commoratus sum. Legi Catonis orationem *De bonis Pulchrae*,[2] et aliam qua tribuno diem dixit. *Io*, inquis puero tuo, *vade quantum potes, de Apollinis bibliothecabus*[3] *has mihi orationes apporta.* Frustra mittis, nam et isti libri me secuti sunt. Igitur Tiberianus bibliothecarius tibi subigitandus est; aliquid in eam rem insumendum, quod mihi ille, ut ad urbem venero, aequa divisione impertiat. Sed ego orationibus his perlectis, paululum misere scripsi, quod aut lymphis aut Volcano dicarem: ἀληθῶς ἀτυχῶς σήμερον γέγραπταί μοι, venatoris plane aut vindemiatoris studiolum, qui

---

[1] Another MS. (quoted in margin of Cod.) has *carissime*.

[2] m² of Cod. has *Dulchae*.

[3] m² corrects to the singular; but there were two libraries in the Temple of Apollo, one for Latin and the other for Greek.

M. CORNELIUS FRONTO

M. Aurelius to Fronto

? 144–145 A.D.

Hail, most reverend master.

1. We are well. By a satisfactory arrangement of meals I worked from three o'clock a.m. till eight. For the next hour I paced about in slippers most contentedly before my bedroom. Then putting on my boots and donning my cloak—for we had been told to come in that dress—I went off to pay my respects to my Lord.

2. We set out for the chase[1] and did doughty deeds. We did hear say that boars had been bagged, for we were not lucky enough to see any. However, we climbed quite a steep hill; then in the afternoon we came home. I to my books: so taking off my boots and doffing my dress I passed nearly two hours on my couch, reading Cato's speech *On the property of Pulchra*,[2] and another in which he impeached a tribune. *Ho,* you cry to your boy, *go as fast as you can and fetch me those speeches from the libraries of Apollo!*[3] It is no use your sending, for those volumes, among others, have followed me here. So you must get round the librarian of Tiberius's library:[4] a little douceur will be necessary, in which he and I can go shares when I come back to town. Well, these speeches read, I wrote a little wretched stuff, fit to be dedicated to the deities of water and fire: truly to-day I have been unlucky in my writing, the lucubration of a sportsman or a vintager, such as

[1] Marcus was fond of hunting; see Capit. iv. 9. Coins also shew this; see Cohen, 408, and a beautiful medallion in Grueber.

[2] Nothing more is known of this speech.

[3] Built by Augustus; see Hor. *Od.* i. 31; *Ep.* i. 3. 17.

[4] In the Palace of Tiberius.

iubilis suis cubiculum meum perstrepunt, causidicali prorsum odio et taedio. Quid hoc dixi? Immo recte dixi, nam meus quidem magister orator | est.

3. Ego videor mihi perfrixisse: quod mane soleatus ambulavi an quod male scripsi, non scio. Certe homo alioqui pituitosus, hodie tamen multo mucculentior mihi esse videor. Itaque oleum in caput infundam et incipiam dormire: nam in lucernam hodie nullam stillam inicere cogito, ita me equitatio et sternutatio defatigavit. Valebis mihi, magister carissime et dulcissime, quem ego—ausim dicere—magis quam ipsam Romam desidero.

Ad M. Caes. iv. 6 (Naber, p. 69).

HAVE mi magister dulcissime.

1. Nos valemus. Ego aliquantulum prodormivi[1] propter perfrictiunculam, quae videtur sedata esse. Ego ab undecima noctis in tertiam diei partim legi ex *Agricultura* Catonis partim scripsi, minus misere mehercule quam heri. Inde salutato patre meo, aqua mulsa sorbenda usque ad gulam et reiectanda fauces fovi, potius quam dicerem *gargarissavi*: nam est apud[2] Novium, credo, et alibi. Sed faucibus curatis abii ad patrem meum et immolanti adstiti. Deinde

---

[1] Should probably be *perdormivi*.
[2] For Cod. *et ad.*

those whose catches[1] ring through my bedroom, a
noise every whit as hateful and wearisome as that of
the law-courts. What is this I have said? Nay, 'tis
true, for my master is an *orator*.

3. I think I must have taken a chill, whether from
walking about in slippers in the early morning, or
from writing badly, I know not. I only know that,
rheumy enough at all times, I seem to be more
drivelling than ever to-day. So I will pour the oil
on my head and go off to sleep, for not a drop of it
do I intend to pour into my lamp to-day, so tired am
I with riding and sneezing. Farewell for my sake,
dearest and sweetest of masters, whom I would
make bold to say I long to see more than Rome
itself.

MARCUS AURELIUS TO FRONTO

? 144–145 A.D.

HAIL, my sweetest of masters.

1. We are well. I slept somewhat late owing
to my slight cold, which seems now to have subsided.
So from five a.m. till nine I spent the time partly
in reading some of Cato's *Agriculture* and partly in
writing not quite such wretched stuff, by heavens, as
yesterday. Then, after paying my respects to my
father, I relieved my throat, I will not say by gargling
—though the word *gargarisso* is, I believe, found in
Novius and elsewhere—but by swallowing honey
water as far as the gullet and ejecting it again.
After easing my throat I went off to my father and
attended him at a sacrifice.[2]   Then we went to

---

[1] Lucian (*Lexiph.* 2) speaks of τοὺς ἐργάτας λιγυρίζοντας
τὴν θερινὴν ᾠδήν.

[2] Capit. *Vit. Pii,* xi. 5, says Pius always performed the
sacrifice himself.

ad merendam itum. Quid me censes prandisse?
panis tantulum, quom conchim[1] caepas et maenas
bene praegnatas alios vorantes viderem. Deinde
Vat. 185 uvis metendis operam dedi|mus et consudavimus et
iubilavimus et *aliquot,* ut ait auctor, *reliquimus alti-*
pendulos vindemiae superstites. Ab hora sexta domum
rediimus.

2. Paululum studui atque id ineptum. Deinde
cum matercula mea supra torum sedente multum
garrivi. Meus sermo hic erat: *Quid existimas modo*
meum Frontonem facere? Tum illa: *Quid autem tu*
meam Gratiam? Tum ego: *Quid autem passerculam*
nostram Gratiam minusculam? Dum ea fabulamur
atque altercamur, uter alter<utr>um[2] vestrum magis
amaret, discus crepuit, id est, pater meus in balneum
transisse nuntiatus est. Loti igitur in torculari cenavimus: non loti in torculari, sed loti cenavimus; et
rusticos cavillantes audivimus libenter. Inde reversus, priusquam me in latus converto ut stertam, meum
pensum explico et diei rationem meo suavissimo
magistro reddo, quem si possem magis desiderare,
libenter plusculum macerarer. Valebis mihi, Fronto,
ubiubi es, mellitissime, meus amor, mea voluptas.
Quid mihi tecum est? Amo absentem.

[1] Madvig would read *cum conchi <quom>.*
[2] Brakman.

luncheon. What do you think I ate? A wee bit of bread, though I saw others devouring beans, onions, and herrings full of roe. We then worked hard at grape-gathering,[1] and had a good sweat, and were merry and, as the poet says, *still left some clusters hanging high as gleanings of the vintage.*[2] After six o'clock we came home.

2. I did but little work and that to no purpose. Then I had a long chat with my little mother as she sat on the bed. My talk was this: *What do you think my Fronto is now doing?* Then she: *And what do you think my Gratia is doing?* Then I: *And what do you think our little sparrow, the wee Gratia,*[3] *is doing?* Whilst we were chattering in this way and disputing which of us two loved the one or other of you two the better, the gong sounded, an intimation that my father had gone to his bath. So we had supper after we had bathed in the oil-press room; I do not mean bathed in the oil-press room, but when we had bathed, had supper there, and we enjoyed hearing the yokels chaffing one another. After coming back, before I turn over and snore, I get my task done and give my dearest of masters an account of the day's doings, and if I could miss him more, I would not grudge wasting away a little more. Farewell, my Fronto, wherever you are, most honey-sweet, my love, my delight. How is it between you and me? I love you and you are away.

---

[1] Capit. (*ibid.* xi. 2) tells us that Pius *vindemias privati modo cum amicis agebat.*

[2] Possibly from the *Vindemiatores* of Novius.

[3] Fronto's daughter.

Ad M. Caes. iv. 7 (Naber, p. 70).

HAVE mihi magister dulcissime.

Tandem tabellarius proficiscitur, et ego tridui |
acta mea ad te tandem possum dimittere. Nec quicquam dico; ita epistulis prope ad xxx dictandis
spiritum insumpsi. Nam quod proxime tibi de epistulis placuerat, nondum ad patrem meum pertuli.
Sed quom dis iuvantibus ad urbem veniemus, admone
me ut tibi aliquid de hac re narrem : sed quae tua et
mea meteoria est, neque tu me admonebis neque ego
tibi narrabo : utique [1] enim revera opus consulto est.
Vale meum—quid dicam <quom> quidquid dicere
satis non est?—vale, meum desiderium, mea lux,[2]
mea voluptas.

Ad M. Caes. iv. 8 (Naber, p. 71).

MAGISTRO meo salutem.

Adventum tuum mihi frater tuus nuper εὐηγ-
γελίσατο. Cupio mehercule possis venire, quod
<salva>[3] salute tua fiat : spero enim fore ut etiam
valetudini meae conspectus tuus aliquid conferat :
εἰς ὄμματ᾽ εὔνου φωτὸς ἐμβλέψαι γλυκύ, Euripides ait,
opinor. Ego impraesentiarum[4] sic me habeo, ut vel
hinc aestimatu facile sit tibi, quod haec precaria
manu scribo. Sane quidem quod ad vires adtinet,
incipiunt redire : pectoris etiam dolor nullus resi-
duus ; ulcus autem illud ἀπεργα[5] . . . . τῆς ἀρτηρίας.
Nos remedia experimur et nequid opere nostro[6]

---

[1] Klussm. for Cod. *atque*.
[2] These words are not quite certain.   [3] Klussm.
[4] A colloquial contraction for *in praesentia rerum*.
[5] Kiehl suggests ἀπεργάζεται.   [6] = *opera nostra*.

M. CORNELIUS FRONTO

Marcus Aurelius to Fronto

? 144–145 A.D.

Hail, my sweetest of masters.

At last the messenger is starting, and at last I can send you my three days' budget of news. But I cannot *say* anything, to such an extent have I exhausted my breath by dictating nearly thirty letters. For as to your last opinion on the question of letters, I have not yet broached the matter to my father. But when we come, God willing, to Rome, remind me to tell you something on this matter. But you and I are so much up in the clouds that neither will you remind me nor I tell you : and yet, indeed, it really needs consideration. Farewell, my—what shall I say when whatever I say is inadequate ?— farewell my longing, my light, my delight.

M. Aurelius to Fronto

? 144–145 A.D.

To my master, greeting.

Your brother but now brought me the good news of your arrival. Heaven knows I long for you to be able to come, if only your health will allow of it, for I hope that the sight of you may do something for my health also. *Sweet 'tis to look into a friend's kind eyes,* as Euripides,[1] I take it, says. My present condition you can easily gauge by the shakiness of my handwriting. As far as my strength is concerned, it is certainly beginning to come back. The pain in my chest, too, is quite gone ; but the ulcer . . . . the trachea. I am under treatment and taking every care that nothing militates

[1] *Ion*, 732.

Vat. 187 claudat, advigilamus. | Neque enim ulla alia re tolera-
biliora diuturna incommoda fieri sentio, quam con-
scientia curae diligentis et temperantiae medicis
obsequentis.   Turpe alioqui fuerit diutius vitium corporis quam animi studium ad recuperandam sanitatem posse durare.   Vale mi iucundissime magister.
Salutat te mater mea.

Ad M. Caes. **v.** 58 (73) (Naber, p. 92).

Vat 109,
col. 2 | Domino meo.
     Vexatus sum, Domine, nocte diffuso dolore per
umerum et cubitum et genu et talum.   Denique id
ipsum tibi mea manu scribere non potui.

Ad M. Caes. iv. 9 (Naber, p. 71).

Vat. 187,
ad fin.
col. 1 | Domino meo.[1]
     Accepi litteras tuas elegantissime scriptas, qui-
bus tu intervallo desiderium litterarum mearum obor-
tum tibi esse ais.   Est igitur vera Socrati opinio,
"doloribus ferme voluptates connexas esse," quom in
carcere dolorem constricti vinculi voluptate resoluti
compensaret.   Item profecto in nobis, quantum
molestiae absentia, tantum commodi adfert desiderium inritatum.   Nam desiderium ex amore est.
Igitur amor cum desiderio auctus est, quod est in

----

[1]This letter is omitted in the Index (given Naber,
p. 58).

against its success. For I feel that my protracted illness can be made more bearable only by a consciousness of unfailing care and strict obedience[1] to the doctors' orders. Besides, it were shame, indeed, that a disease of the body should outlast a determination of the mind to recover health. Farewell, my most delightful of masters. My mother greets you.

FRONTO TO MARCUS AURELIUS AS CAESAR

To my Lord.   ? 144–145 A.D.

I have been troubled, my Lord, in the night with widespread pains in my shoulder and elbow and knee and ankle. In fact, I have not been able to convey this very news to you in my own writing.

FRONTO TO MARCUS AURELIUS AS CAESAR

To my Lord.   ? 144–145 A.D.

I have received your letter, most charmingly expressed, in which you say that the intermission in my letters has caused a longing for them to arise in you. Socrates was right, then, in his opinion that "pleasures are generally linked to pains," when in his imprisonment he held that the pain caused by the tightness of his chains was made up for by the pleasure of their removal.[2] Precisely so in our case the fondness which absence stimulates brings as much comfort as the absence itself causes affliction. For fond longing comes from love. Therefore, absence makes the heart grow fonder, and this is far

---

[1] We know from Galen (xiv. 216, Kühn) that Marcus was in later life, too, a good and intelligent patient.

[2] In Plato's *Phaedo, ad init.*

amicitia multo optimum.   Tum quod quaeris de valetudine mea, iam prius scripseram tibi, me humeri
dolore vexatum ita vehementer quidem ut illam
ipsam epistulam, qua id significabam, scribendo dare
operam nequirem ; sed uterer contra morem nostrum
End of
Vat. 187
and
Quat. ix. <aliena manu> . . . . |.

Ad M. Caes. iv. 10 (Naber, p. 72).

     <Magistro meo salutem.>
      Haec me in praesentia[1] . . . . <Vale mi
Vat. 142 Fronto caris>|sime.   Mater mea te salutat.   Consulem
nostrum saluta et matronam nostram.

Ad M. Caes. v. 1 (Naber, p. 77).

Vat. 127,
col. 2 | Domino meo.
     Si quicquam nos amas, dormi per istas noctes,
ut forti colore in senatum venias et vehementi latere
legas.

Ad M. Caes. v. 2 (Naber, p. 78).

  Magistro meo.
     Ego te numquam satis amabo : dormiam.

Ad M. Caes. v. 3 (Naber, p. 78).

  Domino meo.
     Miserere, unum verbum de oratione ablega, et
quaeso ne umquam utaris : *dictionem* pro *oratione.*[2]
Vale, Domine, mea gloria immortalis.   Matrem
Dominam saluta.

   [1] These words are from the Index.   Apart from them four
pages are lost from *nostrum* in the previous letter.
   [2] m[1] of Cod. has *orationem.*

the best thing in friendship. Then as to my health,
about which you enquire, I had already written to
you that I was suffering so much pain in the shoulder
that I could not succeed in writing the very letter in
which I mentioned it, but, contrary to my usual
custom, had to employ another hand . . . .

Marcus Aurelius to Fronto

? 144–145 A.D.

To my master, greeting.
These things at present . . . . Farewell, my
dearest Fronto, my mother greets you. Greet our
consul[1] and our lady.

Fronto to Marcus Aurelius as Caesar

145–147 A.D.

To my Lord.
If you have any love at all for me, sleep those
nights that you may come into the Senate[2] with a
good colour and read with a strong voice.

M. Aurelius to Fronto

145–147 A.D.

To my master.
I can never love you enough : I will sleep.

Fronto to Marcus as Caesar

145–147 A.D.

To my Lord.
Pardon me, cancel one word from your speech
and, I entreat you, never use it—*dictio* for *oratio*.
Farewell, my Lord, my everlasting glory. Greet my
Lady your mother.

[1] It is not known who is referred to.
[2] For his speech of thanks as consul (145 A.D.) or as
invested with *Trib. Pot.* (147).

Ad M. Caes. v. 4 (Naber, p. 78).

R<ESCRIPTUM>.

Cras me de hoc verbo tibi, si admonueris, defendam.

Ad M. Caes. v. (Index) (Naber, p. 76).

Vat. 128, line 5

<DOMINO meo.> | Quam fortis advenias[1] . . . . .

<MAGISTRO meo.> Fortes venimus . . . .

<DOMINO meo.> Sume cibum, Domine . . . . .

<MAGISTRO meo.> Sumpsi cibum . . . .

<DOMINO meo.> Si animus Faustinae . . . . . .

<MAGISTRO meo.> Et consilio tuo obsequor . . .

<DOMINO meo.> At hercule compleri tem<pus>

<MAGISTRO meo.> Nimis diu sollicitus . . . . .

<DOMINO meo.> Mirifice ego quidem . . . . . .

<MAGISTRO meo.> In media incommoda . . . .

<DOMINO meo.> Adflictus sum labore . . . . . .

<MAGISTRO meo.> Fatigatio ista tua . . . . . .

<DOMINO meo.> Modo mihi Gratia . . . .

<MAGISTRO meo.> Possit satis pro re ista . . . .

<DOMINO meo.> Caietae substiti . . . .

[1] These fifteen letters have only the opening words preserved. As they were contained (including the beginning of the following letter) in four pages of the Codex, they could only have been four or five lines apiece.

---

[1] Cicero uses it (*De Orat.* i. 33).

M. CORNELIUS FRONTO

Marcus Aurelius to Fronto

Answer.   145–147 A.D.

To-morrow, if you will remind me, I will state my
case for this word.[1]

From the Index

Fronto to Marcus and Marcus to Fronto Alternately
145–147 A.D.

To my Lord.   (Tell me) how strong you feel on
arriving . . . .

To my master.   I arrived quite strong . . . .

To my Lord.   Take food, my Lord . . . .

To my master.   I have taken food [2] . . . .

To my Lord.   If Faustina's [3] courage . . . .

To my master.   I both bow to your advice . . . .

To my Lord.   But, by heaven, the completion of
the time . . . .

To my master.   Too long anxious . . . .

To my Lord.   I indeed (was) wonderfully (pleased)
. . . .

To my master.   Into the midst of worries . . . .

To my Lord.   I have been worn out with work
. . . .

To my master.   That fatigue of yours . . . .

To my Lord.   Lately Gratia . . . .

To my master.   Possibly enough for that matter
. . . .

To my Lord.   I have halted at Caieta [4] . . . .

[2] The first four letters seem to refer to the same occasion
as the four that precede.

[3] The first mention of Faustina in connection with Marcus,
to whom she was married in 145.

[4] A harbour of Latium. Marcus (*Thoughts*, i. *ad fin.*)
mentions a stay there.

Ad M. Caes. **v.** 5 [20] (Naber, p. 78).

<MAGISTRO meo.>

Vat. 106:
Quat. x.
ends
Quantum tu mihi . . . . | in biduo[1] nunc, si
videtur, dentes adprimamus tamen; et quo brevius
iter sit tibi recenti morbo Caietae nos opperire.
Facio delicias, quod ferme evenit quibus quod
cupiunt tandem - in manu est: differunt, affluunt,
gestiunt;[2] ego vero etiam fastidio omnia. Domina
mater te salutat, quam ego hodie rogabo ut ad me
Gratiam perducat—*vel fumum* inquit *patriae* Graius[3]
poeta. Vale mi—omnia mea—magister. Amo me
quod te visurus sum.

Ad M. Caes. **v.** 6 [21] (Naber, p. 78).

DOMINO meo.

Postquam profecti estis, genus dolore arreptus
sum, verum ita modico ut et ingrederer pedetemptim
et vehiculo uterer. Hac nocte vehementior dolor
invasit, ita tamen ut iacens facile patiar, nisi quid
amplius ingruerit. Augustam tuam vexatam audio.
Deis equidem salutem eius commendo. Vale, Domine
dulcissime. Dominam saluta.

[1] Cod. *viduo.* From *defendam* in *Ad M. Caes.* **v.** 4 (p. 190)
four pages are lost.
[2] The margin of Cod. gives *statim diffluunt, affluunt, et
fastidiunt.* [3] Jacobs for *Caius* (Mai).

---

[1] Perhaps the phrase means "belittle" or "make light
of a thing."

M. CORNELIUS FRONTO

M. AURELIUS TO FRONTO

To my master.   145–147 A.D.

. . . . in two days now, if that is best, let us clench our teeth all the same; and as you are just recovering from illness, to shorten the journey, wait for us at Caieta. I begin to be dainty,[1] as generally happens with those who have at last in their grasp what they long for: they are carried away,[2] they feel in affluence, they are exultant: for myself, however, I have even lost the taste for everything. My Lady mother greets you. I shall ask her to-day to bring Gratia to me—*even the smoke of one's fatherland*, as the Greek poet[3] says. Farewell, my—all in all—master. I love myself at the thought of seeing you.

FRONTO TO MARCUS AS CAESAR

To my Lord.   145–147 A.D.

After you had set out, I was seized with pain in the knee, but so slight that I could both walk slowly and use a carriage. To-night the pain has come on more violently, but so that I can easily bear it lying down, if it gets no worse. I hear that your Augusta is poorly. I pray the Gods, indeed, to have care of her health. Farewell, most sweet Lord. Greet my Lady.[4]

---

[2] Hauler (*Wien. Stud.* 25, pt. 1, 1903) takes *differunt* as = *differuntur*, a Plautine usage.

[3] Homer, see above p. 94.

[4] Either Faustina or the mother of Marcus. By Augusta is meant Faustina the younger, who received this title on her marriage to Marcus in 145.

Ad M. Caes. **v.** 10 (25) (Naber, p. 80).

Domino meo.

Modo mihi Victorinus indicat Dominam tuam |
magis caluisse quam heri. Gratia leviora omnia
nuntiabat. Ego te idcirco non vidi, quod ex grave-
dine sum imbecillus. Cras tamen mane domum ad
te veniam. Eadem,[1] si tempestivom erit, etiam
Dominam visitabo.

Ad M. Caes. **v.** 11 (26) (Naber, p. 80).

Magistro meo.

Caluit et hodie Faustina, et quidem id ego
magis hodie videor mihi deprehendisse. Sed dis
iuvantibus aequiorem mihi animum facit ipsa, quod
se tam obtemperanter nobis accommodat. Tu, si
potuisses scilicet, venisses. Quod iam potes et quod
venturum promittis, delector, mi magister. Vale mi
iucundissime magister.

Ad M. Caes. **v.** 7 (22) (Naber, p. 79).

| Magistro meo.

Ludis tu quidem, at mihi peramplam anxietatem
et summam aegritudinem, <acerbissimum> dolorem,
et ignem flagrantissimum litteris his tuis misisti, ne
cenare, ne dormire, ne denique studere libeat.
Verum tu orationis hodiernae tuae habeas aliquod

sc. opera.

M. CORNELIUS FRONTO

Fronto to Marcus as Caesar

To my Lord.   145–147 A.D.

Victorinus[1] has just told me that your Lady is
more feverish than yesterday. Gratia reported that
everything had taken a turn for the better. The
reason that I have not seen you is that I am
indisposed with a bad cold. To-morrow morning,
however, I will come to you at home. At the same
time I will call on your Lady also, if convenient.

Marcus Aurelius to Fronto

To my master.   145–147 A.D.

Faustina has been feverish to-day also, and, in
fact, I fancy I have noticed it more to-day. But the
Gods be thanked she herself makes me less anxious
by being such an obedient patient. Of course you
would have come had you been able. I am rejoiced
that you can come now, and promise to do so, my
master. Farewell, most delightful of masters.

Marcus Aurelius to Fronto

To my master.   *Lorium*, 145–147 A.D.

You indeed are playful,[2] but by this letter of
yours you have sent me immense anxiety and intense
distress, most acute pain and burning fever, so that
I have no heart to sup or sleep or even study. But
you would find some comfort in your speech to-day,

---

[1] Afterwards Fronto's son-in-law.
[2] It is not known what misfortune had befallen Fronto.

solacium; at | ego quid faciam? qui et auditionis iam voluptatem consumpsi, et metuo ne Lorium tardiuscule venias, et doleo quod interim doles. Vale, mi magister, cuius salus meam salutem inlibatam et incolumem facit.

Ad M. Caes. **v.** 8 (23) (Naber, p. 79).

MAGISTRO meo.

Ego dies istos tales transegi. Soror dolore muliebrium partium ita correpta est repente, ut faciem horrendam viderim. Mater autem mea in ea trepidatione imprudens angulo parietis costam inflixit: eo ictu graviter et se et nos adfecit. Ipse quom cubitum irem, scorpionem in lecto offendi: occupavi tamen eum occidere priusquam accumberem. Tu si rectius vales, est solacium. Mater iam levior est, dis volentibus. Vale mi optime dulcissime magister. Domina mea te salutat.

Ad M. Caes. **v.** 9 (24) (Naber, p. 79).

DOMINO meo.

Quom te salvom et illaesum dei praestiterunt, maximas deis gratias ago. Te certum habeo, quom instituta tua reputo, haud perturbatum: ego, quam-

---

[1] Annia Cornificia, born about 123 A.D. She married Ummidius Quadratus.

[2] This would be at Lorium, or somewhere in the country.

whereas I, what am I to do? who have already forestalled the pleasure of hearing it and fear that your visit to Lorium may be delayed, and am in pain because you meanwhile are in pain. Farewell, my master, whose health makes my health unimpaired and assured.

Marcus Aurelius to Fronto

To my master.   145–147 A.D.

This is how I have passed the last few days. My sister[1] was seized suddenly with such pain in the privy parts that it was dreadful to see her. Moreover, my mother, in the flurry of the moment, inadvertently ran her side against a corner of the wall, causing us as well as herself great pain by the accident. For myself, when I went to lie down I came upon a scorpion in my bed[2]; however, I was in time to kill it before lying down upon it. If you are better, that is a consolation. My mother feels easier now, thank the Gods. Farewell, best and sweetest of masters. My Lady[3] greets you.

Fronto to Marcus as Caesar

To my Lord.   145–147 A.D.

I am truly thankful to the Gods that they have kept you safe and unharmed.[4] You, I make no doubt, were unperturbed, for I know your philosophic views; for myself, however much you wiseacres may

---

[3] It is not clear whether this is his mother or Faustina.
[4] If Fronto here refers to the scorpion incident, it is curious that he does not enquire for the rest of the family.

libet vos sapientes me inrideatis, consternatus equidem sum. Vale, Domine dulcissime, et deis curae esto. Dominam saluta.

Ad M. Caes. **v.** 12 (27) (Naber, p. 80).

| Domino meo.

Quomodo manseris, Domine, scire cupio. Ego cervicum dolore arreptus sum. Vale, Domine. Dominam saluta.

Ad M. Caes. **v.** 13 (28) (Naber, p. 80).

Magistro meo salutem.

Noctem sine febre videor transmisisse ; cibum non invitus cepi : nunc ago levissime. Nox quid ferat cognoscemus. Sed, mi magister, cervicum te dolore arreptum quo animo didicerim, profecto ex tua proxima sollicitudine metiris. Vale mi iucundissime magister. Mater mea salutat te.

Ad M. Caes. v. 14 (29) (Naber, **p.** 81).

| Domino meo.

Cervicum, Domine, dolore gravissimo correptus sum[1] ; de pede dolor decessit. Vale, Domine optime. Dominam saluta.

[1] Schwierczina for Cod. *gravi sum correptus sum.*

laugh at me, I confess I was thoroughly shocked. Farewell, my most sweet Lord, and may the Gods have you in their keeping. Greet my Lady.

Fronto to Marcus as Caesar

To my Lord.   145–147 A.D.

I am anxious to know, my Lord, how you are keeping. I have been seized with pain in the neck. Farewell, my Lord. Greet your Lady.

Marcus Aurelius to Fronto

To my master, greeting.   145–147 A.D.

I think I have got through the night without fever. I have taken food without repugnance, and am doing very nicely now. We shall see what the night brings. But, my master, by your late anxiety you can certainly gauge my feelings when I learnt that you had been seized with pain in the neck. Farewell, my most delightful of masters. My mother greets you.

Fronto to Marcus as Caesar

To my Lord.   145–147 A.D.

I have been seized, my Lord, with a most severe pain in the neck. The pain has gone from my foot. Farewell, best of Lords. Greet my Lady.

Ad M. Caes. v. 15 (30) (Naber, p. 81).

MAGISTRO meo salutem.

Cervicum dolores si tertio[1] quoque die remiserint, erit quod meam valetudinem maiorem in modum adiuvet, mi magister. Lavi et hodie et ambulavi paulum, cibi paulo plus sumpsi, nondum tamen libente stomacho. Vale mi iucundissime magister. Mater mea te salutat.

Ad M. Caes. v. 16 (31) (Naber, p. 81).

MAGISTRO meo salutem.

Quod[2] tibi etiam tum cervices doluerint, quom[3] mihi scriberes, non possum aequo animo ferre, neque sane volo aut debeo. Ego autem, iuvantibus votum tuum deis, lavi hodie et cibi quantum sat erat cepi; vino etiam libenter usus sum. Vale mi iucundissime magister. Mater mea te salutat.

Ad M. Caes. v. 17 (32) (Naber, p. 81).

DOMINO meo.

Dolores quidem cervicum nihil remiserunt, sed animo bene fuit quom te balneo et vino libenter usum cognovi. Vale, Domine. Dominam saluta.

---

[1] Cod. *tertia.*   [2] Schopen for Cod. *quom.*
[3] *ibid.* for *quo.*

M. CORNELIUS FRONTO

To my master, greeting.   145–147 A.D.

If the pains in your neck get better, even in two days' time, it will help on my convalescence more than anything, my master. I have had a bath and to-day even done a little walking and taken a little more food, but not as yet without discomfort. Farewell, my most delightful of masters. My mother greets you.

Marcus Aurelius to Fronto

To my master, greeting.   145–147 A.D.

I cannot but be distressed that at the very time when you were writing to me your neck was so painful, nor indeed do I wish to be, nor ought I to be, other than distressed. As for me, thanks be to the Gods and your prayers, I have bathed to-day, and taken sufficient food, and wine too I have used with relish. Farewell, my most delightful of masters. My mother greets you.

Fronto to Marcus as Caesar

To my Lord.   145–147 A.D.

The pains in my neck are no easier, but my mind was set at rest as soon as I knew that you had been able to take a bath and relish your wine. Farewell, my Lord. Greet your Lady.

Ad M. Caes. iv. 11 (Naber, p. 72).

| Caesar Frontoni.

Volentibus dis spem salutis nancisci videmur : alvi fluxus constitit, febriculae depulsae : macies tamen pertenuis, et tussiculae nonnihil restat. Profecto intelligis de parvola nostra Faustina haec me tibi scribere, pro qua satis egimus. Tibi valetudo an pro meo voto se accommodet, fac sciam, mi magister.

Ad M. Caes. iv. 12 (Naber, p. 72).

Fronto Caesari.

1. Ut ego, di boni, consternatus sum lecto initio epistulae tuae ! quod ita scriptum fuit ut tuum aliquod valetudinis periculum significari suspicarer. Postquam deinde illud periculum, quod quasi tuum principio litterarum tuarum acceperam, filiae tuae Faustinae fuisse aperuisti, quantum mihi permutatus pavor ! Nec permutatus modo, verum etiam nescio quo pacto nonnihil sublevatus. Dicas licet : *leviusne tibi visum est filiae meae periculum quam meum ? Tibine ita visum, qui praefers Faustinam id tibi esse quod lucem serenam, quod diem festum, quod spem propin-*

quam, quod votum | *impetratum, quod gaudium integrum, quod laudem nobilem atque incolumem ?* Equidem ego quid mihi legenti litteras tuas subvenerit scio ; qua vero id ratione evenerit nescio : nescio, inquam, cur magis ad tuum quam ad tuae filiae periculum consternatus sim ; nisi forte, tametsi paria sint, graviora

M. CORNELIUS FRONTO

Caesar to Fronto.

Thank the Gods we seem to have some hopes of recovery. The diarrhoea is stopped, the feverish attacks got rid of; but the emaciation is extreme, and there is still some cough. You understand, of course, that I am telling you of our little Faustina[1] who has kept us busy enough. Mind you let me know, my master, if, as I heartily pray, your health is improving.

Fronto to Caesar.

1. Good heavens! how shocked I was on reading the beginning of your letter! It was written in such a way that I thought some danger to your health was meant. Then, when the danger, which at the beginning of your note I had taken to be yours, was shewn to be your daughter Faustina's, how transformed was my apprehension. Yet not merely transformed, but in some subtle way a little relieved. You may say, *Did my daughter's danger seem of less account to you than mine? Could it so seem to you, who protest that "Faustina is to you as a limpid light, as a gala day, as a near and dear hope, as a wish fulfilled, as an unalloyed delight, as a glory noble and assured"?* I know, indeed, what came into my mind on reading your letter, but why it came to be so I do not know: I do not know, I say, why I was more shocked at your danger than at your daughter's, unless, perchance, though things be

---

[1] Annia Galeria Faustina, born probably early in 146. She died in infancy, and Herodes set up an inscription to her at Olympia (Dessau, ii. 8803).

tamen videntur quae ad aures prius accidunt.[1] Quae
denique huiusce rei ratio, tu facilius scias, qui de
natura et sensibus hominum scis amplius aliquid
meliusque didicisti. Ego qui a meo magistro et
parente Athenodoto ad exempla et imagines quas-
dam rerum, quas ille εἰκόνας appellabat, apte animo
comprehendundas accommodandasque mediocriter
institutus sum, hanc huiusce rei imaginem repperisse
videor, cur meus translatus metus levior sit mihi
visus : simile solere onus grave humero gestantibus,
quom illud onus in sinistrum ab dextro humero
transtulere, quamquam nihil de pondere deminutum,
tamen ut oneris translatio videatur etiam elevatio.[2]

Vat. 132

2. Nunc quoniam postrema parte epistulae tuae,
quae meliuscule iam valere Faustinam nuntiasti,|
omnem mihi prorsus metum ac sollicitudinem depu-
listi, non alienum tempus videtur de meo adversus
te amore remissius aliquid tecum et liberalius fabu-
landi ; nam ferme metu magno et pavore relevatis
conceditur ludere aliquid atque ineptire. Ego quanto
opere te diligam, non minus [3] de gravibus et seriis
experimentis quam plerisque etiam frivolis sentio.
Quae aut cuiusmodi sint haec frivola indicabo.

3. Siquando te *somno leni,* ut poeta ait, *placidoque
revinctus* video in somniis, numquam est quin am-
plectar et exosculer : tum pro argumento cuiusque
somnii aut fleo ubertim aut exulto laetitia aliqua et

---

[1] The margin of Cod. gives *accedunt.*
[2] Read in the margin of Cod. as *relevatio.*
[3] Should not this be *magis* ?

equally bad, yet those seem worse which are the
first to fall on our ears. What is, in fact, the cause
of this you are more likely to know, for about the
nature and feelings of men your knowledge is somewhat wider than mine, and you have learnt your
lesson better. Tolerably well trained as I was by
my master and parent Athenodotus in the nice
apprehension by the mind and application of illus-
trations and, as it were, similes of things, which he
called εἰκόνες, I think I have hit upon the following
simile of this kind, to explain the fact that the
transference of my fear seemed an alleviation of it—
that much the same thing happens to those who,
carrying a heavy weight on their shoulder, transfer
it from the right shoulder to the left, so that, though
the burden remains as it was, yet the transference
of the pressure seems even a relief.

2. Now, since you have quite dispelled all my fear
and anxiety by the last part of your letter, in which
you announced that Faustina was now somewhat
better,[1] it seems the very time for a little easy and
unconstrained chat with you on my love for you; for
those who are freed from a great fear and apprehension are generally allowed to indulge in a little play-
fulness and frivolity. I feel how dearly I love you,
as much from weighty and serious proofs as also from
many trifles. What these trifles are, and of what
nature, I will point out.

3. Whenever "with soft slumber's chains around
me," as the poet says, I see you in my dreams, there
is never a time but I embrace and kiss you: then,
according to the tenor of each dream, I either weep
copiously or am transported with some great joy and

---

[1] This does not seem to be found in the preceding letter.

voluptate.   Hoc unum ex *Annalibus* sumptum amoris mei argumentum poeticum et sane somniculosum. Accipe aliud rixatorium iam hoc et iurgiosum.   Nonnumquam ego te coram paucissimis et familiarissimis meis gravioribus verbis absentem insectatus sum : olim hoc quom tristior quam par erat in coetu[1] hominum progrederere, vel quom in theatro tu libros vel in convivio lectitabas—nec equidem tum[2] theatris, necdum[3] conviviis abstinebam—tum igitur ego te durum et intempestivom hominem, odiosum | etiam nonnumquam ira percitus appellabam.   Quod si quis alius eodem te convicio audiente me detrectaret, aequo animo audire non poteram.   Ita mihi facilius erat ipsum loqui quam alios de te secius quid dicere perpeti : ita ut Gratiam meam filiam facilius ipse percusserim quam ab alio percuti viderim.

Vat. 131

4. Tertium de meis frivolis addam.   Scis ut in omnibus argentariis mensulis pergulis tabernis protectis vestibulis fenestris usquequaque ubique imagines vestrae sint volgo propositae, male illae quidem pictae pleraeque et crassa, lutea immo, Minerva fictae sculptaeve ; quom interim numquam tua imago tam dissimilis ad oculos meos in itinere accidit, ut non ex ore meo excusserit[4] rictum osculi et somn\<i\>um.†

---

[1] Heindorf prefers *coctum*.   [2] For Cod. *ego dum tu*.

[3] The *dum* is added over the line by m² in the Codex.

[4] Horace, *Sat.* v. 4, 35, has the phrase *excutere risum*, "to raise a smile." For Cod. *somnum* perhaps *savium* could be read.

pleasure. This is one proof of my love, taken from the *Annals*,[1] a poetical and certainly a dreamy one. Listen to another, a quarrelsome and contentious one this time. I have occasionally inveighed against you behind your back in somewhat strong terms before a very few of my most intimate friends. Time was I did this, when you went about in public gatherings with too serious a face,[2] as when you used to read books either in the theatre[3] or at a banquet—nor was I then refraining from theatres, nor as yet from banquets—on such occasions, then, I would call you an austere[4] and unreasonable, even at times, stung by anger, a disagreeable sort of person. But if anyone else found fault with you in my hearing with similar detraction, I could not listen to him with any patience. So it was easier for me to say this of you myself than to suffer others to speak any ill of you: just as I could more easily strike my daughter Gratia myself than see her struck by another.

4. I will add the third of my trifles. You know how in all money-changer's bureaus, booths, bookstalls, eaves, porches, windows, anywhere and everywhere there are likenesses of you exposed to view, badly enough painted most of them to be sure, and modelled or carved in a plain, not to say sorry, style of art, yet at the same time your likeness, however much a caricature, never when I go out meets my eyes without making me part my lips for a smile and dream of you.

---

[1] Of Ennius.   [2] *cp.* Capit. *Vit. Marci*, iv. 8, 10.

[3] *ibid.* xv. 1, and *cp. Thoughts*, vi. 46.

[4] Capit. xxii. 5: *quia durus videbatur ex vhilosophiae iustitutione.*

5. Nunc ut frivolis finem faciam et convertar ad serium, hae litterae tuae cum primis indicio mihi fuerunt, quanto opere te diligam, quom magis perturbatus sum ad tuum quam ad filiae tuae periculum : quom alioqui te quidem mihi, filiam vero tuam etiam tibi, ut par est, superstitem cupiam. Sed heus tu videbis ne delator existas neve indicio pareas apud filiam, quasi vero ego te | quam illam magis diligam. Nam periculum est ne ex ea re filia tua commota, ut est gravis et prisca femina, poscenti mihi manus et plantas ad saviandum ea causa iratior subtrahat aut gravatius porrigat : cuius ego, di boni ! manus parvolas plantasque illas pinguiculas tum libentius exosculabor quam tuas cervices regias tuumque os probum et facetum.

Vat. 138

Ad M. Caes. v. 28 (43) (Naber, p. 84).

Vat. 80,
ad fin.

| Magistro meo.

Dies mihi totus vacuus erit. Siquid umquam me amasti, hodie ama et uberem mi materiam mitte, oro et rogo καὶ ἀντιβολῶ καὶ δέομαι καὶ ἱκετεύω. In illa enim centumvirali non inveni praeter ἐπιφωνήματα.

Vat. 79

Vale, optime magister. | Domina mea te salutat. Volebam aliquid, ubi clamari debeat, scribere. Fave mi et quaere clamosam ὑπόθεσιν.

---

[1] *Uber* (= *grandis*, Quintilian, xii. 10. 58) corresponds to the Greek ἁδρός, and characterises the epideictic kind of oratory.

[2] Cic. *Ad Att.* i. 19 uses this word as equivalent to *acclamationes*, *i.e.* approval by acclamation ; but ἐπιφώνημα

5. Now to call a truce to my trifles and to return to seriousness; this letter of yours served in no small degree to shew the depth of my love for you, since I was more shocked at your danger than your daughter's, whereas, in other respects, I should wish you, indeed, to survive for my sake, but your daughter also for yours, as is right. But hark you, see that you do not turn informer or appear as a witness before your daughter, to make her think that I love you more than her; for there is a danger of your daughter being put out in consequence, as she is a serious and old-fashioned lady, and when I ask for her hands and feet to kiss, of her drawing them away from pique at this, or tendering them grudgingly: whose tiny hands and plump little feet I shall then kiss, by heaven, with more zest than your royal neck and your honest and merry lips.

Marcus Aurelius to Fronto

145–147 A.D.

To my master.

I shall have the whole day free. If you have ever loved me at all, love me to-day, and send me a rich [1] subject, I ask and request and beseech and entreat and implore. For in that law-court subject I found nothing but exclamations.[2] Farewell, best of masters. My Lady greets you. I want something where there ought to be shouts of approval. Humour me and pick out a " shouting " subject.

also stands for *exclamatio*, a rhetorical term for apostrophizing something to excite pity or anger (see *Auct. ad Herenn.* iv. 15. 22). Quintilian however uses it (viii. 5) for the summing up in a concise, telling form of a narrative or proof.

Ad M. Caes. v. 22 (37) (Naber, p. 82).

Vat. 102,
ad fin.

| DOMINO meo.

Ego prodormivi.[1] Materiam misi tibi: res seria
est. Consul populi Romani posita praetexta mani-
cam induit, leonem inter iuvenes quinquatribus per-
cussit populo Romano spectante. Apud censores ex-

Vat. 101 postulat<ur>. | Διασκεύασον, αὔξησον. Vale, Domine
dulcissime. Dominam saluta.

Ad M. Caes. v. 23 (38) (Naber, p. 82).

RESCRIPTUM.

Quando id factum et an Romae? Num illud
dicis in Albano factum sub Domitiano? Praeterea
in hac materia diutius laborandum est ut factum
credatur, quam ut irascatur. Ἀπίθανος ὑπόθεσις videtur mihi, quom plane maluerim,[2] qualem petieram.†
Rescribe statim de tempore.

---

[1] Should probably be *perdormivi*.
[2] Crossley for Cod. *quod plane baluceis*. J. W. E. Pearce
suggests *plane ἀνεβάλου*. Perhaps add *eam*.

---

[1] The word *Quinquatrus* means "falling on the fifth
day" (*i.e.* after the ides of March, viz. March 19), but
the feast also lasted five days. A lesser festival of the

M. CORNELIUS FRONTO

To my Lord.   145–147 A.D.

I have slept late. I have sent you a theme: the case is a serious one. A consul of the Roman people, laying aside his robes, has donned a coat of mail and among the young men at the feast of Minerva[1] has slain a lion in the sight of the Roman people. He is denounced before the Censors. Put into shape and develop. Farewell, most sweet Lord. Greet your Lady.

From Marcus Aurelius to Fronto

145–147 A.D.

Answer.

When did it occur and was it at Rome? Do you mean that the event took place under Domitian at his Alban Villa?[2] Besides in such a theme it will take longer labour to make the fact credible than to be angered at it. It seems to me an improbable subject. I certainly should have preferred one such as I asked for. Let me know the date by return.

---

same name fell on June 13. Suetonius (*Domit.* 4) says that Domitian celebrated the feast yearly at his villa at Albanum.

[2] Afterwards became the town of Albanum. Dio, lxvii. 1, describes it. He tells us (lxvii. 14, § 6) that Acilius Glabrio (supposed to have become subsequently a Christian) fought with wild beasts (*cp.* Juvenal, 4, 95). Suetonius (*Domit.* 10) informs us that he was put to death by Domitian.

Ad M. Caes. v. 24 (39) (Naber, p. 83).

Magistro meo salutem.

Vindemias laetas <eas>que quam firmissimo corpore agere te, mi magister, opto. Me adlevant nuntii de Domnula mea, commodiora dis iuvantibus indicantes. Vale mi iucundissime magister.

Ad M. Caes. v. 25 (40) (Naber, p. 83).

Domino meo.

In hortis vindemias ago. Commode valeo. Aegre tamen insisto dolore digitorum in sinistro pede. Pro Faustina mane cotidie deos appello. Scis[1] enim me pro tua salute optare ac precari. Vale mi Domine dulcissime. Dominam saluta.

Ad M. Caes. v. 26 (Naber, p. 83).

Magistro meo.

Ego adeo perscripsi—tu mitte aliud quod scribam—sed librarius meus non praesto fuit qui transcriberet. Scripsi autem non ex mea sententia, nam et festinavi et tua ista valetudo aliquantulum detrivit mihi. Sed veniam cras petam, quom mittam. Vale mi dulcissime magister. Domina mea mater

Vat. 80

---

[1] Rob. Ellis for Cod. *scio.* Query supply *sic.*

M. CORNELIUS FRONTO

Marcus Aurelius to Fronto

145–147 A.D.

To my master, greeting.

That you should keep a happy vintage, and that in the best of health, is my wish, my master. I am much relieved by the news of my little lady [1] telling me, the Gods be praised, that she is better. Farewell, my most delightful of masters.

Fronto to Marcus as Caesar

145–147 A.D.

To my Lord.

I am keeping the vintage in my "gardens." [2] I am fairly well, but I cannot walk with comfort owing to pain in the toes of my left foot. Every morning I pray the Gods for Faustina, for you know that by so doing I wish and pray for your health. Farewell, my most sweet Lord. Greet my Lady.

Marcus Aurelius to Fronto

145–147 A.D.

To my master.

As far as I am concerned, the writing is finished —so send me something else to write—but my secretary was not at hand to copy out what I wrote. However, what I wrote was not to my mind, as I was hurried, and your being poorly took a good deal out of me. But I will ask your indulgence to-morrow, when I send it. Farewell, my sweetest of masters. The Lady my mother sends you greeting

[1] Apparently the daughter, not the wife, of Marcus.

[2] Probably his residence on the Esquiline, the *Horti Maecenatiani.*

salutem tibi dicit. Nomen tribuni plebis, cui imposuit notam Acilius censor, quem scripsi,[1] mitte mihi.

Ad M. Caes. v. 27 (42) (Naber, p. 83).

DOMINO meo.

Tardius tibi, Domine, rescribo; tardius enim libellum tuum aperui, quoniam ad agendum ad forum ibam. Ego commodius me habeo: tamen ulcusculum altius est. Vale, Domine dulcissime. Dominam saluta.

M. Lucilius tribunus plebis hominem liberum civem Romanum, quom collegae mitti iuberent, adversus eorum sententiam ipsusque[2] vi in carcerem compegit. Ob eam rem a censoribus notatur. Divide primum causam, εἶτα εἰς ἑκάτερα τὰ μέρη ἐπιχείρησον καὶ κατηγορῶν καὶ ἀπολογούμενος. Vale, Domine, lux omnium tuorum. Matrem Dominam saluta.

Ad M. Caes. iv. 13 (Naber, p. 75).

Vat. 138, ad med. | MAGISTRO meo.

C. Aufidius animos tollit, arbitratum suum in caelum fert, negat se hominem iustiorem, ne quid immoderatius dicam, ex Umbria ullum alium Romam venisse. Quid quaeris? Iudicem se quam oratorem

---

[1] Query *scripsti.*

[2] So Cod. says Brakman, but Mai says *ipsius.*

---

[1] A Lucilius was trib. pl. in 94, but no Acilius appears as censor at that date. This letter seems to be an answer to

Let me have the name of the people's tribune against whom Acilius the censor, of whom I wrote, set a mark.

Fronto to Marcus as Caesar

To my Lord.   145-147 a.d.

My answer to you, my Lord, has been somewhat delayed, for I delayed to open your letter, as I was on my way to the forum to plead. I feel better, but the little sore is deeper. Farewell, my sweetest of Lords. Greet my Lady.

M. Lucilius,[1] a tribune of the people, against the decision of his colleagues and with his own hand cast into prison by force a Roman citizen, though they ordered his discharge. For that action he was "marked" by the Censors. First divide the case, then try your hand on either side both as accuser and defender. Farewell, my Lord, the light of all your friends. Greet your lady mother.

Marcus Aurelius to Fronto

To my master.   145-147 a.d.

Gaius Aufidius[2] gives himself airs, extols his own judgment to the skies, says that not another man more just than himself ever came from Umbria, for I must not exaggerate, to Rome. What need of more? He would rather win praise as a judge

the preceding one, but it gives details of the theme which we should expect to have been given when it was first set.

[2] Victorinus, later Fronto's son-in-law. For his incorruptibility see Dio, lxxii. 11. The family came from Pisaurum in Umbria.

volt laudari. Quom rideo, despicit : facile esse ait
oscitantem iudici assidere, ceterum quidem iudicare
praeclarum opus. Haec in me. Sed tamen negotium belle se dedit. Bene est : gaudeo. Tuus ad-
ventus me quom beat tum sollicitat. Cur beet,
nemo quaerat ; quam ob rem sollicitet, ego medius
fidius fatebor tibi. Nam quod scribendum dedisti,
ne paululum quidem operae ei, quamvis otiosus,
dedi. Aristonis libri me hac tempestate bene accipiunt, atque eidem habent male : quom docent
meliora, tum scilicet bene accipiunt ; quom vero os-

tendunt quantum ab his melioribus ingenium | meum
relictum sit, nimis quam saepe erubescit discipulus
tuus sibique succenset, quod viginti quinque natus
annos nihildum bonarum opinionum et puriarum [2]
rationum animo hauserim. Itaque poenas do, irascor,
tristis sum, ζηλοτυπῶ, cibo careo. His nunc ego
curis devinctus obsequium scribendi cotidie in diem
posterum protuli. Sed iam aliquid comminiscar ; et
quod orator quidam Atticus Atheniensium contionem
monebat, *nonnumquam permittendum legibus dormire,*
libris Aristonis propitiatis paulisper quiescere conce-
dam, meque ad istum histrionum poetam [1] † totum
convertam, lectis prius oratiunculis Tullianis. Scribam autem alterutram partem, nam eadem de re

[1] If the reference is to the preceding letter we should have
expected something like *istum Lucilium tribunum pleb s.*

[2] Nab. has *puriorum.*

[1] A Stoic philosopher, but with leanings to Platonism.
His system, like that of Marcus subsequently, concerned
itself only with ethics.

than as an orator. When I smile, he turns up his
nose. Anyone, he says, can sit yawning beside
a judge, but to be a judge is indeed to do noble
work. This is meant for me! However the affair
has turned out finely; all is well: I rejoice. Your
coming makes me happy and at the same time uneasy. Why happy, it needs not to enquire: wherefore uneasy I will, 'fore heaven, avow to you. For
with plenty of time on my hands I have not given
an atom of it to the task you gave me to write.
Ariston's[1] books just now treat me well and at the
same time make me feel ill. When they teach me a
better way, then, I need not say, they treat me well;
but when they shew me how far short my character
comes of this better way, time and time again does
your pupil blush and is angry with himself, for that,
twenty-five years old as I am,[2] no draught has my
soul yet drunk of noble doctrines and purer principles.
Therefore I do penance, am wroth with myself, am
sad, compare myself with others, starve myself. A
prey to these thoughts at this time, I have put off
each day till the morrow the duty of writing. But
now I will think out something, and as a certain
Athenian orator once warned an assembly of his
countrymen, that *the laws must sometimes be allowed to
sleep*,[3] I will make my peace with Ariston's works
and allow them to lie still awhile, and after reading
some of Tully's minor speeches I will devote myself
entirely to your stage poet.[4] However, I can only
write on one side or the other, for as to my defend-

[2] This was written, therefore, between April 26, 146, and
April 26, 147.
[3] See Plut. *Ages.* 30.
[4] Supposed by some to be Plautus.

diversa tueri numquam prorsus ita dormiet Aristo
uti id permittat. Vale mi optime et honestissime
magister. Domina mea te salutat.

Ad M. Caes. **v.** 29 (44) (Naber, p. 84).

Vat. 79,
ad init | Domino meo.

Perendie, Domine, te videbo : sum enim adhuc
a cubito et cervice infirmus. Fer me, obsecro, nimia
et ardua a te postulantem : ita in animum meum
induxi posse <te> efficere quantum contenderis.
Nec deprecor quin me oderis, nisi quantum postulo
perfeceris, si ut facis animum et studium accom-
modaveris. Vale, Domine, anima mea mihi potior.
Dominam matrem saluta.

Ad M. Caes. iii. 13 (Naber, p. 50).

Vat. 111,
ad init. | Domino meo.

1. Quod poetis concessum est ὀνοματοποιεῖν,
verba nova fingere, quo facilius quod sentiunt ex-
primant, id mihi necessarium est ad gaudium meum
expromendum. Nam solitis et usitatis verbis non
sum contentus : ita amentius [1] gaudeo quam ut ser-
mone volgato significare laetitiam animi mei possim,
tot mihi a te in tam paucis diebus epistulas scriptas,

---

[1] For Cod. *amantius.*

---

[1] Here came the parting of the ways, and philosophy and
his teacher Rusticus definitely vanquished Fronto and
rhetoric. See *Thoughts*, i. 7 and 17, § 4.

ing both sides of the question, Ariston will, I am sure, never sleep so soundly as to allow me to do that![1] Farewell, best and most honoured of masters. My Lady greets you.

Fronto to Marcus as Caesar

145–147 A.D.

To my Lord.

I cannot see you, my Lord, till the day after to-morrow; for I am still laid up with pain in the elbow and neck. Bear with me, I beseech you, if what I ask of you is too great and difficult, so rooted in my mind is the conviction that you can succeed in all your endeavours. And I will let you hate me, if you do not accomplish all that I ask, provided that you apply, as you do, heart and mind to it. Farewell, my Lord, dearer to me than my life. Greet my Lady your mother.

Fronto to Marcus as Caesar

145–147 A.D.

To my Lord.

1. The coining of new words, or onomatopoeia, which is allowed to poets to enable them more easily to express their thoughts, is a necessity to me for describing my joy. For customary and habitual words do not satisfy me; so transported am I with joy that I cannot in ordinary language signify the gladness of my heart at your having written me so many letters in so few days,[2] composed too with

---

[2] Philost. (*Vit. Soph.* 242, Kays.) tells us that Marcus sometimes wrote to Herodes three letters in one day.

easque tam eleganter tam amice tam blande tam
effuse tam flagranter compositas, quamquam [1] tot
negotiis tot [2] officiis, tot rescribendis per provincias
litteris destringerere.   At enim proposueram—nihil
enim mihi a te occultum aut dissimulatum retinere
fas est—ita, inquam, proposueram vel desidiae culpam a te subire rarius scribendo tibi potius quam te
multis rebus occupatum epistulis meis onerarem et
ad scribendum provocarem, quom tu cotidie ultro
scripsisti mihi.   Sed quid dico *cotidie* ?   Ergo iam hic
mihi ὀνοματοποιίας opus est.   Nam cotidie foret, si
singulas epistulas per dies singulos scripsisses ; quom

Vat. 242:
Quat.
vii.
vero plures epistulae sint quam dies, | verbum
istud *cotidie* minus significat.   Nec est, Domine,
cur [3] mihi tristior sis, quod [4] omnino veritus sim ne
tibi litterae meae crebriores oneri [5] essent : nam
quo mihi amantior es, tanto me laborum tuorum
parciorem et occupationum tuarum modestiorem
esse oportet.

2. Quid est mihi osculo tuo suavius ?   Ille mihi
suavis odor, ille fructus in tuo collo atque osculo
situs est.   Attamen proxime quom proficiscerere,
quom iam pater tuus vehiculum conscendisset, te
salutantium et exosculantium turba diutius morare-
tur, profuit [6] ut te solus ex omnibus non complecterer
nec exoscularer.   Item in ceteris aliis rebus omnibus numquam equidem mea commoda tuis utilitatibus

---

[1] Ehrenthal for Cod. *cum clam.*
[2] For Cod. *quod* in both places.
[3] For Cod. *quod.*   [4] For Cod. *cur.*
[5] For Cod. *oncris.*   [6] Mai : *prope fuit.*

such felicity, such friendship, such kindness, such fulness, such ardour, though you were distracted by so much business, so many duties, so many letters to be answered throughout the provinces.[1] But indeed I had purposed—for I must not keep anything hidden or dissembled from you—I had purposed, I say, to incur even the reproach of laziness from you by writing to you less often, rather than to trouble you, amid your many engagements, with my letters and tempt you to write, whereas you of your own accord have written to me daily. But why do I say *daily*? It is just here that the need of word-coining comes in. For it would be *daily*, if you had written one letter a day; since however, there are more letters than days, that word *daily* falls short of the meaning. Nor is there need, my Lord, for you to be vexed with me for actually fearing that my too frequent letters should be a burden to you; for the more you love me, the more chary should I be of adding to your work, and the more forbearing in respect of your occupations.

2. What is sweeter to me than your kiss? That sweet fragrance, that delight dwells for me in your neck, on your lips. Yet the last time you were setting out, when your father had already got into the carriage, but you were delayed by the crowd of those who were saying good-bye and kissing you, it was to your advantage that I alone of all did not embrace or kiss you. So too in all other things, I will never set my convenience before your interests,

[1] The expression points to a time after Marcus had been invested with the *Trib. Pot.* and Proconsular Imperium.

anteponam; quia si opus sit, meo gravissimo labore atque negotio tuum levissimum otium redimam.

3. Igitur cogitans, quantum ex epistulis scribendis laboris caperes, proposueram parcius te appellare, quom tu cotidie scripsisti mihi. Quas ego epistulas quom acciperem, simile patiebar quod amator patitur, qui delicias suas videat currere ad se per iter asperum et periculosum. Namque is simul advenientem | gaudet, simul periculum revereatur.[1] Unde displicet mihi fabula histrionibus celebrata, ubi amans amantem puella iuvenem nocte lumine accenso stans in turri natantem in mari opperitur. Nam ego potius[2] te caruero, tametsi amore tuo ardeo, potius quam te ad[3] hoc noctis natare tantum profundi patiar, ne luna occidat, ne ventus lucernam interimat, ne quid ibi ex frigore impliciscare,[4] ne fluctus ne vadus ne piscis aliquo[5] noxsit. Haec oratio amanti plus[6] decuit et melior et salubrior fuit non alieno capitali periculo sectari voluptatis usuram brevem ac poenitendam.

4. Nunc ut a fabula ad verum convertar, id ego non mediocriter anxius eram, ne necessariis laboribus tuis ego insuper aliquod molestiae atque oneris imponerem, si praeter eas epistulas, quas ad plurimos necessario munere cotidie rescribis, ego quoque ad rescribendum fatigarem. Nam me carere omni fructu amoris tui malim, quam te ne minimum quidem incommodi voluptatis meae gratia subire.

---

[1] Jacobs for Cod. *veneretur*.   [2] Query *prorsus*.
[3] C. F. W. Müller suggests the old form *ted* for these two words.   [4] Jacobs for Cod. *impliciscar*.
[5] *sc. modo* or read *aliqua*.   [6] Orelli: *amantibus*.

for, if need were, with heaviest toil and service of mine I would purchase your slightest ease.

3. Considering therefore, how much labour the writing of letters imposed upon you, I had determined to address you more sparingly, when you wrote daily to me. When I got those letters of yours I was in similar plight to a lover, who sees his darling running towards him along a rough and dangerous pathway. For he rejoices at the loved one's coming at the same time that he fears the danger. Consequently I do not care for the story,[1] which is such a favourite with actors, where a loving girl standing by night in a turret with a lighted taper in her hand, awaits her young lover as he swims the straits. For though I burn with love for you, I would rather be severed utterly from you than let you swim so deep a sea so late at night, for fear the moon should set, the wind dash out your light, the cold benumb your senses there, a wave, a reef, a sea-beast in some way work you harm. This language were more fitting for a lover and better and more sound—not at the peril of another's life to seek to enjoy a pleasure short in duration and fraught with regret.

4. Now to turn from fiction to reality, my especial anxiety was lest I should add to your unavoidable labours some superfluous trouble and burden, if besides those letters which your unavoidable duties require you to write daily to very many correspondents, I too should weary you with answering my letters. For I should prefer to sacrifice every advantage of your love, rather than that you should suffer the slightest inconvenience to gratify my pleasure.

[1] Obviously of Hero and Leander.

Ad M. Caes. v. 18 (33) (Naber, p. 81).

Domino meo.

Gravissimo dolore inguinis sum arreptus, | quo omnis dolor a dorso et lumbis incubuit. Vale, Domine. Dominam saluta.

Ad M. Caes. v. 19 (34) (Naber, p. 81).

Magistro meo salutem.

Doluisse te inguina cognosco, mi magister, et quom recordor quantam vexationem tibi iste dolor adferre soleat, gravissimam sollicitudinem patior. Sed me levat quod spero illo spatio, quo perferebatur huc[1] nuntius, potuisse cedere fomentis et remediis illam vim doloris. Nos aestivos calores adhuc experimur, sed quom parvolae nostrae, dixisse liceat, commode valeant, mera salubritate et verna temperie frui existimamus. Vale mi optime magister.

Ad M. Caes. v. 50 (65) (Naber, p. 90).

| Domino meo.

Ego gravissime arreptus sum iterum ab altero inguine.

[1] For Cod. *hoc.*

M. CORNELIUS FRONTO

FRONTO TO MARCUS AS CAESAR.

To my Lord.   ? 148–149 A.D.

I have been seized with very severe pain in the groin. All the pain from the back and loins has concentrated itself there. Farewell, my Lord. Greet my Lady.

MARCUS AURELIUS TO FRONTO.

To my master, greeting.   ? 148–149 A.D.

You tell me that you have pain in the groin, my master. Remembering what distress that pain generally causes you, I feel the most serious anxiety. But I comfort myself with the hope that in the interval required for bringing the news here, the intensity of the pain may have yielded to fomentations and remedies. We are still experiencing summer heat. But since our little girls[1]—we mustn't boast—are quite well, we think that we are enjoying the healthiest of weather and the balmy temperature of spring. Farewell, my best of masters.

FRONTO TO MARCUS AS CAESAR.

To my Lord.   ? 148–149 A.D.

I have been seized with very severe pains again in the other side of the groin.

---

[1] Annia Galeria Faustina and Annia Lucilla, who was born about 148. A son born between the two died soon after birth in 147. See *C.I.G.* 3176.

Ad M. Caes. v. 51 (66) (Naber, p. 91).

RESCRIPTUM.

Quom haec scribas mihi, mi magister, credo intelligis sollicitissimum me vota facere pro salute tua : cuius dis iuvantibus cito compotes erimus. Vale mi magister iucundissime.

Ad M. Caes. **v.** 20 (35) (Naber, p. 82).

| DOMINO meo.

Patri tuo fac notum de infirmitate mea. An me quoque scribere ei debere putes, scribe mihi.

Ad M. Caes. v. 21 (36) (Naber p. 82).

RESCRIPTUM.

Statim, mi magister, indicabo Domino meo necessitatem huius quietis tuae. Velim tamen et a te scribi. Vale mi optime et iucundissime magister.

Ad Antoninum Pium, 5 (Naber, p. 167).

| ANTONINO PIO AUGUSTO Fronto.

Carius[1] <quam> vitae meae parte adpicisci[2] cupio ut te complecterer felicissimo et optatissimo initi imperii die, quem ego diem natalem salutis dignitatis securitatis meae existimo. Sed dolor humeri gravis, cervicis vero multo gravissimus ita me

[1] This word is added from the Index (Naber, p. 163).
[2] Bücheler compares Terence, *Phor*. I. iii. 14, and reads *depicisci*. Niebuhr dispenses with the *quam* supplied by Heindorf and reads *adipisci*.

M. CORNELIUS FRONTO

Marcus Aurelius to Fronto.

? 148–149 a.d.

Answer.

When you write thus to me, my master, you
are aware, I am sure, that I am most anxious and
offer up prayers for your health; of which, please
heaven, we shall speedily be assured. Farewell, my
most delightful of masters.

Fronto to Marcus as Caesar.

? 148–149 a.d.

To my Lord.

Please acquaint your father with my illness.
Tell me if you think I also should write to him.

Marcus Aurelius to Fronto.

? 148–149 a.d.

Answer.

I will let my Lord know at once that your
health necessitates this rest for you. But please
write to him yourself as well. Farewell, my best and
most delightful of masters.

? 148–149 a.d.

Fronto to Antoninus Pius Augustus.

More dearly than with a portion of my life
would I bargain to embrace you on this most happy
and wished-for anniversary of your accession,[1] a day
which I count as the birthday of my own health,
reputation, and safety. But severe pain in my
shoulder, and much more severe in my neck, have

[1] July 1, 138.

adflixit, ut adhuc usque vix inclinare me vel erigere vel convertere possim : ita immobili cervice utor. Sed apud Lares Penates deosque familiares meos et reddidi et suscepi vota, et precatus sum, uti anno insequenti bis te complecterer isto die, bis pectus tuum et manus exoscularer praeteriti simul et praesentis anni vicem perficiens.

Ad Antoninum Pium, 6 (Naber, p. 167).

AB Augusto rescriptum.

Quom bene perspectas habeam sincerissimas in me adfectiones tuas, tum et ex meo animo non difficile credo,[1] mi Fronto carissime, vel praecipue hunc diem, quo me suscipere hanc stationem placuit, a te potissimum vere religioseque celebrari. Et ego quidem et vota tua et te mente, ut par est, Ambr. 347 representavi. | . . . .[2]

Ad M. Caes. v. 30 (45) (Naber, p. 84).

Vat. 79, ad med, | DOMINO meo.

Annum novum faustum tibi et ad omnia, quae recte cupis, prosperum cum tibi tum Domino nostro patri tuo et matri et uxori et filiae ceterisque omnibus, quos merito diligis, precor. Metui ego invalido

---

[1] Brakman's reading of the Codex.
[2] Probably only a line or two of this letter is lost, the gap here covering part of *Ad Pium*, 7.

so crippled me, that I am still scarcely able to bend, sit upright, or turn myself, so rigid must I keep my neck. But before my Lares, Penates, and household gods have I discharged and renewed my vows,[1] and prayed that next year I might embrace you twice on this anniversary, twice kiss your neck and hands, fulfilling at once the office of the past and the present year.

ANTONINUS PIUS TO FRONTO.

ANSWER by Augustus. ? 148-149 A.D.

As I have well ascertained the entire sincerity of your feelings towards me, so I find no difficulty, I assure you, my dearest Fronto, in believing that this day in particular, on which it was ordained for me to assume this station, is kept with true and scrupulous devotion by you above all others. And I indeed have with my mind's eye, as was right, pictured you and your vows . . . .

FRONTO TO MARCUS AS CAESAR.

To my Lord. ? 148-149 A.D.

A happy New Year and a prosperous in all things that you rightly desire to you and our Lord your Father, and your mother and your wife and daughter,[2] and to all others who deservedly share your affection—that is my prayer! In my still feeble

---

[1] If this letter is correctly dated, these *vota* would be the *decennalia*. See *Coins of Pius*, Cohen, 226-229.

[2] As only one daughter is now mentioned, the little Faustina must have died, leaving Lucilla alone.

adhuc corpore turbae et impressioni me committere.
Si dei iuvabunt, perendie vos vota nuncupantes videbo.
Vale mi Domine dulcissime.   Dominam saluta.

Ad M. Caes. v. 31 (46) (Naber, p. 85).

Magistro meo salutem.

Et ipse prospere sis ingressus annum! Omne
votum tuum Dei tibi ad usum tuum, qui noster idem
erit, devertant atque, ut facis, pro ami|cis bene optes,
ceteris bene velis.   Quae [1] pro me precatus es scio te
<ex animo> precatum.   Quod [a] turba cavisti, tibi
et meae curae consuluisti.   Quietius idem fiet perendie, si di <velint.   Gratia> tua <tuo> officio functa
est.   Nescio an <Dominam> suam salutaverit.   Vale
mi dulcissime magister.   Mater mea te salutat.

Vat. 94

Ad M. Caes. v. 32 (47) (Naber, p. 85).

Magistro meo.

Et nunc sanus et deinceps validus laetus com-
pos omnium votorum agas [2] diem natalem, mi magister; quae mea precatio sollemnis semper auctior fit,
quanto magis accedit et mihi firmitas ad diligendum
et aetas suavissimae familiaritatis nostrae.   Vale mi
magister iucundissime mihi.   Mater mea te salutat.
Gratiae salutem dic <et fer osculum parvolae tuae
Gratiae.>[3]

---

[1] Half a line is left blank in the Cod. before *quae*.
[2] Mai for Cod. *magis*.
[3] I have added these words: see end of next letter.

state of health I was afraid to trust myself to the crowd and crush. I shall see you, please God, the day after to-morrow offering up your vows. Farewell, my most sweet Lord. Greet my Lady.

To my master, greeting.   ? 148–149 A.D.

May you also have entered upon a prosperous year, and may the Gods turn to your advantage, which will be ours also, every prayer of yours! May you pray, as you do, for the good of your friends and wish for the good of all others! Your prayers for me I know have been heartfelt. In fighting shy of the crowd, you have consulted both your safety and my anxiety. The ceremony will be repeated on a quieter scale the day after to-morrow, if the Gods will. Your Gratia has done your part for you. I do not know if she has greeted her Lady. Farewell, my sweetest of masters. My mother sends you her greeting.

MARCUS AURELIUS TO FRONTO.

To my master.   ? 148–149 A.D.

May you keep your birthday, my master, both sound in health now and strong in all years to come, happy, and with all your wishes granted; which yearly prayer of mine grows ever more comprehensive as my capacity for affection increases and the period of our most sweet intercourse lengthens! Farewell, my master most delightful to me. My mother greets you. Give Gratia a greeting and your little Gratia a kiss from me.

231

Ad M. Caes. v. 33 (48) (Naber, p. 85).

DOMINO meo.

Quaecumque mihi precatus es, omnia in tua salute locata sunt. Mihi sanitas, bona valetudo, laetitia, res prosperae meae ibi sunt, quom tu corpore animo rumore tam incolumi uteris, tam carus patri, tam dulcis matri, tam sanctus uxori, tam frater bonus ac benignus. Haec sunt quae me cum hac valetudine tamen cupientem vitae faciunt. Absque te satis su|perque et aetatis et laboris et artis et gloriae, dolorum vero et aegritudinum aliquanto plusquam satis superque.

Vat. 98

Filiae meae iussu tuo osculum dedi. Numquam mihi tam suavis tamque saviata visa est. Dominam saluta, Domine dulcissime. Vale et fer osculum matronae tuae.

Ad M. Caes. v. 34 (49) (Naber, p. 86).

DOMINO meo.

Saenius Pompeianus in plurimis causis a me defensus, postquam publicum Africae redemit, plurimis causis rem familiarem nostram adiuvat. Commendo eum tibi, quom ratio eius a Domino nostro patre tuo tractabitur, benignitatem ingenitam tibi,

---

[1] This the first allusion to Lucius Verus, the other adopted son of Pius, afterwards joint-emperor with Marcus.

[2] Lucilla, the daughter of Marcus, must be meant.

M. CORNELIUS FRONTO

Fronto to Marcus as Caesar.

To my Lord.   ? 148-149 A.D.

All the blessings you have prayed for me are
bound up with your welfare. Health of body and
mind, happiness, prosperity, are all mine, as long as
you enjoy a body, a mind, a reputation so hale and
well, while you are so dear to your father, so sweet
to your mother, so blameless a husband, so good and
kind a brother.[1] It is this which makes me cling
to life, in spite of my ill-health. Apart from you I
have had enough and to spare of life and toil, of
profession and fame, but of pains and infirmities
something more than enough and to spare.

I gave my daughter the kiss you sent her: never
has she seemed to me so kissing-ripe, never so
kissed. Greet my Lady, my most sweet Lord.
Farewell, and give your little matron[2] a kiss
from me.

Fronto to Marcus as Caesar.

To my Lord.   ? 149-153 A.D.

Saenius Pompeianus,[3] whom I have defended in
many cases, since he took up the contract for farm-
ing the taxes of Africa, is from many causes a
stand-by in my affairs. I commend him to you that,
when his accounts are scrutinised by our Lord your
Father, you may be induced both by my recommen-

---

[3] There is an inscription (*C. I. L.* **vi.** 8588 ; *cp.* viii. 997) by
his wife, Fuficia Clymena, to Q. Saenius Pompeianus as
conductor IIII publicorum Africae, i.e., farmer of four public
revenues of Africa (see Orelli, *Inscr. Lat.* 6650).

quam omnibus ex more tuo tribuis, ut huic et mea
commendatione et tua consuetudine ductus impertias.
Vale, Domine dulcissime.

Ad M. Caes. **v.** 35 (50) (Naber, p. 86).

RESCRIPTUM.

Pompeianus meritis isdem, quibus te sibi con-
ciliavit, me quoque promeruit. Quare cupio omnia
ei ex indulgentia Domini mei patris obsecundare.
Nam ea quae tibi ex sententia procedunt, gaudia
sunt mea. Vale mi magister iucundissime. Faustina
et parvolae nostrae te salutant.

Ad M. Caes. v. 36 (51) (Naber, p. 86).

MAGISTRO meo.

Si te in provincia, mi magister, adierit Themis-
tocles quidam, qui se Apollonio magistro | meo
philosophiae dicat cognitum, eum <scito> esse [1] qui
hac hieme Romam venerit et mihi voluntate magistri
per filium Apollonium sit demonstratus: ei tu, mi
magister, velim quod possis bene facias, bene suadeas. Nam ius et aequom omnibus Asianis erit apud
te paratissimum : sed consilium, comitatem, quaeque

Vat. 104

---

[1] Mai for Cod. *sese.*

---

[1] Lucilla and Arria Fudilla, the latter born about 150 A.D.
[2] Asia. Fronto was consul in 143, and the usual interval
between the consulship and proconsulate at this time was

dation and your own constant practice to extend to
him that characteristic kindness, which you habitually show to all.   Farewell, my sweetest Lord.

MARCUS AURELIUS TO FRONTO.

ANSWER.   ? 149–153 A.D.

Pompeianus has won my esteem also by the
same deserts which have endeared him to you.   So
I desire that in accordance with the Lord my father's
indulgent ways everything should second his wishes.
For whatever falls out as you desire is a joy to me.
Farewell, my most delightful of masters.   Faustina
and our little girls[1] greet you.

MARCUS AURELIUS TO FRONTO.

To my master.   ? 153–154 A.D.

If in your province,[2] my master, you come
across a certain Themistocles, who says that he is
known to Apollonius my teacher[3] in philosophy,
understand that he is a person who came to Rome this
winter and was brought to my notice by Apollonius
the son, at his father's request.   May I ask you, my
master, to befriend him, and advise him, as far as
you can.   For you will, I know, be always most
ready to do what is just and proper by all Asians,
but counsel and courtesy and all those personal

---

twelve to fifteen years.   But Fronto may have had his appointment accelerated in consideration of his age or health.

[3] Marcus speaks very highly of him (*Thoughts*, i. 8 ; 17, § 4),
and Epiphanius calls him ἑταῖρος ᾿Αντωνίνου.   But see
Capit. *Vit. Pii*, x. § 4, and Lucian, *Demonax*, § 31.

amicis sine ullo cuiusquam incommodo propria im-
pertire fides ac religio proconsulis permittit, peto
Themistocli libens impertias. **Vale mi iucun**dissime
magister. Rescripto nihil opus est.

Ad Antoninum Pium, 8 (Naber, p. 169).

Antonino Pio Augusto Fronto.

1. Omnem operam me dedisse, sanctissime Imperator, et impenso studio cupisse fungi proconsulari
munere res ipsa testis est. Nam et de iure sor-
tiendi, quoad incertum fuit, disceptavi et, postquam
iure liberorum prior alius apparuit, eam quae mihi
remansit splendidissimam provinciam pro electa

Ambr. 332:
Quat. **xxxi.**
ends

habui. Post illa quaecumque ad instruendam | pro-
vinciam adtinerent, quo facilius a me tanta negotia
per amicorum copias obirentur, sedulo praeparavi.
Propinquos et amicos meos, quorum fidem et integritatem cognoveram, domo accivi. Alexandriam ad
familiares meos scripsi ut Athenas festinarent, ibique me opperirentur, iisque Graecarum epistularum
curam doctissimis viris detuli. Ex Cilicia etiam
splendidos viros, quod magna mihi in ea provincia
amicorum copia est, quom publice privatimque semper negotia Cilicum apud te defenderim, ut venirent
hortatus sum. Ex Mauretania quoque virum aman-
tissimum mihique mutuo carum, Iulium Senem, ad
me vocavi, cuius non modo fide et diligentia, sed
etiam militari industria circa quaerendos et conti-
nendos latrones adiuvarer.

---

[1] Cirta, in Numidia, where he was born.

civilities, which both honour and conscience permit
a proconsul to shew his friends, so long as no one
else is injured thereby—these I ask you freely to
extend to Themistocles. Farewell, my most delightful of masters. No answer is required.

? 153–154 A.D.

FRONTO to Antoninus Pius Augustus.

1. The facts testify, most reverend Emperor,
that I have spared no pains and earnestly desired to
discharge the duties of proconsul. For as long as
the matter was undecided, I claimed my rights under
the lot and, when by virtue of having more children
another proved to have the prior claim, I was as satisfied, as if I had chosen it, with that most splendid
province which was left to me. Then I took active
steps to enlist the help of my friends in all that
concerned the ordering of the province. Relations
and friends of mine, of whose loyalty and integrity
I was assured, I called from home[1] to assist me.
I wrote to my intimates at Alexandria[2] to repair
with all speed to Athens and await me there, and I
deputed the management of my Greek correspondence to those most learned men. From Cilicia
too I called upon eminent citizens to join me, for,
owing to my always having advocated the public and
private interests of Cilicians before you, I had hosts
of friends in that province. From Mauretania also
I summoned to my side Julius Senex, a man whose
love for me was no less than mine for him, that I
might avail myself not only of his loyalty and diligence, but also of his military activity in the hunting
down and suppressing of brigands.

[2] Where he probably studied in his youth.

2. Haec omnia feci spe fretus posse me victu tenui et aqua potanda malam valetudinem qua impedior, si non omnino sedare, certe ad maius intervallum reiectos eius impetus mitigare. Ita evenit ut solito diutius bene valerem et fortis vigerem, adeo ut duas amicorum causas non minimi laboris apud te tutatus sim. Ingruit deinde tanta vis valetudinis,

Ambr. 331 quae mihi ostenderet omnem spem illam | <frustra fuisse> . . . .[1]

Ad M. Caes. **v.** 37 (52) (Naber, p. 87).

Vat. 104,
ad med.

| Domino meo.

Aridelus iste, qui tibi litteras meas reddit, a pueritia me curavit a studio perdicum usque ad seria officia. Libertus vester est; procurabit[2] vobis industrie; est enim homo frugi et sobrius et acer et diligens. Petit nunc procurationem ex forma suo loco ac iusto tempore. Faveto ei, Domine, quod poteris. Si formam non cognosces hominis, ubi ad nomen Arideli ventum fuerit, memento a me tibi Aridelum commendatum. Vale, Domine dulcissime. Dominam saluta.

---

[1] The lost parts at the end of this letter and at the beginning of *Ad Pium*, 9, cover one page.

[2] Cod. *procuravit*, but *b* and *v* are used interchangeably.

2. All this I did, buoyed up by the hope that by abstemiousness and water-drinking I might, if not wholly relieve the ill-health from which I suffered, yet at all events mitigate its attacks by postponing them for a longer period. The result was that I had a lengthier spell of health than usual, and felt strong and vigorous, so much so that I was able to appear before you on behalf of two of my friends in cases that entailed very considerable labour. Then I was assailed by so severe an attack of illness as shewed me that all my hopes had been illusory . . . .

Fronto to Marcus as Caesar

? 153–154 A.D.

To my Lord.

This Aridelus, who is taking my letter to you, has attended to all my wants since I was a boy, from a passion for partridges to important duties. He is a freedman of yours; you will find him a diligent procurator, for he is honest, temperate, brisk, and industrious. He is now a candidate for a procuratorship[1] in due form, being of suitable position and regulation age. Assist him, my Lord, with your interest, as far as may be. If you do not recognize his person, when you come to the name Aridelus, remember that Aridelus has been commended to you by me. Farewell, most sweet Lord. Greet your Lady.

---

[1] A procurator might be (1) a collector of the imperial revenues, (2) a steward, (3) an overseer of any kind, as agent or manager.

Ad M. Caes. v. 38 (53) (Naber, p. 87).

Domino meo.

Utrum facti virtus ornaverit orationem, an| oratio factum nobilissimum aequiparaverit, incertus sum : certe quidem eiusdem <haec> dicta cuius illa facta. Sed et fratris tui oratio me delectavit, nam et ornata fuit et cordata. Et certum habeo eum minimum spatii habuisse ad meditandum.

Ad M. Caes. v. 39 (54) (Naber, p. 87).

Rescriptum,

Reversus a convivio patris libellum tuum accepi, dimisso iam, ut cognosco, eo per quem fuerat adlatus. Rescribo igitur vespera multa quod tu legas die crastino. Orationem patris mei parem materiae suae visam tibi nihil mirum est, mi magister. Fratris autem gratiarum actio mihi eo laudabilior est, quo minus ad meditandum, ut coniectas, habuit spatii. Vale mi iucundissime magister. Mater mea te salutat.

Ad M. Caes. v. 40 (55) (Naber, p. 87).

Domino meo.

Cholera usque eo adflictus sum ut vocem amitterem, singultirem, suspirio angerer,[1] postremo venae

---

[1] Schopen for Cod. *agerer.*

M. CORNELIUS FRONTO

Fronto to Marcus as Caesar

? 153–154 A.D.

To my Lord.

Whether the merit of the act set off the speech,[1] or the speech did not fall short of a most noble act, I can hardly say: yet of this I am sure, that these words had the same author as those deeds. But your brother's speech [2] also delighted me, for it was polished and politic, and I feel sure he had very little time for preparing it.

Marcus Aurelius to Fronto

? 153–154 A.D.

Answer.

On my return from a banquet of my father's I got your letter, and learn that the messenger who brought it has already gone. So I am writing this quite late in the evening, that you may read it to-morrow. It is no matter of surprise, my master, that my father's speech should seem to you worthy of the subject. But my brother's speech of thanks is in my opinion the more praiseworthy in that, as you surmise, he had but little time to prepare it. Farewell, my most delightful of masters. My mother greets you.

Fronto to Marcus as Caesar

? 154–156 A.D.

To my Lord.

I have had such a choleraic attack [3] that I lost my voice, gasped and struggled for breath; finally,

---

[1] Of Pius.

[2] Of thanks, possibly for the consulship in 154.

[3] What the specific disease was is not clear.

deficerent, sine ullo pulsu venarum animo male fieret ;
denique conclamatus sum a nostris ; neque sensi
aliquamdiu : ne balneo quidem aut frigida aut cibo
recreandi me ac fovendi medicis tempus aut occasio
data, nisi post vesperam micularum minimum cum
vino destillatum gluttivi. Ita | focilatus totus
sum.[1] Postea per continuum triduum vocem non
recuperavi. Sed nunc deis iuvantibus commodissime
valeo, facilius ambulo, clarius clamito : denique, si
dei iuvabunt, cras vehiculo vectari destino. Si facile
silicem toleravero, quantum pote ad te curram. Tum
vixero quom te videro. Ad VII Kal. Roma profi-
ciscar, si dei iuvabunt, Vale, Domine dulcissime,
desiderantissime, causa optima vitae meae. Dominam saluta.

Ad. M. Caes. v. 41 (56) (Naber, p. 88).

MAGISTRO meo salutem.

Post tempus te videre cupiebam ; quid tu censes
post periculum ? quod suffugisse te, mi magister,
iterum deis ago gratias lectis tuis litteris, quae me
rursum quasi renovant : quom commemorares quo in
loco fueris, consternarunt. Sed habeo te dis volentibus, et ut promittis propediem videbo : et bene
spero de bona longa valetudine. Salutat te mater
mea. Vale mi iucundissime magister.

[1] The Cod. repeats *sum* after *focilatus*. Query *<sensim>*.

Vat. 86

my circulation failed and the pulse being impercep-
tible I became unconscious; in fact, I was given up
by my family as dead and remained insensible for
some time. The doctors were given no time or
opportunity to revive or relieve me even with a
warm bath or cold water or food, except that after
nightfall I swallowed a few morsels of bread soaked
in wine. Thus I was gradually brought quite round.
For three whole days after I did not recover my
voice. But now by God's help I am getting on very
comfortably. I walk with more ease and my voice
is stronger and more distinct; in fine, I purpose,
please God, to take a drive to-morrow. If I find I
can stand the flint paving well, I will hasten to you
as fast as I can. Only when I see you shall I live.
I will set out from Rome, please God, on the 7th day
before the Kalends. Farewell, my Lord, most sweet,
most missed, my best reason for living. Greet your
Lady.

Marcus Aurelius to Fronto

? 154–156 A.D.

To my master, greeting.

After your absence I was longing to see you :
what think you [1] after your danger? for your escape
from which, my master, I thank the Gods a second
time after reading your letter, which again, as it
were, reassures me : it struck me with consternation
when you gave me an account of your condition.
But the Gods be thanked I have you still and, as you
promise, shall see you again soon : and I have good
hopes of your continued convalescence. My mother
greets you. Farewell, my most delightful master.

sc. " must my feeling be."

Ad M. Caes. **v.** 42 (57) (Naber, p. 88).

Domino meo.

Plurimos natales dies liberum tuorum prosperis
tuis rebus ut celebres parentibus probatus, populo
acceptus, amicis pergratus,[1] fortuna et genere et loco
tuo dignus, omni vita mea redemisse cupiam, non hac
modo | exigua vita quae mihi superest, sed illa etiam
quam vixi, si quo modo <in> integrum redigi ac pro
te tuisque liberum tuorum commodis in solutum
dependi potest. Si facile ingredi possem, hic erat
dies quo cum primis complecti te cuperem, sed con-
cedendum est pedibus scilicet, quando ipsi parum
procedunt. Ego de aquarum usu delibero. Si cer-
tius quid statuero, faciam tibi notum. Vale mi
Domine dulcissime. Faustinam tuam meis verbis
appella et gratulare, et matronas nostras meo nomine
exosculare sed, uti ego soleo, cum plantis illis et
manibus. Dominam saluta.

Vat. 85

Ad M. Caes. v. 43 (58) (Naber, p. 89).

Magistro meo salutem.

Salvos esto nobis, salva sit tibi domus tua, salva
nostra ; quae, si animum nostrum spectes, una est
domus. Recte scio autem, si vel difficulter ingredi

---

[1] Cornelissen for Cod. *probatus.*

M. CORNELIUS FRONTO

FRONTO TO MARCUS AS CAESAR

To my Lord.   ? 154–156 A.D.

That you may keep many birthdays of your
children with all happiness, the pride of your
parents, the darling of the people, the beloved of
your friends, worthy of your fortune, your lineage,
and your station, gladly would I give my whole life,
not that meagre portion of it only that now remains
to me, but also what I have already lived, if in any
way it could be restored to me entire, and expended
as the repayment of a debt for the benefit of yourself and your children. If I could walk with comfort, this were the day on which I would wish among
the first[1] to embrace you; but I must, as you see,
make my feet some concession, since they have not
much procession in them. I am thinking of trying
waters. If I come any nearer a decision, I will
let you know. Farewell, my sweetest Lord. Give
your Faustina a message from me and congratulate
her[2] and kiss our little ladies in my name and, as
I always do, their feet and hands as well. Greet
your Lady.[3]

MARCUS AURELIUS TO FRONTO

To my master, greeting.   ? 154–156 A.D.

May you be preserved to us! May your house
be preserved, and ours! which, if you look at our
feelings, is but one house. I know well you would

[1] Or, "above all."
[2] On the birthday of one of the children; see next letter.
[3] The mother of Marcus.

posses, venturum te·ad nos fuisse. Sed venies saepe
et tecum celebrabimus, si dei volent, omnia festa
nostra. Vale, mi magister iucundissime. Mater mea
te salutat.

Ad M. Caes. v. 44 (59) (Naber, p. 89).

Domino meo.

    Pueri dum e balneis me sellula, ut adsolent,
advehunt, imprudentius ad ostium balnei fervens
adflixerunt. Ita genum mihi simul abrasum | et
ambustum est : postea etiam inguen ex ulcere ex-
titit. Visum medicis ut lectulo me tenerem. Hanc
causam, si tibi videbitur, etiam Domino patri tuo
indicabis, si tamen videbitur. Etiam[1] cras mihi
adsistendum erit familiari. Hodierno igitur otio et
quiete labori me crastino praeparabo. Victorinus
noster aget, ne me acturum putes. Vale, Domine
dulcissime. Dominam saluta.

Vat. 100

Ad M. Caes. v. 45 (60) (Naber, p. 90).

Magistro meo salutem.

    Auxisti curas mihi, quas opto quam primum
releves, sedatis tibi doloribus genus et inguinis. Me
autem infirmitas Dominae meae matris quiescere non
sinit. Eo accedit adpropinquatio partus Faustinae.
Sed confidere dis debemus. Vale, mi magister iucundissime mihi. Mater mea te salutat.

        Eussner reads *si tibi videbitur, etiam ipse.*

have come to us, if you could have walked even with difficulty. But you will come often and join us, if the Gods will, in keeping all our fêtes. Farewell, my most delightful of masters. My mother greets you.

FRONTO TO MARCUS AS CAESAR

? 154–156 A.D.

To my Lord.

While my attendants were carrying me here as usual from the baths in a sedan-chair, they dashed me somewhat carelessly against the scorching entrance to the bath. So my knee was both scraped and scorched : afterwards, too, a swelling came up on the sore place. The doctors advised my keeping in bed. Should you think fit, please also give my Lord your father this reason, but only if you think fit. To-morrow too, I must support an intimate friend in court. So by to-day's idleness and rest I shall get myself ready for to-morrow's duties. Our Victorinus will do the pleading, for do not suppose that I shall plead. Farewell, sweetest of Lords. Greet my Lady.

MARCUS AURELIUS TO FRONTO

? 154–156 A.D.

To my master, greeting.

You have added to my anxieties, which I hope you will as soon as possible relieve by the subsidence of the pains in the knee and the swelling. As for me, my Lady mother's illness gives me no rest. There is, besides, the near approach of Faustina's lying-in. But we must have faith in the Gods. Farewell, my most delightful of masters. My mother greets you.

Ad M. Caes. **v.** 46 (61) (Naber, p. 90).

DOMINO meo.
Ipso die quo[1] proficisci destinabam, genus dolo-
rem sensi. Spero in paucis diebus me recte fore.
Vale, Domine optime. Dominam saluta.

Ad M. Caes. **v.** 47 (62) (Naber, p. 90).

MAGISTRO meo salutem.
Nunc denique opto, mi magister, iucundiora indices. Nam doluisse te in id tempus, quo mihi
scribebas, litterae declarant. Haec obambulans dic-
tavi. Nam eum motum in praesentia ratio corpusculi
desiderabat. Vindemiarum | autem gratiam nunc
demum integram sentiam, quom tua valetudo placa-
tior esse nobis coeperit. Vale mi iucundissime
magister.

Vat. 99

Ad M. Caes. **v.** 48 (63) (Naber, p. 90).

DOMINO meo.
Plantae, Domine, dolore impedior. Ideo vos
per istos dies non salutavi. Vale, Domine optime.
Dominam saluta.

Ad M. Caes. **v.** 49 (64) (Naber, p. 90).

MAGISTRO meo.
Quom salubre tibi est facile progredi, tunc et
nobis conspectus tuus erit iucundus. Id ut quam
primum eveniat et dolor plantae quiescat, di iuvent.
Vale mi optime magister.

[1] For Cod. *ipsa . . . qua.*

M. CORNELIUS FRONTO

Fronto to Marcus as Caesar

To my Lord.   ? 154–156 A.D.

The very day on which I proposed to start I felt a pain in my knee. I hope to be all right in a day or two. Farewell, my best of Lords. Greet my Lady.

Marcus Aurelius to Fronto

To my master, greeting.   ? 154–156 A.D

By this time, at all events, my master, I hope you can send better news, for your letter says that you were in pain up to the time when you wrote. I have dictated this, walking about. For the state of my wretched body requires that exercise just now. But I shall only feel the full benefit of the vintage season when we find your health beginning to mend. Farewell, my most delightful of masters.

Fronto to Marcus as Caesar

To my Lord.   ? 154–156 A.D.

I am laid up with pain in the sole of my foot. That is why I have not paid you my respects these past days. Farewell, best of Lords. Greet my Lady.

Marcus Aurelius to Fronto

To my master.   ? 154–156 A.D.

When you are well enough to walk comfortably, then we also shall be delighted to see you. May the Gods bring that about as soon as possible, and the pain in your foot be better. Farewell, my best of masters.

Ad M. Caes. **v.** 52 (67) (Naber, p. 91).

Vat. 99, ad fin.

| Domino meo.

Decem tanta te amo. Filiam tuam vidi. Videor mihi te simul et Faustinam infantes vidisse : tantum boni ex utriusque voltu est commixtum. Decem tanta te amo. Vale, Domine dulcissime. Dominam saluta.

Ad M. Caes. **v.** 53 (68) (Naber, p. 91).

Magistro meo.

Et nos Gratiam, quod tui similis est, magis Vat. 110: Quat xi. amamus. Facile ergo intellegimus | quanta apud te sit filiolae nostrae conciliatrix similitudo utriusque nostri, et omnino quod eam vidisti est iucundum mihi. Vale mi optime magister.

Ad M. Caes. **v.** 54 (69) (Naber, p. 91).

Domino meo.

Tertius est dies, quod per noctem morsus ventris cum profluvio patior. Hac vero nocte ita sum vexatus, uti prodire non potuerim, sed lectulo me teneam. Medici suadent balneo uti. Multos natales tuos ut celebres a deis precatus sum. Vale, Domine. Dominam saluta.

---

[1] Probably Domitia Faustina, who died as an infant. See inscription on the *Moles Hadriana*, Orelli 672 = Willm. 964. Cornificia, the next daughter, was not born till about 159.

M. CORNELIUS FRONTO

Fronto to Marcus as Caesar

To my Lord.   ? 154–156 A.D.

I love you ten times as much—I have seen your daughter![1] I seem to have seen you as well as Faustina in your infancy : so much that is good in both your faces is blended in hers. I love you ten times as much. Farewell, sweetest of Lords. Greet your Lady.

Marcus Aurelius to Fronto

To my master.   ? 154–156 A.D.

We too love Gratia the more for her likeness to you.[2] So we can easily understand how our little girl's likeness to both of us endears her to you, and in every way it is a delight to me that you have seen her. Farewell, my best of masters.

Fronto to Marcus as Caesar

To my Lord.   ? 154–156 A.D.

This is the third day that I have been troubled all night long with griping in the stomach and diarrhoea. Last night, indeed, I suffered so much that I have not been able to go out, but am keeping my bed. The doctors recommend a bath. I have prayed the Gods to give you many happy returns of the day.[3] Farewell, my Lord. Greet your Lady.

---

[2] Ehrenthal thinks that Marcus should have said : "We too love you the more because Gratia is like you. So we can understand how our likeness to our baby endears us to you."   [3] April 26 (? 156).

Ad M. Caes. **v.** 55 (70) (Naber, **p.** 91).

MAGISTRO meo.

Tu quoque intelligis, mi magister, quid ego pro
me optem : sanum et validum te deinceps et hunc
diem tuum sollemnem et ceteros vel nobiscum vel
nobis utique securis pro te quam diutissime cele-
brare. Ceterum ego coniectavi statim fuisse eiusmodi aliquid quam ob rem te non viderim. Et, si
dicendum est, delector potius talem querellam corpusculi quam dolores aliquos intercessisse. Praeterea de profluvio isto bene spero, nam etsi nunc te
exhauserit, tamen dis volentibus confido salubriter
sponte provenisse alvum tibi verno tempore, quom
alii id consulto movent et machinantur. Vale, mi
iucundis|sime magister. Mater mea te salutat.

Vat. 109

Ad M. Caes. **v.** 56 (71) (Naber, **p.** 92).

DOMINO meo.

Fauces miseras habeo, unde etiam calui per
noctem. In genu dolor est modicus. Vale, Domine.
Dominam saluta.

Ad M. Caes. **v.** 57 (72) (Naber, **p.** 92).

MAGISTRO meo.

Iam habeo quod primum et praecipuum desid-
erabam : desisse febriculam colligo ex litteris tuis.

M. CORNELIUS FRONTO

Marcus Aurelius to Fronto

To my master.   ? 154–156 A.D.

You also know, my master, what I on my part
wish: that you should be hale and strong hence-
forth, and keep this your solemn day[1] and all
future ones for as many years as possible either
with us or, at all events, without giving us any
anxiety on your behalf. Of course, I guessed at
once that there was some reason of this kind for
our not seeing you. And I must confess that I am
thankful that the cause was such a complaint of your
body rather than some other pains. Besides I
have great hopes of that flux, for though it prostrate
you for the time, yet I trust, if the Gods will, that
your bowels have naturally and to the good of your
health felt the "motions of the spring," while others
contrive and bring this about by design. Farewell,
my most delightful of masters. My mother greets
you.

Fronto to Marcus as Caesar

To my Lord.   ? 154–156 A.D.

I have a wretched sore throat, which also made
me feverish all the night. My knee pains me a
little. Farewell, my Lord. Greet your Lady.

Marcus Aurelius to Fronto

To my master.   ? 154–156 A.D.

I now learn what I wished first and foremost to
hear. I gather from your letter that the feverishness

[1] Viz. Marcus's birthday.

Nunc, mi magister, quod ad fauces adtinet, brevi temperantia aspelletur,[1] et mihi a te levior [2] nuntius veniet. Vale mi magister iucundissime. Mater mea te salutat.

Ad Antoninum Pium, 3 (Naber, p. 164).

Ambr. 341, *ad fin.* | Antonino Pio Augusto Fronto.

1. Si evenire posset, Imp., ut amici ac familiares nostri nostris moribus cuncta agerent, maxime vellem ; tum, si non moribus, at saltem ut consiliis ubique nostris uterentur. Sed quoniam suum [3] cuiusque ingenium vitam gubernat, fateor aegre ferre me, Ambr. 356 quod amicus meus | Niger Censorius testamento suo, quo me heredem instituit, parum verbis temperavit. Id ego factum eius improbus sim, si defendendo purgare postulem ; immemor amicitiae, nisi saltem deprecando sublevem.

2. Fuit sine dubio Niger Censorius verborum suorum impos et minus consideratus, sed idem multarum rerum frugi vir et fortis et innocens. Tuae clementiae est, Imp., unicam hominis verborum culpam cum ceteris eius recte factis ponderare.

3. Ego quidem quom ad amicitiam eius accessi,

---

[1] Schopen for Cod. *appelletur.*
[2] Cod. has *at plenior.* The *levior* is by Brakman.
[3] m[3] in the margin of Cod. gives *suam.*

---

[1] Lucilla, the mother of Marcus, died about 156. This is the last mention of her.

M. CORNELIUS FRONTO

has gone. Now, my master, as for the sore throat, it will be got rid of by a little abstinence, and we shall soon have better news from you. Farewell, my most delightful of masters. My mother[1] greets you.

? 154–156 A.D.

FRONTO to Antoninus Pius Augustus.

1. If it could be brought about, Imperator, that our friends and relations should in all cases act by our principles of conduct, there is nothing I should desire more; next I would have them follow, if not our principles yet at least our advice on every occasion. But since each man's own character governs his life, I can only confess that I am sorry my friend Niger Censorius[2] used such intemperate language in his will, in which he made me his heir. If I claimed to clear him by justifying his action, I should be unprincipled; I should be disloyal to my friend if I did not at least say what I could in his excuse.

2. It cannot be denied that Niger Censorius was unrestrained and ill-advised in his language, but at the same time in many respects he was an honest man and manly and blameless. It will accord with your clemency, Imperator, if you set his other creditable actions against his solitary misconduct in word.

3. When I first came to be his friend, his strenuous

---

[2] Nothing is known of Censorius, but Gavius Maximus, whom he attacked, probably died in 157. The tone of this letter is much more formal and less familiar than the previous ones to Pius, and this may be evidence of an earlier date. But Fronto had a difficult task to perform, and his letter is a model of tact.

<iam ei amorem aliorum>[1] strenua opera domi belli-
que promeruerant.   Ut ceteros eius amicos omittam,
Turboni Marcio et Erucio Claro erat familiarissimus,
qui duo egregii viri alter equestris alter senatorii
ordinis primarii fuerunt.   Postea vero ex tuis etiam
iudiciis ei plurimum et honorum et auctoritatis acces-
serat.   Talis ego viri amicitiam appetivi.

4. Haud sciam an quis dicat debuisse me amicitiam cum eo desinere,[2] postquam cognoveram gratiam
eius apud animum tuum imminutam.   Numquam ita
animatus fui, Imp., ut coeptas in rebus prosperis
amicitias, siquid adversi increpuisset, desererem.   Et

Ambr. 355 omnino—cur enim non sententiam | animi mei ex-
promam?—ego eum qui te non amabit hostis numero
habebo ; quem vero tu minus amabis, miserum potius
quam hostem iudicabo.   De[3] . . . . permultum
refert improbes aliquem an oderis . . . . <so>ciis
et consiliis indigebat.   Atque utinam Niger, sicut in
plerisque mihi post paruit, ita consilium meum in
testamento <conficiendo>[4] rogasset!   Haud umquam
tantam maculam memoriae suae inussisset verbis
immoderatis ipsum se potius quam alios laedentibus.

5. Nec . . . . .[5] intervallum intercessisset quo
Ambr. 346 . . . . . | virum illo ipso tempore quo offendit : sed
amando ita offendit ut pleraque animalia, quibus

---

[1] Nothing can be read in the Codex except *a . . . crem
c . . . m.*

[2] For Cod. *desinire.*   Query *deserere* as below.

[3] From here eighteen lines are lost, the one sentence
(*permultum*, etc.) given being from the margin of the Codex.

[4] Mai.

[5] One line lost, and after *quo* nine and a half lines.

achievements, civil and military, had already won him the love of others. Not to mention his other friends, he was on the most intimate terms with Marcius Turbo[1] and Erucius Clarus,[2] who were both eminent men in the first rank, the one of the Knights, the other of the Senators. Subsequently, however, a great accession of honours and authority accrued to him from your courts[3] also. Such was the man whose friendship I coveted.

4. Possibly some might say that I ought to have given up my friendship with him when I realized that he was not held by you in the same favour as before. But, Imperator, I was never of such a mind as to cast off a friendship formed in prosperity as soon as a whisper of adversity was audible. And in any case—for why should I not say what is in my mind?—I shall hold as an enemy one who bears you no love, but one for whom you have but little love I shall count as an unfortunate rather than as an enemy . . . . There is a very great difference between blaming a man and hating him . . . . was in want of friends and advice. And would that Niger, as in most things subsequently he was guided by me, so had asked my advice in drawing up his will! Never would he have seared his memory with such a stain by reckless words that injured himself more than anyone else.

5. Nor . . . . would an interval have intervened . . . . a man at the very time of his offence. But he offends from very love, just as most animals that

---

[1] He was *praef. praet.* under Hadrian from 119–135 A.D.

[2] Consul II. in 146, and then *praef. urbi.*

[3] Or do the words mean "from your marks of approbation"?

abest ars et sedulitas educandi, ova atque catulos suos unguibus aut dentibus male contrectant, nec odio sed imperitia nutricandi obterunt.

6. Ego certe deos superos inferosque et fidem arcanam humanae amicitiae testor, me semper auctorem fuisse cuius [1] . . . . me . . . . animo . . . . utraque causas . . . . et sane . . . . | hominem . . . . eum incidisse magis doleas sed fideliter quem in eodem <agere> velle in quo . . . . et sane . . . . expectari poterat in eo quem <corre>xerat. Nec <moverat> tanta benignitas et tot beneficia . . . . tibi autem non . . . . equidem . . . . cumque habeat suum finem. Res autem istas, quas nec <tacere> voluimus nec <negare e re> credimus et, si dei aequi sint, veras et congruentes simplicitati nostrae amicitiae, semper adsequamur.

Ambr. 345

Ad Antoninum Pium, 7 (Naber, p. 168).

| <Gavio Maximo Fronto>
Cum gravitatem [2] . . . . Dolor iracundiae coniunctus mentem hominis perturbavit . . . . Virtutibus ceteris iracundia venenum ac pernicies fuit [3] . . . . <Sed nemo meum erga Nigrum amorem improbet>[4] | qui non tuum ante reprehenderit. Postremo neque ego Nigrum propter te amare

Ambr. 347 or 354, both illegible except margin

Ambr. 353

---

[1] The mutilated portions of this letter cover about forty lines. The position of the isolated words *me* to *sane* is doubtful, as Mai (see Naber, p. 166, note 6) inserts them in his two editions in separate places. All the added words are by Mai, except *e re*, which are suggested by Rob. Ellis.

[2] From the Index to *Ad Amicos* (ii. 5). See Naber, p. 189.

lack skill and perseverance in maternal duties injure their eggs and their young with talons or teeth, maltreating them not from malice but from want of experience in nursing.

6. I at least call to witness the Gods above and the Gods below and the hidden loyalties of human friendship, that I have ever been the author . . . .

. . . .
. . . .
. . . .
. . . .

Nor has he been influenced by kindness so great and benefits so many . . . . whenever he has his own end.   But let us always strive for those things, which we have neither been willing to pass over in silence nor think it right to deny, and such things, if the Gods are just, as are true and in accord with the straightforward nature of our friendship.

? 154–156 A.D.

FRONTO to Gavius Maximus.[1]

. . . . Grief added to anger upset the man's mental balance . . . . Anger poisoned and ruined his other virtues . . . . But let no one find fault with my love for Niger, who is not prepared to blame yours first.   Lastly, I did not begin to love Niger on your account, that I should on your

---

[1] He was *praef. praet.* 141-157, and therefore, we may suppose, a personal friend of Pius.

---

[3] These two sentences are from the margin of Cod. Ambr. 354.

[4] Added by Mai, except *improbet*, for which he gives *vituperet*.

coeperam, ut propter te eundem amare desinerem,
neque tu me a Nigro tibi traditum diligere coepisti.
Quam ob rem tecum quaeso, ne quid obsit amicitia
nobis, quae[1] nihil profuit. Iam si dicendum sit,
deos testor me saepe vidisse Nigrum Censorium
ubertim flentem desiderio tui atque huius discidii
dolore.

Sed erit fortasse tempus aliud, quod[2] ego memoriae
eius placem te ac mitigem. Interim, ne quid loci
malignis hominibus adversus me apud aures tuas
pateat, <tibi spondeo in perpetuum meam>[3] fidem,
quam quom firmam et sinceram cum Censorio serva-
verim, multo magis profecto tecum perpetuam atque
incorruptam retinere conitar.

Ad Antoninum Pium, 4 (Naber, p. 167).[4]

Ambr. 345,
ad med.

| Domino meo Caesari.

Niger Censorius diem suum obiit. Quincuncem
bonorum suorum nobis reliquit testamento cetera
honesto, quod ad verba vero adtinet inconsiderato :
in quo irae magis quam decori suo consuluit. Inclementius enim progressus est in Gavium Maximum
clarissimum et nobis observandum virum.

Ob eam rem necessarium visum scribere me
Domino nostro patri tuo et ipsi Gavio Maximo diffi-
cillimae quidem rationis epistulas : in quibus et
factum Nigri mei, quod improbabam, non repre-
hendere nequibam, et tamen amici atque heredis

---

[1] Mai for Cod. *qui*. Kluss. prefers *quibus*.

[2] Naber reads *quo*.

[3] Mähly, but he reads *perpetuum* without *in*. Cod. *perperam*.

[4] This letter is omitted in the Index of *Letters to Pius*,
but is found among them. It is clearly to Marcus.

account cease to love him; nor did you begin to
have a liking for me through Niger's introduction.
Wherefore, I beseech you, let not a friendship now
be a hindrance which was never a help to us. Now,
if I must say so, let the Gods witness that I have
often seen Niger Censorius weeping copiously for
want of you and for distress at this dissension.

But perhaps I shall have another opportunity of
mollifying you and reconciling you to his memory.
Meanwhile, lest your ears be open to any attacks by
ill-disposed persons on me, I pledge to you my
lasting loyalty, which, as I kept it truly and
faithfully with Censorius, much more assuredly shall
I strive to preserve lasting and unimpaired with you.

Fronto to Marcus.

154–156 A.D.

To my Lord Caesar.

Niger Censorius is dead, leaving me heir to five-
twelfths of his estate by a will in all other respects
unexceptionable but, as far as its language is concerned, ill-advised, since in this he followed the
dictates of anger rather than consulted his self-
respect. For he inveighed in unmeasured terms
against Gavius Maximus, a man of senatorial rank
and entitled to my regard.

In consequence I have thought it necessary to
write to our Lord your Father and to Gavius Maximus himself letters of a very difficult tenor. For,
whereas I could not but find fault with the action of
my friend Niger, which I myself disapproved of, I
wished at the same time, as was right, not to fail in

Ambr. 348

officium, ut par erat, retinere cupiebam. Haec ego te, ut mea omnia cetera, scire volui, conatus | mehercules ad te quoque de eadem re prolixiores litteras scribere : sed recordanti cuncta mihi melius visum non obtundere te neque a potioribus avocare.

Ad Antoninum Pium, 9 (Naber, p. 170).

Ambr. 330,
ad med.

| \<Antonino Pio Augusto Fronto\>.

Ambr. 329

1. . . . . amicorum meorum fecit modestia ne quid improbe peterem [1] . . . . | Equitis Romani unius contubernalis mei Sextii Calpurnii dignitatem rogatu meo exornasti duabus iam procurationibus datis. Ea ego duarum procurationum beneficia quater numero : bis quom dedisti procurationes, itemque bis quom excusationes recepisti.

2. Supplicavi iam tibi per biennium pro Appiano amico meo, cum quo mihi et vetus consuetudo et studiorum usus prope cotidianus intercedit. Quin ipsum quoque certum habeo et affirmare ausim eadem modestia usurum qua Calpurnius Iulianus meus usus est. Dignitatis enim suae in senectute ornandae causa, non ambitione aut procuratoris stipendii cupiditate optat adipisci hunc honorem.

---

[1] From the margin of Ambr. 330.

[1] Fronto had pupils who lived with him, such as the two sons of Sardius Saturninus, mentioned below.

[2] This was the historian Appian, who tells us in the Preface to his *History* that he received such an appointment

my duty as friend and heir. I was anxious that you should know of this, as of all else that concerns me, and, by heaven, I began a lengthy letter to you on this subject; but on thinking everything over I decided not to importune you or call you away from more important business.

? 157–161 A.D.

Fronto to Antoninus Pius Augustus.

1. . . . . . The modesty of my friends has ensured that I should make no unworthy request for them . . . . you have at my request enhanced the dignity of one Roman knight, Sextius Calpurnius, who lived with me,[1] by the grant of two procuratorships already. I count these two procuratorships as favours four times given: twice when you granted them, and twice when you permitted them to be declined.

2. For two years now I have been your suppliant for my friend Appianus,[2] between whom and myself there has been both a long-standing intimacy and almost daily practice of mutual studies. Moreover, I feel certain and would be bold to affirm, that he will shew the same modesty that my friend Calpurnius Julianus has. For it is to enhance his dignity in old age that he desires to attain this distinction, and not from ambition or coveting the salary of a procurator.

from Marcus and Lucius, when emperors. These procurators were set over every department of state and of the imperial household. They managed the emperor's domains, his mines, etc., the corn-supply, the water-supply, and the alimentary institutions. In the imperial provinces the procurators were fiscal officers. The procurator *a rationibus* was the highest of these officials, and corresponded to a Secretary of State.

Quom primum pro Appiano petivi, ita benigne admisisti preces meas ut sperare deberem.

Proximo superiore anno petenti mihi propitius multa respondisti, illud vero etiam comiter, futurum ut quom Appiano me rogante procurationem dedisses, causidicorum scatebra exoreretur idem petentium. Meministi etiam quem de Graecia propitius et ridens nominaveris. Sed multa distant: aetas, orbitas, cui leniendae solaciis opus est. | Ausim dicere honestatem quoque et probitatem inter duos bonos viros nonnihil tamen distare: quod propterea facilius dico, quoniam illum, cui amicum meum antepono, non nominavi.

Ambr. 340

3. Postremo dicam, quomodo simplicitas mea et veritas me dicere hortantur et fiducia amoris erga te mei, profecto aequius esse illum quoque propter me impetrare. Memento etiam, Domine Imperator, quom ille meo exemplo petet, me biennio hoc petisse. Igitur illi quoque, si videbitur, post biennium dato. Fecerit exemplo nostro, si ipse quoque se tibi impetraverit excusare.

Epist. Graec. 4 (Naber, p. 244).

Ambr. 160, ad init.

| Παρὰ Ἀππιανοῦ Φρόντωνι.

1. Οὐδὲ σήμερον ἐδυνήθην σε ἰδεῖν διὰ τὴν γαστέρα νυκτὸς ἐνοχλοῦσαν ἕως ἄρτι κοιμηθείς. ἃ δὲ ἀγρυπνῶν

---

[1] *i.e.* that the Greek as well as Appian should be granted his request.

[2] See Fronto's letter throwing up his proconsulship, p. 236.

When I first made request for Appianus, you gave my petition so kindly a hearing that I had a right to hope.

When I renewed my request the next, which was last, year, your answer contained much that was gracious, one thing even in a vein of pleasantry, that the moment you gave Appianus the procuratorship at my request, a flood of pleaders would gush forth asking a like favour. You remember too the native of Greece whom you graciously and smilingly mentioned. But the cases are far from parallel : there is age, there is childlessness, which calls for consolations to relieve it. I would make bold to add that, though both are good men, yet in worth and integrity one has some advantage over the other ; and I may say this the more freely, in that I have not named him whom I put second to my friend.

3. Lastly I will say, as I am prompted to do by plain dealing and truth as well as by the assurance of my love towards you, that surely it is fairer that the other [1] also should gain his wish on my account. Remember too, my Lord Imperator, when he follows my example in petitioning, that I have petitioned these two years. Then let him too, if so it please you, be gratified after two years. He will but be following my example, if he also then get permission to be excused.[2]

From Appianus to Fronto.[3]

? 157–161 A.D.

1. I could not see you to-day either, as owing to gastric trouble last night I have only just got up. What I was puzzling over in my wakeful

---

[3] It appears that Appian had sent Fronto a present of two slaves, which Fronto returned. Appian now sends them again, with this letter.

ἠπόρουν, οὐ κατέσχον οὐδ' ἀνεβαλόμην, ἀλλ' ἐκ πολλῶν ὀλίγα σοι γέγραφα. σὺ δέ, εἰ μὲν δίκαιά ἐστιν, ὡς δικαίοις, εἰ δὲ σχολαστικά, ὡς ἁπλοῖς, εἰ δὲ μή, ἀλλ' ἔμοιγε ὡς λυπουμένῳ καὶ παρακαλοῦντι πείσθητι καὶ εἶξον.

2. Εἰκὸς ἕπεσθαι τοῖς κοινοῖς τὰ ἰδιωτικά. εὐθύνομεν γοῦν τὰ ἴδια πρὸς ἐκεῖνα καὶ ὁ νόμος οὕτω κελεύει. πῶς οὖν αἱ μὲν πόλεις οὐκ ὀκνοῦσι λαμβάνουσαι παρὰ τῶν διδόντων ἀναθήματά τε καὶ χρήματα καὶ ἀργύριον αὐτὸ πολιτῶν τε καὶ ξένων, ἤδη δέ τινας καὶ αὐτούς πως ὑποδιδόντας, φίλος δὲ δὴ παρὰ φίλου λαβεῖν ὀκνεῖ παρακαλοῦντος; καὶ οἱ θεοὶ δὲ τῷ νόμῳ τῶν πόλεων προσίενται [1] ταῦτα παρὰ τῶν ἀνθρώπων [2] καὶ δεικνύουσιν οἱ θησαυροὶ τῶν θεῶν. καὶ οἱ φίλιοι δὲ ἐκ τῶν διαθηκῶν λαμβάνειν οὐκ ὀκνοῦσιν. καὶ διὰ τί οὖν ἐκ μὲν διαθηκῆς ἄν τις λάβοι, παρὰ δὲ τῶν περιόντων οὐ λάβοι, ὁπότε καὶ μεῖζον τοῦτ' [3] ἔχει τὸ δεῖγμα τῆς προθυμίας; οἱ μὲν γὰρ ἄλλον ἄλλου προτιθέασιν, οἱ δὲ περιόντες ἑαυτῶν τοὺς φίλους προτιθέασιν. καὶ ἥδιον παρὰ τοῦ περιόντος λαβεῖν, ὅτι καὶ μαρτυρῆσαι περιόντι δυνατόν ἐστι καὶ ἀμείψασθαι. πάλιν ξένιον μὲν οὔτε θεοῖς οὔτε πόλει πέμπεται, τὰ σεμνότερα δ' ἀεὶ τοῖς σεμνοτέροις.

3. Ἀλλ' οὐκ εἰσὶ ταῦ|τα βαρύτερα λαμβάνειν; τί γάρ ἐστι φιλίας καὶ τιμῆς βαρύτερον, ὧν οὐδ' ἴσως γε [4] ἄρειον οὐδέν ἐστιν; τί δὲ καὶ βαρὺ ἦν ὅλως ἢ τί ἂν ἐγὼ βαρὺ

---

[1] Heinαorf for Cod. προσθεναι.
[2] Jacobs for Cod. ἀνδρῶν.
[3] Naber for Cod. ταῦτ'.
[4] Studemund for Cod. ἴσος γ'.

hours I am not keeping back or putting off, but
have written you a few out of my many thoughts.
And you, if they are just, give ear and assent to
them as just; if they are pedantic, as sincere; but
in any case do so to me, as aggrieved and a suppliant.

2. It is but natural that the individual should
take pattern by the community. At any rate we
direct our private affairs on the lines of public ones
and the law bids us do this. How is it then, that
states do not shrink from receiving from the donors,
native and alien, offerings and property and money
itself, and in some cases even a free gift of their
persons, but a friend shrinks from receiving a gift
from a friend when he entreats it? And the Gods
too by the law of cities accept these gifts from men,
as the treasuries of the Gods testify. Aye friends
too do not shrink from taking under wills. And why,
pray, should a man take under a will, but take
nothing from the living, when the latter gift is an
even greater proof of affection. For the testator
prefers one man to another, but the living donor
prefers his friend to himself. And it is sweeter to
receive a gift from the living, because it is possible
both to acknowledge it to a living person and to
make a return. Again a trifling gift[1] is not made
to Gods or cities, but nobler things are always for
the more noble.

3. But, you will say, does not their acceptance
bring a heavier obligation? Why, what can be a
heavier one than friendship and honour, than which
things there is perhaps nothing better? And what
was there here even heavy at all, or what should

[1] Martial heads his thirteenth book of epigrams *Xenia*,
from the little complimentary gifts made to guests and friends.

ἔχοιμι; οὐδ' ἂν μὲν ἐργασαίμην οὐδὲν οὐδὲ πριαίμην
οὐδέποτε, †δέον τινα μισθὸν ἴσον ¹† ἐξ οἴκου, φασίν, ἐς
οἶκον μετελθεῖν. ἐννόησον δὲ κἀκεῖνο, ὅση μὲν ἡδονὴ τῷ
πέμψαντι ληφθέντων, ὅση δὲ λύπη μὴ ληφθέντων ἐπιγίγ-
νεται. εἰ τὸ καθαρὸν . . . .² καὶ μετὰ πολὺ προσιέναι
σοι. πιστεύοις δὲ δίκαιον εἶναι τὸν νόμον τῶν τε πόλεων
καὶ θεῶν καὶ φίλων . . . .³ φίλων δὲ οὐ τοσοῦτον ἐπι-
δεικνύντων θράσος εὐνοίας, ἀλλὰ †κρυπτόντων⁴ ὑπὸ
δέους,† ἔπεμψα τὸ πρὶν ἐπιτρέψῃς. σὺ δὲ μὴ δεύτερον
ἀποπέμψῃς,⁵ ᾧ γε ἔδει μηδ' ἅπαξ.

Epist. Graec. 5 (Naber, p. 246).

Ἀππιανῷ παρὰ Φρόντωνος.

1. Οὐκ ἀπορήσειεν ἂν οὐδ' ἐκεῖνος πιθανῶν λόγων,
ὅστις πρὸς τὸ πρῶτον ἐνθύμημα τῶν ὑπὸ σοῦ προτεθέντων
ἐνίσταιτο, ὡς μὴ δέοι ἕπεσθαι τοῖς κοινοῖς τὰ ἴδια. πολλὰ
γὰρ ἔθη καὶ νόμιμα κοινῇ ταῖς πόλεσιν καὶ ἰδίᾳ τοῖς καθ'
ἕκαστον εὑρήσομεν οὐχ ὅμοια. μάθοις δὲ ἂν προσέχων
ταῖς τε δίκαις καὶ τοῖς ἀγῶσιν τοῖς δημοσίοις καὶ τοῖς
ἰδιωτικοῖς· ἔνθα οὔτε ὁ τόπος τῶν δικαστηρίων οὔτε τῶν

Ambr. 138

δικαζόντων ὁ ἀριθμὸς οὔτε ἡ τά|ξις τῶν φάσεων καὶ
κλήσεων οὔτε τοῦ ὕδατος τὸ μέτρον, οὐδὲ τὰ προστιμή-
ματα τῶν κατεγνωσμένων τὰ αὐτά, ἀλλὰ πλεῖστον ὅσον

---

¹ Du Rieu reads the faint traces in the Codex as μεολ . . .
αμεκηνειχον.   ² Twelve letters are lost.
³ About eighteen letters are lost.
⁴ Jacobs for Cod. ναιτοντων (according to du Rieu).   Mai

I count heavy? I would not traffic in anything nor
buy anything, that necessitated an equivalent return passing, as they say, from house to house.
Consider this point also, what pleasure acceptance
gives the sender, and what mortification follows
upon non-acceptance . . . . even after many days
to come to you. Pray believe that the law of Gods
and cities and friends is a just one . . . . but as
friends do not parade such a forwardness of good-
will but from diffidence conceal it, I send before
you give permission. Do not you send back my
gift a second time, as you ought not to have done
even the first time.

To Appian from Fronto.

? 157–161 A.D.

1. Even he would have no lack of plausible arguments who, in answer to the first of the propositions
submitted by you, should object that private conduct
ought *not* to conform to that of states. For we
shall find many customs and usages publicly established in cities and privately practised by individuals
to be dissimilar. You can easily convince yourself
of this by looking at the litigation and disputes
between public bodies and between individuals, wherein neither the venue of the court nor the number of
the judges nor the order of the pleas and summonses
nor the allowance of time for the speakers nor the
penalties of conviction are the same, but there is

---

read the Codex καὶ τούτων ὑποδέουσι. The οὐ τοσοῦτον is
Naber's correction of Mai's οὐχ ὡς τοῦτον.
    ⁵ Niebuhr for Cod. μηδὲ τιμη . . .

διήνεγκεν τὰ δημόσια τῶν ἰδίων. καὶ ὅτι τῆς μὲν πόλεως
ἀναπεπτάσθαι προσήκει τὰς πύλας εἰσιέναι τε τῷ βου-
λομένῳ καὶ ἐξιέναι ὅποτε βούλοιτο· ἑκάστῳ δὲ ἡμῶν τῶν
ἰδιωτῶν εἰ μὴ φυλάττοι τὰς θύρας καὶ πάνυ ἐγρηγοροίη ὁ
θυρωρός, εἴργων μὲν τῆς εἰσόδου τοὺς μηδὲν προσήκοντας,
τοῖς δὲ οἰκέταις αὖ[1] ἐπιτρέπων ἀδεῶς ὅποτε βούλοιντο
ἔξω βαδίζειν, οὐκ ἂν ὀρθῶς οἰκουροῖτο τὰ κατὰ τὴν οἰκίαν.
καὶ στοαὶ δὲ καὶ ἄλση καὶ βωμοὶ καὶ γυμνάσια καὶ λουτρὰ
τὰ μὲν δημόσια πᾶσιν καὶ προῖκα ἀνεῖται, τὰ δὲ τῶν
ἰδιωτῶν ὑπὸ σιδηρᾷ κλειδὶ καί τινι θυροφύλακι,[2] καὶ
μισθὸν ἐκλέγουσιν παρὰ τῶν λουσαμένων. οὐδὲ τὰ δεῖπνα
δὲ ὅμοια τὰ ἰδιωτικὰ καὶ τὰ ἐν Πρυτανείῳ· οὐδὲ ὁ ἵππος ὅ
τε ἰδιωτικὸς καὶ ὁ δημόσιος· οὐδὲ ἡ πορφύρα τῶν ἀρχόντων
καὶ τῶν δημοτῶν· οὐδὲ ὁ στέφανος ὁ τῶν ῥόδων τῶν
οἴκοθεν καὶ ὁ τῆς ἐλαίας τῆς Ὀλυμπίασιν.

2. Ἅμα ταῦτα μὲν ἐάσειν μοι δοκῶ καὶ χαριεῖσθαί σοι
τὸ δεῖν ἕπεσθαι τοῖς δημοσίοις τὰ ἰδιωτικά. χαρισάμενος
δὲ τοῦτο οὐκέτι χαρισαίμην ἂν τοῦθ' †ὅ ⟨γε π⟩εῖσαί ⟨με
θ⟩έλεις, ⟨ὅτι καὶ⟩ ἐμὲ πρέπει ἕπεσθαι.† τί δὴ τοῦτό

ἐστιν, ἐγὼ | φράσω. τὸ μὲν ἀμφισβητούμενον ἡμῖν,
οἶμαι, τοῦτο ἦν, εἰ χρὴ μεγάλα καὶ πολλῆς τιμῆς ἄξια
δῶρα παρὰ τῶν φίλων δέχεσθαι. ταῦτα προστάσσων εἰς
παράδειγμα ἐκάλεις τὸ τὰς πόλεις μεγάλα δῶρα παρ'
ἀλλήλων προσίεσθαι, αὐτὸ δὴ τὸ ἀμφισβητούμενον
σφετεριζόμενος, ὦ φιλότης. ὁ γὰρ τοὺς ἰδιώτας ἐγὼ
φάσκων μὴ δεῖν μεγάλα δῶρα παρ' ἀλλήλων λαμβάνειν,
τὸ αὐτὸ τοῦτο ἂν εἴποιμι καὶ περὶ τῶν πόλεων, ὡς οὐδὲ
τὰς πόλεις δέοι λαμβάνειν· σὺ δέ, ὡς τοῦτο προσῆκον

---

[1] For Cod. οὐκ.   [2] Naber for Cod. Σύρῳ φύλακι.

every difference between the public cases and the private. Again the gates of a city must be opened wide for any to enter at will and, when he will, to go out. But for each one of us as individuals, if his doorkeeper guard not his door and be ever on the watch, debarring from ingress those who have no business there, but on the other hand permitting the inmates to go out freely whenever they wish, the safeguarding of the house could not be properly effected. So also porticoes and groves and altars and gymnasia, and baths, if public ones, are thrown open free to all, but if private, are kept under strong lock and key with a door-keeper to boot, and a fee is exacted from the bathers. Nor yet are banquets in private houses and in the Town-Hall the same; nor a horse if it belong to a private person or to the state; nor the purple robe of the magistrate and of the townsman; nor the garland of home-grown roses and the wreath of olive at Olympia.

2. At the same time I think that I will waive this and concede to you that private conduct must needs conform to public. But conceding this, I would not go further and concede what you would fain persuade me of, that *I* must conform to it. I will explain what I mean. The point in dispute between us, I take it, was this, whether one ought to accept great and valuable gifts from friends. Justifying this, you pointed to the example of cities accepting great gifts one from another, taking for granted, my dear friend, the very point in dispute. For alleging as I do that individuals ought not to take great gifts from one another, I would say exactly the same of cities, that they ought not to take them either; but you, begging the question

ταῖς πόλεσιν λαβών, εἰς ἀπόδειξιν φέρεις τοῦ καὶ τοῖς
ἰδιώταις προσήκοντος. τὸ δὲ ζητούμενον μὴ δεῖν ἐξ αὐτῶν
τῶν ἀμφισβητουμένων ἀποδεικνύειν φήσαις ἄν. εἰ δὲ
τοῦτο φῇς, ὅτι λαμβάνουσι πολλαὶ πόλεις τὰ τοιαῦτα
δῶρα, φαίη ἂν ὅτι καὶ τῶν ἰδιωτῶν πολλοὶ λαμβάνουσι
τὰ τοιαῦτα, ζητοῦμεν δὲ εἰ ὀρθῶς καὶ προσηκόντως λαμ-
βάνουσιν. τοῦτο δὲ τὸ ζήτημα ἀπὸ τῶν ἰδιωτῶν ἀρξά-
μενον διήκει καὶ πρὸς τὰς πόλεις. τοῦτο μὲν οὖν δίκαια
ποιῶν ἐν ζητήματος μέρει διαλείψεις ἀμφισβητήσιμον, τὸ
τῶν πόλεων λέγω. οὐδὲ γὰρ οὐδ' ἐκεῖνό σ' ἀγνοεῖν οἶμαι,
ὡς αἱ πλεῖσταί γε τῶν εὐδοξοτάτων καὶ εὐνομουμένων[1]
πόλεων οὐκ ἐδέξαντο τὰ μεγάλα δῶρα· ὥσπερ ἡ Ῥωμαίων
πόλις πολλὰ πολλάκις παρὰ | πλείστων πεμπόμενα οὐ
προσήκατο, ἡ δὲ τὴν Ἀθηναίων βαρύτερα τῶν προση-
κόντων ἐκλέγουσα, οὐ πάνυ τι ὤνατο.

3. Τὸ δέ γε τῶν θεῶν παράδειγμα, ὅτι δῶρα καὶ ἀναθή-
ματα θεοὶ δέχονται, καὶ πάνυ σοι διὰ βραχέων εἰρημένον,
ἐν ἴσῳ τάχει ἀπολύσασθαι πειράσομαι. οὐδὲ γὰρ προσ-
κυνεῖσθαι[2] μοι προσῆκεν μήτε θεῷ μήτε αὖ βασιλεῖ
Περσῶν ὄντι.

4. Πιθανώτατον δὲ νὴ Δία τὸ τῶν διαθηκῶν ὑπήνεγκας,
τί δή ποτε ἐκ διαθηκῶν καὶ τὰ μεγάλα λαμβάνοντες παρὰ
τῶν ζώντων τηλικαῦτα[3] οὐ προσησόμεθα· φθάνεις δὲ τὴν
αἰτίαν αὐτὸς ὑποβάλλων. οἱ μὲν γάρ, ὡς σὺ φῇς, ἄλλον
ἄλλου προτιθέασιν οἱ κατὰ διαθήκας χαριζόμενοι· φημὶ δὴ
παρὰ τούτων λαμβάνειν προσήκειν. οἱ δὲ αὖ ζῶντες, ὡς
σὺ φῇς, ἑαυτῶν τοὺς φίλους οἷς χαρίζονται προτιμῶσιν·
δι' αὐτὸ δὴ τοῦτο φημὶ δεῖν τὰ πεμπόμενα μὴ προσίεσθαι.

---

[1] Niebuhr for Cod. εὐνοουμενων.
[2] Mai for Cod. προσκεινεισθαι.
[3] Brakman says the Codex reads σπουδαια.

Ambr. 144

that this is right for cities, adduce it as a proof of what is right for individuals. You must admit that one ought not to prove the question at issue by means of the very points in dispute. But if you say that many states accept such gifts, I will answer that many individuals also accept them, but that the question is whether it is right and fit that they should accept them. And this question beginning with individuals extends to cities also. This point, therefore, I mean the action of cities, you must in all fairness leave on one side, as part of the question in dispute. For I take it you are not unaware that the majority of the most famous and well-ordered cities have never accepted great gifts; as, for example, the City of Rome has rejected many such many a time from very many senders, but Athens exacting heavier gifts than befitted was not at all benefited thereby.

3. As to your example from the Gods, that they receive gifts and offerings, which you touched on quite briefly, I will endeavour to dismiss it no less shortly. As I am neither God nor the Persian King, it was not fitting even to pay me homage.

4. The most plausible argument you brought forward, by heaven, was the one from wills—why is it that, when we take even large bequests under wills, we should not accept such from the living? The reason is suggested already by yourself. For those who benefit their friends in their wills prefer, as you say, one legatee to another: from them I admit that it is right to take. The living on the other hand prefer, as you say, the friends whom they benefit to themselves. For this very reason I say that what is offered should not be

βαρὺ γὰρ ὄντως καὶ ὑπεροπτικὸν καὶ τυραννικόν, ὡς
ἀληθῶς, τὸ δέχεσθαι τὰς τοιαύτας προτιμήσεις, ἐν αἷς ὁ
τιμῶν ἕτερον δῆλός ἐστιν αὐτὸς αὑτὸν τιμάζων καὶ ἐν
δευτέρῳ τιθεὶς τοῦ προτετιμημένου. οὐδὲ γὰρ ἵππον
ἀναβαίην ἄν, ἀφ' οὗ καταβὰς αὐτός τις καὶ βαδίζων ἐμὲ
δὴ[1] ἱππάζεσθαι ἀξιοίη· οὐδὲ ἐν θεάτρῳ καθεζοίμην ἄν,
ἄλλου μοι ὑπανισταμένου, οὐδὲ ἱμάτιον δεξαίμην ἂν ἐν
χειμῶνος ὥρᾳ, εἴ τις ἀποδυόμενος | ῥιγῴη μὲν αὐτός, ἐμὲ δὲ
ἀμφιεννύοι. οἰκειότερος γὰρ αὐτὸς ἕκαστος αὑτῷ καὶ
προτιμᾶσθαι πρὸς αὑτοῦ δικαιότερος.

5. Φῂς δὲ ξένια μὴ πέμπεσθαι θεοῖς. ἢ οὐχὶ ξένια τὰ
ψαιστὰ <τὰ> πόπανα καὶ τὸ μέλι καὶ ὁ οἶνος ὁ σπενδό-
μενος καὶ τὸ γάλα καὶ τὰ σπλάγχνα τὰ τῶν ἱερείων; καὶ ὁ
λιβανωτὸς δὲ ξένιον θεοῦ.

6. Ταῦτα μὲν πρὸς τὰ ὑπὸ σοῦ σοφῶς καὶ πιθανῶς πάνυ
δημοσίων τε καὶ θείων καὶ διαθηκῶν πέρι προτεθέντα
ἐνθυμήματα. τὰ δὲ παρ' ἐμοῦ ταῦτα εἰρήσθω διὰ βραχέων·
ὅσα αἰτεῖν ἀναιδὲς καὶ φιλοκερδὲς καὶ πλεονεκτικόν, ταῦτα
καὶ παρ' ἑκόντος[2] λαμβάνειν ὁμοίως ἀναιδοῦς τινος καὶ
φιλοκερδοῦς ἀνδρὸς καὶ πλεονέκτου· αἰτεῖν δέ γε τὰ
μεγάλα ἀναιδές, πολὺ δὴ μᾶλλόν γε λαμβάνειν. καὶ
οὐδὲν διήνεγκεν εἰ παρ' ἑκόντος λαμβάνοι τις ἢ ἀρνοῦντος·
οὐ μὲν γὰρ δεῖ αἰτεῖν,[3] ἀλλ' οὐδὲ λαμβάνειν.† οὐδέ γε τὰ
τοιαῦτα δῶρα χρή τινα ἑλέσθαι, ἃ τοὺς μὲν πέμποντας
πενεστέρους ἀποδείξει, τοὺς δὲ λαμβάνοντας πλουσιω-
τέρους παρασκευάσει. ἑκάτερον δὲ τοῦτο ἐν τοῖς μεγάλοις
δώροις ἔνεστιν. εἰ γοῦν ἀποτιμήσεις γίγνοιντο, σὺ μὲν ὁ

---

[1] Cod. δε; if δὲ is kept, read βαδίζοι.
[2] Naber for Cod. παρέχοντος.
[3] For Cod. (according to Studemund) τι<να ἢ ἀρνοῦντος
οὐκ ἐν τῷ> αἰτεῖν.

accepted. For it is in reality no light thing and savours, to tell the truth, of arrogance and tyranny to receive such marks of preference, wherein he, that does another honour, manifestly does himself dishonour, and sets him whom he has honoured above himself. For I would not even mount a horse, if the rider dismounting and going on foot asked me to ride; nor would I sit down in a theatre, if another gave up his seat to me; nor in wintry weather accept a man's cloak, if by stripping himself and shivering he kept me warmly wrapped. For each man is his own nearer concern and more deserving of honour at his own hands.

5. You say that trifling gifts are not sent to the Gods. What, are not these trifling gifts—the little barley-cakes and the honey and the libation-wine and the milk and the organs of the victims? Aye, and the frankincense is a trifling gift to a God.

6. So much for the propositions so cleverly and plausibly urged by you touching things public and things divine and touching wills. But for myself let me briefly say this: whatever it is shameless and greedy and covetous to ask for, it is no less characteristic of the shameless, the greedy, and the covetous man to accept even from a voluntary giver. To ask for big gifts is shameless, far more to accept them. And it is all one whether we take from a willing or a reluctant giver; for it is not right to ask, but it is not right to take either. Nor should a man accept such gifts as shall leave the sender poorer and render the receiver richer. And great gifts involve both these results. At any rate in the case of a property valuation, you who sent these two

πέμψας τοὺς δύο τούτους παῖδας μικροτέραν, ἐγὼ δὲ ὁ
λαβὼν μείζω τὴν οὐσίαν ἀποφανοῦμαι. οὐ γάρ ἐστιν
Ambr. 151 εὐκαταφρόνητος οὔτε ἐν ἀποτιμήσει χρημάτων οὔτε | ἐν
ἀντιδόσει οὐσίας οὔτε ἐν ἀπογραφῇ τέλους οὔτε ἐν κατα-
βολῇ φόρου ὁ τῶν δύο δούλων ἀριθμός.

7. Ὁ δὲ τὰ βαρύτερα δῶρα πέμπων οὐχ ἧττον λυπεῖ
τοῦ βαρεῖαν πέμποντος ἐπὶ τὸν σισφαιρίζοντα ἢ μεγάλην
κύλην προπίνοντος τῷ συμπότῃ· εἰς γὰρ μέθην οὐκ εἰς
ἡδονὴν προπίνειν ἔοικεν. ὥσπερ δὲ τὸν οἶνον ἐν τοῖς
σώφροσιν συμποσίοις ὁρῶμεν κιρνάμενον ἀκράτῳ μὲν
πάνυ ὀλίγῳ, πλείστῳ δὲ τῷ ὕδατι, οὕτω δὴ καὶ τὰ δῶρα
κιρνάναι προσῆκεν πολλῇ μὲν φιλοφροσύνῃ, ἐλαχίστῳ δὲ
ἀναλώματι. τίσιν γὰρ ἂν φαίημεν ἁρμόττειν τὰ πολυτελῆ
δῶρα; ἆρά γε τοῖς πένησιν; ἀλλὰ πέμπειν οὐ δύνανται· ἢ
τοῖς πλουσίοις; ἀλλὰ λαμβάνειν οὐ δέονται. τοῖς μὲν
οὖν μεγάλοις δώροις τὸ συνεχὲς οὐ πρόσεστιν, ἢ ἐκπεσεῖν
ἀνάγκη τῶν ὑπαρχόντων, εἴ τις μεγάλα τε πέμποι καὶ
πολλάκις. τοῖς δὲ μικροῖς δώροις τό τε συνεχὲς πρόσεστιν
καὶ τὸ ἀμεταγνωστόν, εἰ <καὶ μικρὰ δεῖ τε>λέσαι μικρὰ
πέμψαντι.†

8. Ὁμολογήσαις δ' ἂν καὶ τοῦτο, ὡς, εἴ τις ἑαυτῷ μὲν
ἔπαινον παρασκευάζοι, ἕτερον δὲ ἐπαίου ἀποστεροίη, οὐ
δίκαιος. σὺ δὲ μεγάλα δῶρα πέμπων σαυτῷ μὲν ἔπαινον
παρασκευάζεις ὡς μεγαλοφρόνως χαριζόμενος, ἐμὲ δὲ
ἐπαίνου ἀποστερεῖς προσίεσθαι βιαζόμενος. δόξαιμι γὰρ
Ambr. 152 ἂν | καὶ αὐτὸς μεγαλόφρων τὰ τηλικαῦτα μὴ προσέμενος.
ἐν δὲ τοῖς μικροῖς τῶν δώρων ἴσος ὁ ἔπαινος τῷ μὲν

slaves would declare your property as less and I who received them as more. For the item of these two slaves is no negligible one, either in valuation of goods or in exchange of properties [1] or in assessment for taxation or in payment of tribute.

7. He that sends too heavy a gift offends no less than he who sends his fellow ball-player too heavy a return or toasts his fellow guest with a big cup. For he would seem to toast him for debauch not for delight. But just as in temperate banquets we see the wine mixed in the proportion of a great deal of water to quite a little wine, so should gifts be a blend of much loving-kindness and very little outlay. For whom can we say that costly gifts befit? The poor? But they cannot send them. The rich? But they do not need them. Moreover, great gifts cannot be given continuously; or, if a man send great gifts and often, he must come to the end of his resources. But small gifts admit of being given continuously and with no compunction, since a man need make but a small acknowledgment to one who has sent a small gift.

8. This too you would confess, that a man acts unjustly, if he so acquire praise for himself as to rob another of his. But you in sending great gifts acquire to yourself praise for large-hearted generosity, but you rob me of praise by constraining me to accept favours. For I too might shew large-heartedness by refusing to accept such. But in small gifts the apportionment of praise is equal, in that the

[1] At Athens a man, who thought himself unfairly taxed compared with another, could claim a re-assessment for both or an exchange of properties between them (ἀντιδόσις).

πέμψαντι ὅτι οὐκ ἠμέλησεν, τῷ δὲ λαβόντι ὅτι οὐχ ὑπερη-
φάνησεν. ματευσαίμην δ' ἄν, εἰ καί σοι χαλεπῶς χρώ-
μενος,[1]† ὡς καὶ σὺ αὐτὸ τοῦτο δῶρον ἐμοῦ πέμψαντος οὐκ
ἂν ἔλαβες, πῶς παρὰ σοῦ τοὺς πεμφθέντας παῖδας ἡδό-
μενος προσείμην ἄν; . . . . [2] Γλαῦκος πάλαι . . . . [3]
χρύσεα τῶν χαλκείων καὶ τὰ ἑκατόμβοια τῶν ἐννεαβοίων
ἀμείβοντος. πᾶσα μὲν γὰρ ἀνάγκη τὸν ἀμειβόμενον ἢ
πολὺ πλέονος ἄξια ἀντιπέμπειν καὶ Ὁμήρῳ μάρτυρι τὰς
φρένας δοκεῖν ὑπὸ τοῦ Διὸς βεβλάφθαι, ἢ τὰ μείω ἀντι-
πέμποντα μὴ δίκαια ποιεῖν. τρίτον δὲ καὶ δικαιότατον, ἃ
πέμπεται τῷ αὐτῷ μέτρῳ καὶ τοῖς ἴσοις[4] δώροις ἀμεί-
βεσθαι. τοῦτο δὲ ὁ ποιῶν ὁμοιότατος ἐμοί, τῷ αὐτὰ δὴ
τὰ πεμφθέντα ἀποπέμποντι.

Ἀλλὰ ταῦτα μὲν φίλῳ πρὸς τὸν φίλτατον πεπαίχθω.
†τροφεῖ<α> δὲ <τῶν παίδων> καὶ λογιζομένῳ μείζονα
τὸν καρπόν σοι νῦν παρέξει.[5]†

Ad Amicos, i. 3 (Naber, p. 175).

Ambr. 336,
ad fin. col. 1

| FRONTO Lolliano Avito salutem.

Montanum Licinium—ita te reducem complectar,
quo iure iurando mea tuaque salus aeque continetur—
sic diligo ut non temere quemquam eorum, quiscum
mihi hospitii iura sunt, Montano meo anteponam.

---

[1] Studemund reads the Codex εικοτι τω χαληπο χρωμενος;
du Rieu as εικοντας νωητιω χρωμενοι.

[2] Two lines are lost here.   [3] Seven lines lost.

[4] Naber reads κατά γε Ἡσίοδον, after Jacobs, for καὶ τοῖς ἴσοις.

[5] I have followed Mai except for the bracketed words.
After this letter the corrector adds Feliciter, as if his task
was ended.

sender did not neglect to send, and the recipient did not disdain, the gift. But I would ask, pressing you perhaps rather hard, how can I receive with delight the slaves sent from you, whereas you would not have accepted an identical present, had I sent it? . . . . It would have been Glaucus[1] of old over again . . . . "exchanging gold for bronze and a hundred oxen's worth for that of nine." For it is inevitable that the exchanger of presents should either send in return gifts of much greater value and, as Homer testifies, seem bereft of his senses by Zeus, or act inequitably by sending a meaner gift in return. The third and most equitable rule is to requite what is sent according to the same measure and with equal gifts.[2] He that did this would be as like as possible to me, for I am sending back the very things that were sent.

But enough of this pleasantry from a friend to a very dear friend. The cost of the keep of these slaves will now, if you calculate it, give you a little the best of the bargain

? 157–161 A.D.

Fronto to Lollianus Avitus,[3] greeting.

Licinius Montanus—" so may I have you safe back in my arms," and this is an oath which equally involves my weal and yours—is one whom I love so dearly that there is no one of those, who have shared my home with me, whom I could easily prefer to my

---

[1] Hom. *Il.* vi. 236.

[2] *cp.* Hesiod, *W. and D.* 349, 354 : εὖ μὲν μετρεῖσθαι παρὰ γείτονος, εὖ δ' ἀποδοῦναι | αὐτῷ τῷ μέτρῳ.

[3] Proconsul of Africa 156–159. Apuleius also (*Apol.* 94 f.) wrote to Avitus a letter of recommendation, eulogizing him in language that reminds us of Fronto.

Quotienscumque Romam venit, in meo contubernio
fuit, meis aedibus usus est ; una nobis mensa semper : postremo omnium paene rerum consiliorumque
communicatio et societas fuit. Huic tantum honorem haberi a te velim quantum tuo hospiti contubernali
consiliario tributum ab altero postulares. O<mnium
litterarum et> bonarum artium sectator est meus
Montanus, tum doctrina et facundia est eleganti.
Etsi sentio me meo artificio nimium favere quod ipse

Ambr. 335   nihil studio eloquentiae antetulerit . . . . . . | . .

Apud me antiquissimum locum laudis eloquentia
possidet [1] . . . . Ex summis benignitatis opibus
tribuas . . . . Nihil postulavit pro sua verecundia
nisi quod probum honestumque sit et tibi datu et sibi

Ambr. 334   postulatu [2] . . . . | . . Frugi probus philostorgus,
cuius rei nomen apud Romanos nullum est [3] . . . .

Ambr. 333   . . | . . Is adeo [4] postulat asylum in ora, denique
iustas res istas. Igitur non maris sed aurae cupidus
<est> . . . . Facundissimo omnium quae tua nobili-
tas est [5] . . . . let. Cavillantes eundem audio aegre
abstractum tristem contubernio meo, quod pectoris
valetudine correptus laetissimo caelo posse redire ab
Cirta patria serio videatur, quod ut fiat optes. Quom

---

[1] From the margin of Cod.
[2] *Ibid.*   [3] *Ibid.*
[4] For all the rest of this letter see Hauler, *Wien. Stud.*
38, pp. 379–381 (1916).
[5] From the margin of the Codex.

Montanus. As often as he came to Rome he was my guest, my house was at his disposal, he always shared my table; in fact there was between us a community and fellowship in almost all our acts and counsels. Please pay him such attention as you would expect to be shewn by another to your intimate friend, the sharer of your home and your counsels. My Montanus is devoted to all letters and noble accomplishments, besides being a man of learning and cultured eloquence. Although I feel that I am biased in favour of my own craft, because he has himself preferred nothing to the study of eloquence . . . . With me eloquence holds the most honoured place . . . . From your utmost stores of good-nature grant . . . . He has asked nothing, as was to be expected of his modesty, except what is right and honourable for you to give and for him to ask . . . . Worthy, upright, rich in natural affection,[1] a quality for which the Romans have no word . . . . He indeed asks for a health-resort on the coast, and lastly those reasonable adjuncts. Consequently it is not the sea but the air that he is desirous of . . . . The most eloquent of all, such is your nobleness . . . . I hear that some speak captiously of his having been torn away with grief and reluctance from my home-circle, because seized as he was with an affection of the chest, there seemed a real possibility that the extreme salubrity of the climate would enable him to return from his native city Cirta. Pray that it may be so. Since I love him for my

---

[1] Fronto tells us elsewhere (*Ad. Ver.* ii. 7, and *cp.* Marcus, *Thoughts*, i. 11) that φιλοστοργία was practically non-existent, at least among the patricians of Rome. The word means affection between the members of a family. *Cp.* Ep. Romans, I. 30.

eum inter paucissimos ultro amem, fac mihi caro
fruaris, eum praesentem accipias et propitia cura
ambias et auxilium summum ei amicis consiliis
\<fera\>s.   Post hospitis salutem corpusque examines
saepius cupio[1] . . . . ita celebratus[2] es . . . .

Ad Amicos, ii. 4 (Naber, p. 191).

Ambr.
291 col.
2, and
339 *ad
fin*.

| Cornelio Repentino Fronto salutem.

    Fecisti, frater Contucci, pro tua perpetua consuet-
udine et benignitate, quod Fabianum spectatum in
officiis civilibus, frequentem in foro,[3] meum familiarem ita tutatus es ut ei existimationem incolumem
conservares.   Meritis tibi parem gratiam referundam

About
here
Ambr.
338

dei immortales prospe\<re praestent\> . . |[4] . .
. . . . neque mox habebis tibi nobiles: teneto
potius eos satis aperto odio plenos fuisse[5] . . . .

Ad Amicos, i. 1 (Naber, p. 172).

Ambr.
328

| Fronto Claudio Severo salutem.

    1. Commendandi mos initio dicitur benivolentia
ortus, quom suum quisque amicum alii amico suo

---

[1] Hauler says five lines more of the letter remain, in which
Fronto sends greetings to his friends, and thanks Lollianus
by anticipation for his trouble.

[2] This is the marginal variant for a word in the text which
Hauler reads as *cenobatus* or *cenobator* and explains as *xenoda-
tor* (ξενοδώτης) ; but Mai read it *generatus*.

[3] Niebuhr for Cod. *forum*.

[4] About one column is lost, but in this Hauler (*Wien. Stud.*
33, pp. 174 ff.) says he has deciphered some other lines,
which he does not, however, give.

part as I do very few, please use him as one who is
dear to me, welcome him when he comes and win
his love with your gracious care for him and give him
the best of help with friendly counsel. Afterwards I
desire you often to test the health and condition of
your guest . . . .

? 157–161 A.D.

FRONTO to Cornelius Repentinus,[1] greeting.

You have acted, brother Contuccius, according
to your never-failing habit and kindness in so effectually safeguarding the good name of Fabianus, a
man of tried experience in civil duties, constant in
attendance at the forum, and my close friend.   May
the immortal Gods ensure to you with all happiness a
recompense equal to your kindness . . . .
nor will you soon find (such among) the nobles :
hold rather that they were full of sufficiently un-
disguised hatred . . . .

? 157–161 A.D.

FRONTO to Claudius Severus,[2] greeting.

1. The custom of recommendation is said in the
first instance to have sprung from good will, when
every man wished to have his own friend made

---

[1] Corn. Repentinus Contuccius was *praef. praet.* with Fur.
Victorinus for the year 159, and probably died that year.
As the *praef. praet.* had judicial powers, the case of Fabianus
may have come before him.

[2] Probably the consul of 146, and the father-in-law of
Marcus's daughter ,Fadilla.   In his *Thoughts*, i. 14, Marcus
mentions the latter as "having confidence in the love of his
friends."

---

[5] After a gap of a few lines comes a note of the corrector,
Legi emendavi qui supra.

demonstratum conciliatumque vellet. Paulatim iste mos progressus est, ut etiam eos qui in publico vel privato iudicio disceptarent, nec tamen improba res videretur, iudicibus ipsis aut iis qui consilio adessent, commendare<nt>[1] : non, opinor, ad iustitiam iudicis labefactandam vel de vera sententia deducendam. Sed <ut>[2] iste in ipsis iudiciis mos inveteratus erat causa perorata laudatores adhibere, qui quid de reo[3] existimarent pro sua opinione cum fide expromerent, item istae commendantium litterae laudationis munere fungi visae sunt.

2. Quorsum hoc tam ex alto prohoemium ? Ne me existimasses parum considerasse gravitatem auctoritatemque tuam commendando Corneliano Sulpicio familiarissimo meo, qui propediem causam apud vos dicturus est. Sed, ut dixi, veteris instituti exemplo necessarium meum laudare apud te ausus sum.

3. Industrius vir est, strenuus, ingenio libero et liberali, patriae amantissimus, innocentia fretus magis quam confidens, litterarum studio et bonarum | artium elegantia mihi <acceptissimus>[4] . . . .

4. | . . . . quicum mihi . . . . <in>tercedit. Neque forte aut temere necessitudine ista sumus

Ambr. 327, followed by 326

Ambr. 325

---

[1] Schopen ; but the word lacks a subject. Perhaps *fas esset* has dropped out before *commendare*.

[2] Schopen.

[3] Naber for Cod. *quidquid ergo*.

[4] Heindorf. Two pages are lost, and five lines at the beginning of p. 326. The marginal corrector notes on p. 327 that Fronto used *iusso*, not *iussu*.

known to another friend and rendered intimate with him. Then the custom gradually grew up of giving such recommendations in the case of those persons even who were parties to a public or private trial, provided however that the case was not a flagrant one, to the actual judges or their assessors on the bench : not, I take it, to undermine the fairness of the judge or to lead him aside from giving true judgment. But as there had long established itself in the very courts of law this custom of bringing forward, when the case had been heard out, witnesses to character to give in all honesty their own private opinion of the defendant, so these commendatory letters seemed to discharge the function of a testimony to character.

2. Wherefore this preface going back so far? That you may not think that I have had but scant regard for your dignity and authority in recommending Sulpicius Cornelianus,[1] a most intimate friend of mine, who is very shortly to plead his case before you. But as I have said, following a long-established precedent, I venture to speak in praise of my friend before you.

3. The man is hard-working, energetic, of a free and free-handed nature, a true patriot, relying on his innocence rather than presuming on it, to me a most congenial friend from his devotion to literature and his taste in the liberal arts . . . .
. . . .

4. . . . . Nor did this close relationship between us arise casually or by chance,

---

[1] Phrynichus in his Ἐκλογή speaks highly of a Sulp. Cornelianus, and says that Marcus and Lucius put all the affairs of the Greeks in his charge συνεργὸν αὐτὸν ἑλόμενοι τῆς Βασιλείας.

copulati, nec ultro me amicitiam Corneliani adpetisse fateor. Laus ad me de ingenio eius iam[1] pervaserat, quam veram ad aures meas accidisse usu didici multisque documentis expertus sum. Habitavimus una, studuimus una, iocum seriumque participavimus, fidei consiliique periculum fecimus : omnibus modis amicitia nostra et voluptati nobis et usui fuit. Quam ob rem, quantum plurimum possum, tantum quaeso ut carissimo mihi homini in causa faveas . . . .[2] citavit ad accusationem nostri ordinis virum. Sed lectis concilii commentariis . . . . plane . . . . facit . . . .[3] <propul>sare conisus est. Sollicitudo amici[4] me a . . . . multis eum verbis commendare : sed fidum amorem nostri spondet < . . . . quic> quid postulem†, orationem vobis unum meum verbum visum iri.

Ad Amicos, i. 2 (Naber, p. 174.)

Φρόντων ᾿Απ<πίῳ> ᾿Απολλωνίδῃ.

Ambr. 336 Κοριγηλιανὸν Σουλπίκιον φιλεῖν ἠρξάμην ἡσθ|εὶς τῷ τε τρόπῳ τἀ⌐δρὸς καὶ τοῖς λόγοις· πέφυκεν γὰρ πρὸς λόγους ἄριστα. οὐκ ἂν δ᾿ ἔξαρνος εἴην τὰ πρῶτα παρ᾿ ἐμοὶ φέρισθαι τὴν ἐκ παιδείας φιλίαν συσταθεῖσαν· παιδείαν δὲ ταύτην λέγω τὴν τῶν ῥητόρων· αὕτη γὰρ δοκεῖ

---

[1] Cod. apparently has *a* before perv. Schwierczina prefers *fama*.
[2] Three lines lost.   [3] About two lines lost in these gaps.
[4] Mai gives *animi,* but doubtfully. After *me a* three letters are lost.

and I am free to confess that I did not go out of my
way to seek the friendship of Cornelianus. I had
already heard his character spoken of with praise,
and that it was a true report which reached my ears
I have learnt by experience and verified with many
proofs. We have lived together, studied together,
shared alike in things grave and gay, put our loyalty
and our counsels to the proof. In every way our
friendship has conduced to our pleasure and our
profit. Wherefore I appeal to you as earnestly as I
can to give this very dear friend of mine a favourable
hearing in his case . . . . summoned for trial a
member of our order. But the notes of the *Consilium*[1]
being read . . . . tried to
rebut it. Anxiety for my friend (makes) me commend him at such length: but our friendship is a
guarantee of your loyal love for me and (will bring
it about that), whatever I ask, a whole speech should
seem to you but one word.

FRONTO TO APPIUS APOLLONIDES.

? 157–161 A.D.

DELIGHT in the character and eloquence of the
man first made me love Sulpicius Cornelianus. For
he has the greatest aptitude for eloquence; and I
will not deny that the friendship which is grounded
on culture takes the highest place with me, and the
culture I mean here is that of the orator. For this

---

[1] If the MS. *concilii* may be so translated. The *Consilium*
was a body of officials and assessors attending the judges at a
trial.

μοι ἀνθρωπίνη τις εἶναι· ἡ δὲ τῶν φιλοσόφων θεία τις
ἔστω. βοήθησον οὖν τὰ δυνατὰ Κοριηλιανῷ ἀγαθῷ ἀνδρὶ
κἀμοὶ φίλῳ <καὶ λογίῳ> [1] καὶ οὐ φιλοσόφῳ.

Ad Amicos, i. 4 (Naber, p. 176).

AEGRILIO PLARIANO salutem.

  Iulium Aquilinum virum, si quid mihi credis,

doctis|simum facundissimum, philosophiae disciplinis
ad optimas artes, eloquentiae studiis ad egregiam
facundiam eximie [2] eruditum, commendo tibi quam
possum studiosissime. Decet a te gravissimo et sap-
ientissimo viro tam doctum tamque elegantem virum
non modo protegi sed etiam provehi et illustrari.
Est etiam, si quid mihi credis, Aquilinus eiusmodi
vir ut in tui ornamentis aeque ac nostri merito
numerandus sit. Non dubitabis ita esse ut dico, si
eum audire disputantem de Platonicis disciplinis
dignatus fueris. Perspicies pro tua prudentia in-
tellegentiaque summa <non> minorem fama, lucu
lentissimum verborum adparatu, maxima frequentia
sententiarum. Quom haec ita esse deprehenderis,
scito amplius esse in hominis moribus, tanta probitate
est et verecundia : maximi concursus ad audiendum
eum Romae saepe facti sunt. Plurimi nostri ordinis viri facundiam eius non modo probant sed

---

[1] Naber.
[2] Niebuhr for Cod. *ex iure* ; query *e puero.*

seems to me to be human; as for philosophy's, let
it be divine. Do your utmost then for Cornelianus,
who is a good man and a friend of mine and
eloquent and no philosopher.

? 157–161 A.D.

To Aegrilius Plarianus, greeting.

I commend to you with all possible cordiality
Julius Aquilinus,[1] a man, if you have any faith in
my judgment, most learned, most eloquent, excep-
tionally trained by the teachings of philosophy to
the noblest accomplishments and by the study of eloquence to a matchless facility of speech. A man so
learned and so cultured should naturally find from a
man of your serious character and wisdom not only
protection but advancement and honour. Aquilinus
is also, believe me, a man of such a character that he
deserves to be accounted an ornament to yourself
no less than to me. You will not doubt that it is
as I say, if you once deign to hear him discuss the
doctrines of Plato. With your perspicacity and
good sense you will find him not unequal to his high
fame, most conspicuous for the magnificence[2] of
his language and the immense abundance of his
thoughts. When you have realized the truth of this,
know that there is still more behind in the man's
character, so great are his integrity and his modesty.
Crowds of people constantly gathered to hear him
at Rome. There are numbers of senators who not
only applaud his eloquence, but also admire his

[1] Nothing is known for certain of him. Plarianus was
leg. pr. pr. of Africa in 159. For him see *C.I.L.* viii. 800,
1177.
[2] *cp.* the use of *adparatus* in Hor. *Od.* i. 38. Dio, lxxii.
11, § 2, uses the expression παρασκευὴ τῶν λόγων.

eius [1] etiam admirantur.   Officio necessario inductus
est ut hinc proficisceretur ad consolandam conso-
brinam suam casu gravi adflictam.   Quantumcumque
Aquilino meo honoris tribueris, id te mihi tribuere
existimato.

Ad Amicos, i. 5 (Naber, p. 177).

| Fronto Claudio Iuliano salutem.

   Cuperemus profecto, mi Naucelli carissime, eo
nos fato praeditos ut, si mihi liberi etiam virilis
sexus nati fuissent, eorumque aetas hoc potissimum
tempore ad munia militaria fungenda adolesceret,
quo tempore tu provinciam cum exercitu adminis-
trares, uti sub te mei liberi stipendia mererent.
Non longe aberit quin hoc, quod uterque cuperemus,
evenerit.   Nam Faustinianum Statiani mei filium,
non minus diligo neque minus eum diligi cupio,
quam si ex me genitus esset.   Is nunc sub te mere-
bit.   Tu studium meliore bono <pensabis>.[2]   Quantum ex tua benivolentia Faustinianus ornamenti
adsequetur, tantum tu voluptatis ex Faustiniani
elegantia capies.   Quam doctus sit, mihi crede ;
quam rei militaris peritus, praedicant omnes sub
quibus meruit.   Sed tum demum doctrinae indus-
triaeque suae fructum sese percepisse putabit, ubi se
tibi probavit.   Fac periculum [3] in militiae muneribus,
fac periculum in consiliis iudiciariis, fac periculum in
litteris, omni denique prudentiae et facilitatis [4] usu
vel serio vel remisso, semper et ubique eum parem

---

[1] A substantive may have dropped out or the second
eius be corrupt.   [2] Cod. has *an.* . . .

[3] See Ter. *Eun.* III. ii. 23.

[4] Kiessling prefers *facultatis*.   The author of the *De
Differentiis Verborum* (? Fronto) distinguishes the words
thus : *facultas locupletis, facilitas artificis est.*

M. CORNELIUS FRONTO

. . . . He was obliged to leave Rome by the necessary duty of comforting his lady cousin, who is
suffering under a great misfortune. Any attention
you pay to Aquilinus please consider as paid to me.

? 157–161 A.D.

Fronto to Claudius Julianus, greeting.

We could assuredly wish, my dearest Naucellius,[1]
it had been our happy fortune that, if I had had any
children also of the male sex and these were of an age
for the discharge of military duties at this particular
time, when you are administering a province with
an army, my children should serve under you. This
that each of us would desire will almost be fulfilled.
For I love Faustinianus, the son of my friend
Statianus, not less, and I desire him to be loved no
less, than if he came from my own loins. He is now
to serve under you. Any attention you shew him
will be paid with interest. However much distinction Faustinianus gains by your goodwill, the pleasure
you derive from his refined nature will be no less.
His learning you may trust me for; his military
ability is vouched for by all those under whom he
has served. But he will not think that he has
reaped the full fruit of his learning and industry
until he has earned your approbation. Try him in
military duties, try him in legal consultations, try him
in letters, in a word, in everything that requires
judgment and ability, whether grave or gay, you will
find him always and everywhere equal to himself. As

[1] The other name of Julianus. He was consul in 145, and
therefore proconsul about 157–159.

sui invenies.   Patrem vero eius egregium virum,
nisi tute nosses, satis | ego laudare non possem.
Quin aliquanto minus dixerim, tametsi plurimum
dixero.   Prorsus ego Statiani mei filium qualemcumque diligerem tam hercule quam Faustiniani mei
patrem qualemcumque carum haberem.   Nunc vero
uter utri plus apud me gratiae conciliet ignoro; nisi
quod utrumque impensius alterum alterius gratia
diligo.

Ad Amicos, ii. 11 (Naber, p. 200).

IIIVIRIS ET DECURIONIBUS [1]

QUANTAE mihi curae [2] . . . . | multoque malim
patriae nostrae tutelam auctam quam meam gratiam.
Quare suadeo vobis patronos creare, et decreta in
eam rem mittere ad eos qui nunc fori principem
locum occupant: Aufidium Victorinum, quem in
numero municipum habebitis, si di consilia mea
iuverint, nam. filiam meam despondi ei nec melius
aut mihi in posteritatem aut meae filiae in omnem
vitam consulere potui quam quom talem mihi
generum cum illis moribus tantaque eloquentia elegi;
Servilium quoque Silanum, optimum et facundissi-
mum virum, iure municipis patronum habebitis,

----

[1] *sc. Cirtensibus.* The title is from the Index, as two pages
are lost here.   The letter which preceded this one was also
to the Triumvirs of Cirta (Index, Naber, p. 189; Ambr. 292,
col. 2).

[2] These words are from the Index, but it is possible that
they were the opening words of the other letter, and the
heading *Meae totius gloriae* assigned to the other letter was
the beginning of the letter here given.

to that eminent man, his father, did you not know
him for yourself, I could not praise him highly enough.
Nor could I escape having said a great deal too
little, though I said ever so much. Verily I should
love the son of my Statianus, whatever he were,
just as by heaven I should hold dear the father of
my Faustinianus, whatever he were. Now, however,
I do not know which of the two endears me more
to the other, save that I love each of them more
dearly, the one for the sake of the other.

FRONTO TO THE TRIUMVIRS AND SENATORS OF CIRTA[1]

? 157–161 A.D.

How great are my cares . . . . and I should
much prefer the guardianship of our native country
to be strengthened than my own interests. Wherefore my advice to you is to choose for your patrons,
and send resolutions to that effect to, those who at
present stand highest at the bar—Aufidius Victorinus, whom you will have on your burgess-roll if the
Gods favour my designs, for I have betrothed my
daughter[2] to him, nor could I have better consulted
the interests either of myself in the matter of
posterity or of my daughter in the matter of her
whole life, than when I chose such a son-in-law, a
man of such character and great eloquence; Servilius
Silanus also, an excellent and most eloquent man,
you will have as your patron by burgess right, since

---

[1] Fronto was born at Cirta, now Constantine, in Numidia.
Triumvirs, also in some cases *quattuorviri iuri dicundo*, were
the chief magistrates of *municipia*. Colonies, such as Cirta,
usually had *duumviri*. [2] Gratia.

quom sit <e> vicina et amica civitate Hippone
Regio ; Postumium Festum et morum et eloquentiae
nomine recte patronum vobis feceritis, et ipsum
nostrae provinciae et civitatis non longinquae.
Horum patronorum non mediocrium . . . . oderint
. . . . adesse . . . .[1] adversus rem atque nolint
. . . .[2] dicam, quoad aetas mihi et valetudo integra
fuit, negotia nostra . . . . alius . . . . ⟨is⟩ta aetate

Ambr. 305

. . . .[3] | nostram forensium et iuniorum praesidiis
esse fundatum. Nec genere quantus . . . . nostra
. . . .[4] virum popularem habeamus et virum con-
sularem ius publicum respondentem. Ego quoque,
ut spero, quoad aetatis vis viguit, in officiis civilibus
non obscure versatus sum. Alii quoque plurimi sunt
in senatu Cirtenses clarissimi viri. Postremus est
honor maximus tres vestri cives . . . .[5] sed etiam
suave est . . . . uter quo . . . .[6] sed vos melius
est iam nunc interdum . . . .[7] quantum . . . .[8]

Ad Verum Imp. i. 3 (Naber, p. 116).

Ambr. 426,
col. 2

| Magistro meo.

Est quod ego tecum graviter conquerar, mi
magister, et quidem ut querelam dolor superet, quod
ego te tanto post intervallo nec complexus neque
adfatus sim, quom et in palatium veneris et postquam
ego a Domino meo fratre vixdum discesseram. Equi-

---

[1] From *mediocrium* are five lines.
[2] Two lines and two letters are missing.
[3] About three lines are lost. Mai supplies *coloniam* before
nostram and marks *forensium* as doubtful.
[4] About eight lines lost.
[5] Thirteen lines lost. [6] One word lost.
[7] One word lost. [8] Four lines are lost.

he comes from the neighbouring and friendly state of Hippo Regius[1]; Postumius Festus[2] you cannot do wrong in electing as your patron in consideration of his character and eloquence, himself also a native of our province and of no distant state. Of these no ordinary patrons . . . .
. . . . as long as my strength and health were sound, our business . . . .
. . . . that our city has been established by the help of practised speakers and men in the prime of life . . . . we should have a well-known man and a consular to be responsible for our public interests. I too, as I hope, while young and strong, played no obscure part in civil affairs. There are many other natives of Cirta also in the Senate, entitled to be called most eminent.[3] The last honour is the greatest, three of your citizens . . . .
. . . . but it is better for you now sometimes. . . . .

LUCIUS VERUS TO FRONTO

161 A.D.

To my master.

I have a serious complaint to make against you, my master, and yet that is not so great as my disappointment, that after so long a separation I did not embrace or speak to you, though you both came to the Palace and came when I had only just left the Lord my brother. You may be sure I gave my brother a

---

[1] Now Bona or Beled el Aneb.

[2] A grammarian of whom an inscr. (*C.I.L.* vi. 146) says *orator utraque facundia maximus.* For him see Aul. Gell. xix. 13.

[3] The official title of senators.

dem multum fratrem meum obiurgavi cur me non
revocarit.[1] Neque culpam abnuere ausus est. Quantum, oro te, fuit ante mihi significare, te ad fratrem
meum <venturum> esse, velle me quoque visere,
postremo redire me iubere, uti confabularemur?
quid enim, si me hodie domum arcessas, nonne

omnibus omissis libens curram? | Qui quidem aeger-
rime tulerim quod non cotidie ad te commeem.
Quin gravissimum stationis nostrae id esse arbitrer,
quod veniendi ad te adeo <rara est facultas> . . . .
solus . . . . ad te currissem. Nunc oro saltem, dum
mi<hi nondum vacat ad te>[2] conte<ndere, rescribas
quo<modo valeas: nec diu iam impedient negotia,
quamvis> tum<e>ant, quin te <revisam aut>
. . . . expectem. Vale, mi magister, Vero tuo
carissime et humanissime.

Ad Verum Imp. i. 4 (Naber, p. 117).

Domino meo Vero Augusto.

1. Quod heri, quom in palatium vestri visendi
causa venissem, non te viserim, non mea culpa
evenisse ostendam paulo post. Quod si <volens>[3]
libens scienti animo hoc officium non persolvissem,
haudquaquam me poeniteret. Fuit enim, fuit haec

causa cur tu tam | familiaribus litteris mecum ex-
postulares. Neque tanto opere gauderem si, quom
ad te venissem, summo cum honore a te appellatus

---

[1] Heind. for Cod. *revocavit.*

[2] This and the following additions are by Heindorf, except
nondum for *non.* The mutilated portion is about a column
of the Codex.   [3] So Mai, but query *ipse* for *volens.*

good scolding for not calling me back; and he could
not deny that he was to blame. How easy, prithee,
it would have been to let me know beforehand that
you were coming to see my brother, and would like to
see me as well, or failing that, to have asked me to
return, that we might have a talk. What? if you sent
for me to-day to your house, should I not put everything aside and run to you? Indeed, I have been very
cross that I could not visit you every day. Nay, I
think it is the heaviest penalty of our position that
I so seldom have an opportunity of coming to you
. . . . alone . . . . I should have run to you.
Now at least I beseech you, as I have no leisure yet
to hasten to you, write and tell me how you are:
affairs of state, however pressing, shall not long
prevent me from seeing you again or expecting you
. . . . Farewell, my master, to your Verus most
dear and most kind.

Fronto to Lucius Verus as Emperor

To my Lord Verus Augustus.[1]   161 A.D.

1. That it was no fault of mine that I did not
see you yesterday, when I came to the Palace to see
you both, I will presently shew. But had I myself
deliberately from choice left this duty unpaid, I
should not in the least regret it. For this, this was
the cause of your reproaching me in such a friendly
letter. Nor should I be so greatly pleased, had I
come to you and been welcomed by you with every

---

[1] This letter appears to have been written very soon after
the death of Pius (on March 7, 161). Fronto had been away
four months, possibly on a visit to Africa, where he had
property and friends.

essem, quam nunc gaudeo tanto me iurgio desideratum Namque tu pro tua singulari humanitate omnes nostri ordinis viros, ubi praesto adsunt, honorifice adfaris, non omnes magno opere requiris absentes. Haec denique culpae causa est, in qua malim te mihi graviter irasci quam libenter ignoscere. Irasceris enim quanto desiderantius desideras: a quibus autem aversus fueris, neque irasceris neque desiderabis,[1] si amare desieris. Enimvero quom tu tuusque frater in tantis opibus locati, tanta multitudine omnium generum omniumque ordinum, in quos amorem vestrum dispergitis, circumfusi, mihi quoque partem amoris vestri nonnullam impertiatis, quid me facere oportet, cuius spes opesque omnes in vobis sunt solis sitae? Non ei tum pectus meum . . . . aut ubi illos mihi ante-<positos> . . . . praestare possim quam ut vos illis anteponam. | Sic enim profecto merebor ut vos quoque illos mihi anteponatis.

Ambr. 443

2. Sed ne diutius defensionem meam differam, nulla, ut dixi, mea culpa accidit ut te non convenirem. Nam ex hortis redii Romam ante diem quintam Kal. April. diluculo ut <eo ipso>[2] si possem die longo post tempore domum irem†.[3] Sed eo <quom venissem melius visum> est . . . . nae ego pergerem <quid> ut facerem? *Satin salvae* ut percontarer? an ut complecterer? an ut exoscularer? an ut confabularer? an ego quarto post mense lacrimas vestras spectatum measque ostentatum venirem? Quid igitur postero die feci? Non sum

---

[1] Fresh lines deciphered by Hauler. See *Wien. Stud.* 40, p. 95.

[2] Brakman.

[3] Mai *con* <*venirem*>. Du Rieu sees *consuero* in the Codex.

honour, as I am now that you felt my absence
enough to give me such a scolding. For while with
your characteristic kindliness you give all members
of our order, when they present themselves, an
honourable welcome, yet it is not all of them about
whom you make earnest enquiries when they are
absent. In fact this is the cause of my fault, inasmuch
as I should prefer you to be seriously angry with me
than too ready to pardon. For your anger is the
measure of your regret. But those from whom you
are estranged you will neither be angry with nor
miss, if you have ceased to love them. For indeed,
since you and your brother, set in so great a station,
surrounded by so great a multitude of all sorts and
conditions of men, on whom you lavish your love,
bestow on me too some portion of that love, what
ought I to do, whose hopes and fortunes all on
you alone are centred?[1] . . . . or that I shall be
able to . . . . those who are preferred to me than
that I should prefer you to them. For thus I should
assuredly deserve that you also should prefer them
to me.

2. But not to defer my defence any longer, it
was, as I said, no fault of mine that I did not meet
you. For I returned from my gardens to Rome on
March 28th at dawn, in order that I might if
possible after so long an interval reach home that
very day. But when I had come there, it seemed
better . . . . verily I should hasten to do what?
To ask *Is all well?* to embrace? to kiss? to have a
talk? Or was it that after four months I should
come to look on your tears and exhibit my own?
What then did I do the next day? I did not

---

[1] Terence, *Phorm.* III. i. 6. *Adelphi,* III. ii. 32.

ausus neque fratri tuo neque tibi scribere me ad vos
esse venturum, sed ad libertum Charilam perscripsi
his si recte memini verbis : Ἆρα σήμερον εὔκαιρόν
ἐστιν ἀφικέσθαι με πρὸς αὐτούς ; σύ μοι δήλωσον ὡσανεὶ
ἔμφρων κἀμοὶ φίλος· κἀμοί σε . . . . <Quom ve>ni
Ambr. 446   ego in palatium . . . . . . [1] | . . vestrae pro re nata
occu<pationes> . . . . aliud [2] . . . .

Ad Antoninum Imp. ii. 1 (Naber, p. 104).

Ambr. 239,
col. 1

| MAGISTRO meo.[3]

Ambr. 240   . . . . <legi ex Coe>|lio paululum et ex Ciceronis
oratione, sed quasi furtim, certe quidem raptim :
tantum instat aliud ex alio curarum, quom interim
requies una librum in manus sumere.   Nam parvolae
nostrae nunc apud Matidiam in oppido hospitantur :
igitur vespera ad me ventitare non possunt propter
aurae rigorem. Vale mi optime [4] magister. Dominus
meus frater et filiae cum sua matre, cuius prae
. . . . avis, ex animo tibi salutem dicunt.

Mitte mihi aliquid quod tibi disertissimum videatur, quod legam, vel tuum aut Catonis aut Ciceronis
aut Sallustii aut Gracchi aut poetae alicuius, χρήζω
γὰρ ἀναπαύλης, et maxime hoc genus, quae me lectio

---

[1] About eight lines are lost.
[2] These six words are from the margin of the Codex. Du
Rieu reads *destrae*, not *vestrae*.
[3] A new book begins here, as the words *Legi emendavi* immediately before it shew, but it is not certain whether it is the
second book to Antoninus. More than a column is lost here.
[4] For Cod. *domine*, which seems impossible.

venture to write either to your brother or to you, that I would come to you, but I wrote to your freedman Charilas to the best of my recollection in these words: *Is it convenient for me to come to them to-day? Please tell me as a man of sense and a friend of mine* . . . . when I went into the palace . . . . your occupations under the new circumstances . . . .

Marcus Antoninus as Emperor to Fronto

To my master.   161 A.D.

. . . .
. . . . I have read a little of Coelius and of Cicero's speech, but as it were by stealth, certainly by snatches, so closely does one care tread on the heels of another, my one relaxation the while being to take up a book. For our little daughters are at present lodging with Matidia[1] in the town, so that they cannot come to me in the evening owing to the keenness of the air. Farewell, my best of masters. The Lord my brother and my daughters[2] with their mother, whose . . . . send you their affectionate greetings.

Send me something to read which you think particularly eloquent, either of your own or Cato's or Cicero's or Sallust's or Gracchus's or some poet's, for I need relaxation, and especially of such a kind that the reading of it may uplift me and shake me

---

[1] The great-aunt of Marcus. One of the little daughters must have been Cornificia, born about 159. It is not clear who the other was. Domitia Faustina died before Marcus became emperor, and Sabina was not born yet.

[2] Lucilla and Fadilla.

extollat et diffundat ἐκ τῶν κατειληφυιῶν φροντίδων ;
etiam si qua Lucretii aut Ennii excerpta habes
εὔφωνα <στίχι>α [1] et sicubi ἤθους ἐμφάσεις.

Ad Antoninum Imp. ii. 2 (Naber, p. 105).

DOMINO meo Antonino Augusto Fronto.

Nae ego post homines natos et locutos omnium
facundissimus habear, quom tu, M. Aureli, mea
scripta lectitas et probas | et lucrativa tua in tantis
negotiis tempora meis quoque orationibus legendis
occupare non inutile tibi arbitraris neque infruc-
tuosum.

Quod sive amore inductus etiam ingenio meo
delectaris, beatissimus equidem sum, quod tibi tam
sum carus, ut esse videar etiam disertus; sive ita
censes et ita iudicio tuo et animi sententia decernis,
mihi quoque iam disertus iure videbor, quoniam
videar tibi.

Quod vero patris tui laudes a me in senatu desig-
nato et inito consulatu meo dictas legisti libenter,
minime miror. Namque tu Parthos etiam et Hiberos
sua lingua patrem tuum laudantes pro summis ora-
toribus audias. Nec meam orationem sed patris tui
virtutem miratus es, nec laudatoris verba sed laudati
facta laudasti.

Brakman.

free from the cares that beset me; also if you have
any extracts from Lucretius or Ennius, sonorous
lines if possible, and any that give the impress of
character.[1]

FRONTO to my Lord Antoninus Augustus.

Verily, since the creation of mankind and their
endowment with speech let me be held the most
eloquent of all men, since you, Marcus Aurelius,
study my writings and esteem them, and do not
think it useless or unprofitable to yourself in the
midst of such great affairs to spend your valuable
time in reading my speeches.

But if it is your love for me which makes you
delight even in my abilities, most blest am I in that I
am so dear to you as to seem even eloquent in your
eyes; or if it is your real judgment and considered
opinion that makes you so think, then shall I have
every right to seem eloquent to myself since I seem
so to you.

I am, however, not in the least surprised that you
have found pleasure in reading the praises of your
father, which I uttered in the Senate when consul
designate and again when I had taken up the office.[2]
For you would listen even to the Parthians and
Iberians in their own tongue, so they but praised
your father, as if they were most consummate orators.
It was not my speech you admired but your father's
virtues,[3] nor was it the words of the praiser but the
deeds of the praised that you praised.

[1] See Philost. *Epistles*, 364, Kayser.
[2] In 143. *cp.* above, p. 113.
[3] *cp.* Marcus, *Thoughts*, i. 16; vi. 30.

De tuis autem laudibus, quas in senatu eodem illo die protuli, ita sentias velim : tunc in te eximiam indolem fuisse, nunc summam virtutem ; frugem tunc in segete florentem, nunc messem perfectam et horreo conditam. Sperabam tunc, habeo nunc. Spes in rem convertit.

Quod autem mitti a me tibi postulasti, acceptis <litteris> . . . . | . . Atticis propinque thymum serpyllumque Hymettium ruminantibus viris . . . . vel graves ex orationibus veterum sententias arriperetis vel dulces ex poematis vel ex historia splendidas vel comes ex comoediis vel urbanas ex togatis vel ex Atellanis lepidas et facetas[1] . . . .

Ambr. 234

Ad Verum Imp. i. 2 (Naber, p. 115).

<Magistro meo>.

. . . . <mihi cum >[2] | nostro, Calpurnium dico, contentio est, quem ego facile et omnino spectantibus et te, si spectaveris, teste revincam, Pyladem magistro suo istum tanto meliorem esse, quanto sit Apolausto similior. Sed quod sine ioco dicatur, iube Valerium istum Antonium dare mihi libellum, uti rescriptione quoque nostra gratia sententiae nostrae

Ambr. 426, following Vat. 3

---

[1] These two sentences are from the margin of the Codex.
[2] Added by Naber. It is not known how much is lost, probably not much.

As to my praises of yourself, which I pronounced the same day in the Senate, I would have you look on them in this light, that you then shewed rare natural ability, but now a consummate excellence; that you were then as corn sprouting in a field, but are now as the harvest fully ripe and gathered in the garner. All was hoping then, all is having now. Hope has turned to reality.

What you asked me, however, to send you, on receiving your letter . . . . men of Attica chewing hard-by the cud of their native herbs and the wild thyme of Hymettus . . . . You could pluck either weighty thoughts from the speeches of the ancients or sweet thoughts from their poems, or splendid thoughts from history, or kindly ones from comedies, or courtly ones from the national drama, or witty and humorous ones from the Atellane farces . . . .

Lucius Verus to Fronto

161 a.d.

To my master.

. . . . My friend, I mean Calpurnius, and I are having a dispute, but I shall easily confute him in the presence of all, and with you, too, if you are present, as a witness, that Pylades is superior to his master,[1] by so much as he is more like Apolaustus.[2] But to speak seriously, tell your Valerius Antonius to hand me the petition, that by our reply also

[1] Also called Pylades. They were both *pantomimi*.
[2] Probably a freedman of Verus, named after the great actor Apolaustus (mentioned, Capit. *Vit. Veri*, viii.).

fiat. Epistulam tuam summa cum voluptate et solita cum admiratione legi. Vale, mi magister, Vero tuo dulcissime et carissime.

Ad Verum Imp. i. 5 (Naber, p. 118).

<? DOMINO meo.>[1]

Ambr. 445,
following
446 (see
above, p.
300)

. . . . | percontatum an videre me posset; postquam respondi posse, succidaneum sibi Tranquillum nostrum paravit, quem etiam cenae succidaneum paraverat. Mea parum refert, quis me de caris tibi amicis diligat, nisi quod prior ratio est eius, qui minus est nostris fastidiosus. Ego . . . . Nam is quoque ex tempore eum vidit. Invenit autem me Tranquillus, quom frigeret, etiam nunc vetantem, sed minus . . . . uva . . . . [belli] . . . . dinitates tantas ori<turas>. Ago quanta Tranquilli industriae, qui nisi sciret quanto opere me diligeres, voluntarium hoc negotium sibi numquam expetisset.

Ad Amicos, ii. 1 (Naber, p. 190).

Ambr. 340,
ad init., and
292, col. 2

| VOLUMNIO QUADRATO.

SECRETUM servabo ita ut vis. Legam libenter, itaque ut soleo corrigam, quantum manus, quae infirmissimae sunt, tolerare poterunt. Ex voto studiorum cultum[2] teneto; et si quid vacui temporis detur, exercendo ingenio occupare.

[1] Owing to the condition of the Codex it is impossible to tell whether this is a separate letter or part of *Ad Verum* i. 4, as Naber thinks. Possibly it is a letter to a friend, and not to the Emperor at all.   [2] Heindorf *cursum.*

our verdict may be quashed. I read your letter with the greatest pleasure and with my usual admiration. Farewell, my master, to your Verus sweetest and dearest.

(? To my Lord.)   ? 161 A.D.

.... to enquire whether he could see me; when I answered that he could, he procured our friend Tranquillus[1] as his substitute, whom he had also procured as his substitute at dinner. It makes little difference to me, who of the friends you hold dear has an affection for me, except that I take prior account of him who is less disdainful of my friends. I . . . . for he also saw him at once. Tranquillus however found me, when he had a cold, still forbidding but less (positively the use of) grapes . . . . such great . . . . would arise. How much do I owe to the diligence of Tranquillus, who would never have offered himself for this business, did he not know how much you loved me.

FRONTO TO VOLUMNIUS QUADRATUS.

161 A.D.

I WILL, as you wish, keep your secret. I will gladly read it and correct it in my usual way as far as my hands, which are quite crippled, will permit. Continue in the cultivation of your studies according to your wish, and utilize any spare time you have in practising your talents.

---

[1] Not Suetonius the writer, who would have been seventy years old by 139 A.D.

Ad Amicos, ii. 2 (Naber, p. 190).

VOLUMNIO QUADRATO.

CASTRICIUS noster libellum tuum mihi heri reddidit de balneo egredienti : petii ut mane ad me veniret ad rescriptum accipiendum. Per noctem ita vexatus sum tussi et vigiliis ut necessario in quintam horam dormierim. Ita Castricium nostrum detinui. Ciceronianos emendatos et dis|tinctos habebis ; adnotatos a me leges ipse ; in volgus enim eos exire quare nolim, scribam [1] diligentius.

Ambr. 291

Ad Amicos, ii. 3 (Naber, p. 191).

VOLUMNIO QUADRATO.

LEGAM, fili, libenter orationem istam quam misisti mihi et, si quid videbitur corrigendum, cor|rigam, sed librarii manu, nam mihi manus debilis doloribus non mediocribus. Cum istis tamen doloribus in circum delatus sum. Rursum enim studio circensium teneor . . . .[2] <perp>eram composita sit rhetorice tota.[3]

Ambr. 340
ends :
followed by
339

[1] The reading on Cod. p. 340 is *scrib rem ad te.*

[2] About seventeen lines are lost. Brakman conjectured *perperam.*

[3] m[1] of Cod. has *rhetoricotata*, which m[2] corrects apparently to *rhetorico tota.*

M. CORNELIUS FRONTO

161 A.D.

Our friend Castricius handed me your letter yesterday as I was leaving the baths, and I asked him to come to me for an answer in the morning. During the night I suffered so much from cough and sleeplessness that I was obliged to stay in bed till 11 o'clock. That accounts for my keeping our friend Castricius back. You shall have the books of Cicero corrected and punctuated. Those which I have annotated please keep for your own eye. I will write to you more carefully the reasons why I do not wish them to become public property.

Fronto to Volumnius Quadratus.

161 A.D.

I will gladly, my son, read your speech, which you have sent me, and correct anything that seems to require it, but by the hand of my secretary, for my own hand is useless from severe pain. In spite of the pain, however, I have been carried to the circus. For I am again seized with a passion for the games . . . . be badly composed and wholly in rhetorical style.

THE LOEB CLASSICAL LIBRARY

VOLUMES ALREADY PUBLISHED

Latin Authors

AMMIANUS MARCELLINUS. Translated by J. C. Rolfe. 3 Vols.

APULEIUS: THE GOLDEN ASS (METAMORPHOSES). W. Adlington (1566). Revised by S. Gaselee.

ST. AUGUSTINE: CITY OF GOD. 7 Vols. Vol. I. G. E. McCracken. Vols. II and VII. W. M. Green. Vol. III. D. Wiesen. Vol. IV. P. Levine. Vol. V. E. M. Sanford and W. M. Green. Vol. VI. W. C. Greene.

ST. AUGUSTINE, CONFESSIONS OF. W. Watts (1631). 2 Vols.

ST. AUGUSTINE, SELECT LETTERS. J. H. Baxter.

AUSONIUS. H. G. Evelyn White. 2 Vols.

BEDE. J. E. King. 2 Vols.

BOETHIUS: TRACTS and DE CONSOLATIONE PHILOSOPHIAE. Rev. H. F. Stewart and E. K. Rand. Revised by S. J. Tester.

CAESAR: ALEXANDRIAN, AFRICAN and SPANISH WARS. A. G. Way.

CAESAR: CIVIL WARS. A. G. Peskett.

CAESAR: GALLIC WAR. H. J. Edwards.

CATO: DE RE RUSTICA. VARRO: DE RE RUSTICA. H. B. Ash and W. D. Hooper.

CATULLUS. F. W. Cornish. TIBULLUS. J. B. Postgate. PERVIGILIUM VENERIS. J. W. Mackail.

CELSUS: DE MEDICINA. W. G. Spencer. 3 Vols.

CICERO: BRUTUS and ORATOR. G. L. Hendrickson and H. M. Hubbell.

[CICERO]: AD HERENNIUM. H. Caplan.

CICERO: DE ORATORE, etc. 2 Vols. Vol. I. DE ORATORE, Books I and II. E. W. Sutton and H. Rackham. Vol. II. DE ORATORE, Book III. DE FATO; PARADOXA STOICORUM; DE PARTITIONE ORATORIA. H. Rackham.

CICERO: DE FINIBUS. H. Rackham.

CICERO: DE INVENTIONE, etc. H. M. Hubbell.

CICERO: DE NATURA DEORUM and ACADEMICA. H. Rackham.

CICERO: DE OFFICIIS. Walter Miller.

CICERO: DE REPUBLICA and DE LEGIBUS. Clinton W. Keyes.

Cicero: De Senectute, De Amicitia, De Divinatione. W. A. Falconer.

Cicero: In Catilinam, Pro Flacco, Pro Murena, Pro Sulla. New version by C. Macdonald.

Cicero: Letters to Atticus. E. O. Winstedt. 3 Vols.

Cicero: Letters to His Friends. W. Glynn Williams, M. Cary, M. Henderson. 4 Vols.

Cicero: Philippics. W. C. A. Ker.

Cicero: Pro Archia, Post Reditum, De Domo, De Haruspicum Responsis, Pro Plancio. N. H. Watts.

Cicero: Pro Caecina, Pro Lege Manilia, Pro Cluentio, Pro Rabirio. H. Grose Hodge.

Cicero: Pro Caelio, De Provinciis Consularibus, Pro Balbo. R. Gardner.

Cicero: Pro Milone, In Pisonem, Pro Scauro, Pro Fonteio, Pro Rabirio Postumo, Pro Marcello, Pro Ligario, Pro Rege Deiotaro. N. H. Watts.

Cicero: Pro Quinctio, Pro Roscio Amerino, Pro Roscio Comoedo, Contra Rullum. J. H. Freese.

Cicero: Pro Sestio, In Vatinium. R. Gardner.

Cicero: Tusculan Disputations. J. E. King.

Cicero: Verrine Orations. L. H. G. Greenwood. 2 Vols.

Claudian. M. Platnauer. 2 Vols.

Columella: De Re Rustica. De Arboribus. H. B. Ash, E. S. Forster and E. Heffner. 3 Vols.

Curtius, Q.: History of Alexander. J. C. Rolfe. 2 Vols.

Florus. E. S. Forster. Cornelius Nepos. J. C. Rolfe.

Frontinus: Stratagems and Aqueducts. C. E. Bennett and M. B. McElwain.

Fronto: Correspondence. C. R. Haines. 2 Vols.

Gellius. J. C. Rolfe. 3 Vols.

Horace: Odes and Epodes. C. E. Bennett.

Horace: Satires, Epistles, Ars Poetica. H. R. Fairclough.

Jerome: Selected Letters. F. A. Wright.

Juvenal and Persius. G. G. Ramsay.

Livy. B. O. Foster, F. G. Moore, Evan T. Sage, and A. C. Schlesinger and R. M. Geer (General Index). 14 Vols.

Lucan. J. D. Duff.

Lucretius. W. H. D. Rouse. Revised by M. F. Smith.

Manilius. G. P. Goold.

Martial. W. C. A. Ker. 2 Vols. Revised by E. H. Warmington.

Minor Latin poets: from Publilius Syrus to Rutilius Namatianus, including Grattius, Calpurnius Siculus, Nemesianus, Avianus and others, with " Aetna " and the " Phoenix." J. Wight Duff and Arnold M. Duff.

2

Minucius Felix. Cf. Tertullian.

Ovid: The Art of Love and Other Poems. J. H. Mosley. Revised by G. P. Goold.

Ovid: Fasti. Sir James G. Frazer

Ovid: Heroides and Amores. Grant Showerman. Revised by G. P. Goold

Ovid: Metamorphoses. F. J. Miller. 2 Vols. Vol. 1 revised by G. P. Goold.

Ovid: Tristia and Ex Ponto. A. L. Wheeler.

Persius. Cf. Juvenal.

Pervigilium Veneris. Cf. Catullus.

Petronius. M. Heseltine. Seneca: Apocolocyntosis. W. H. D. Rouse. Revised by E. H. Warmington.

Phaedrus and Babrius (Greek). B. E. Perry.

Plautus. Paul Nixon. 5 Vols.

Pliny: Letters, Panegyricus. Betty Radice. 2 Vols.

Pliny: Natural History. 10 Vols. Vols. I–V and IX. H. Rackham. VI.–VIII. W. H. S. Jones. X. D. E. Eichholz.

Propertius. H. E. Butler.

Prudentius. H. J. Thomson. 2 Vols.

Quintilian. H. E. Butler. 4 Vols.

Remains of Old Latin. E. H. Warmington. 4 Vols. Vol. I. (Ennius and Caecilius) Vol. II. (Livius, Naevius Pacuvius, Accius) Vol. III. (Lucilius and Laws of XII Tables) Vol. IV. (Archaic Inscriptions)

Res Gestae Divi Augusti. Cf. Velleius Paterculus.

Sallust. J. C. Rolfe.

Scriptores Historiae Augustae. D. Magie. 3 Vols.

Seneca, The Elder: Controversiae, Suasoriae. M. Winterbottom. 2 Vols.

Seneca: Apocolocyntosis. Cf. Petronius.

Seneca: Epistulae Morales. R. M. Gummere. 3 Vols.

Seneca: Moral Essays. J. W. Basore. 3 Vols.

Seneca: Tragedies. F. J. Miller. 2 Vols.

Seneca: Naturales Quaestiones. T. H. Corcoran. 2 Vols.

Sidonius: Poems and Letters. W. B. Anderson. 2 Vols.

Silius Italicus. J. D. Duff. 2 Vols.

Statius. J. H. Mozley. 2 Vols.

Suetonius. J. C. Rolfe. 2 Vols.

Tacitus: Dialogus. Sir Wm. Peterson. Agricola and Germania. Maurice Hutton. Revised by M. Winterbottom, R. M. Ogilvie, E. H. Warmington.

Tacitus: Histories and Annals. C. H. Moore and J. Jackson. 4 Vols.

3

TERENCE. John Sargeaunt. 2 Vols.
TERTULLIAN: APOLOGIA and DE SPECTACULIS. T. R. Glover. MINUCIUS FELIX. G. H. Rendall.
TIBULLUS. Cf. CATULLUS.
VALERIUS FLACCUS. J. H. Mozley.
VARRO: DE LINGUA LATINA. R. G. Kent. 2 Vols.
VELLEIUS PATERCULUS and RES GESTAE DIVI AUGUSTI. F. W. Shipley.
VIRGIL. H. R. Fairclough. 2 Vols.
VITRUVIUS: DE ARCHITECTURA. F. Granger. 2 Vols.

Greek Authors

ACHILLES TATIUS. S. Gaselee.
AELIAN: ON THE NATURE OF ANIMALS. A. F. Scholfield. 3 Vols.
AENEAS TACTICUS. ASCLEPIODOTUS and ONASANDER. The Illinois Greek Club.
AESCHINES. C. D. Adams.
AESCHYLUS. H. Weir Smyth. 2 Vols.
ALCIPHRON, AELIAN, PHILOSTRATUS: LETTERS. A. R. Benner and F. H. Fobes.
ANDOCIDES, ANTIPHON. Cf. MINOR ATTIC ORATORS.
APOLLODORUS. Sir James G. Frazer. 2 Vols.
APOLLONIUS RHODIUS. R. C. Seaton.
APOSTOLIC FATHERS. Kirsopp Lake. 2 Vols.
APPIAN: ROMAN HISTORY. Horace White. 4 Vols.
ARATUS. Cf. CALLIMACHUS.
ARISTIDES: ORATIONS. C. A. Behr. Vol. I.
ARISTOPHANES. Benjamin Bickley Rogers. 3 Vols. Verse trans.
ARISTOTLE: ART OF RHETORIC. J. H. Freese.
ARISTOTLE: ATHENIAN CONSTITUTION, EUDEMIAN ETHICS, VICES AND VIRTUES. H. Rackham.
ARISTOTLE: GENERATION OF ANIMALS. A. L. Peck.
ARISTOTLE: HISTORIA ANIMALIUM. A. L. Peck. Vols. I.–II.
ARISTOTLE: METAPHYSICS. H. Tredennick. 2 Vols.
ARISTOTLE: METEOROLOGICA. H. D. P. Lee.
ARISTOTLE: MINOR WORKS. W. S. Hett. On Colours, On Things Heard, On Physiognomies, On Plants, On Marvellous Things Heard, Mechanical Problems, On Indivisible Lines, On Situations and Names of Winds, On Melissus, Xenophanes, and Gorgias.
ARISTOTLE: NICOMACHEAN ETHICS. H. Rackham.

ARISTOTLE: OECONOMICA and MAGNA MORALIA. G. C. Armstrong (with METAPHYSICS, Vol. II).

ARISTOTLE: ON THE HEAVENS. W. K. C. Guthrie.

ARISTOTLE: ON THE SOUL, PARVA NATURALIA, ON BREATH. W. S. Hett.

ARISTOTLE: CATEGORIES, ON INTERPRETATION, PRIOR ANALYTICS. H. P. Cooke and H. Tredennick.

ARISTOTLE: POSTERIOR ANALYTICS, TOPICS. H. Tredennick and E. S. Forster.

ARISTOTLE: ON SOPHISTICAL REFUTATIONS.
On Coming to be and Passing Away, On the Cosmos. E. S. Forster and D. J. Furley.

ARISTOTLE: PARTS OF ANIMALS. A. L. Peck; MOTION AND PROGRESSION OF ANIMALS. E. S. Forster.

ARISTOTLE: PHYSICS. Rev. P. Wicksteed and F. M. Cornford. 2 Vols.

ARISTOTLE: POETICS and LONGINUS. W. Hamilton Fyfe; DEMETRIUS ON STYLE. W. Rhys Roberts.

ARISTOTLE: POLITICS. H. Rackham.

ARISTOTLE: PROBLEMS. W. S. Hett. 2 Vols.

ARISTOTLE: RHETORICA AD ALEXANDRUM (with PROBLEMS. Vol. II). H. Rackham.

ARRIAN: HISTORY OF ALEXANDER and INDICA. Rev. E. Iliffe Robson. 2 Vols. New version P. Brunt.

ATHENAEUS: DEIPNOSOPHISTAE. C. B. Gulick. 7 Vols.

BABRIUS AND PHAEDRUS (Latin). B. E. Perry.

ST. BASIL: LETTERS. R. J. Deferrari. 4 Vols.

CALLIMACHUS: FRAGMENTS. C. A. Trypanis. MUSAEUS: HERO AND LEANDER. T. Gelzer and C. Whitman.

CALLIMACHUS, Hymns and Epigrams, and LYCOPHRON. A. W. Mair; ARATUS. G. R. Mair.

CLEMENT OF ALEXANDRIA. Rev. G. W. Butterworth.

COLLUTHUS. Cf. OPPIAN.

DAPHNIS AND CHLOE. Thornley's Translation revised by J. M. Edmonds: and PARTHENIUS. S. Gaselee.

DEMOSTHENES I.: OLYNTHIACS, PHILIPPICS and MINOR ORATIONS I.–XVII. AND XX. J. H. Vince.

DEMOSTHENES II.: DE CORONA and DE FALSA LEGATIONE. C. A. Vince and J. H. Vince.

DEMOSTHENES III.: MEIDIAS, ANDROTION, ARISTOCRATES, TIMOCRATES and ARISTOGEITON I. and II. J. H. Vince.

DEMOSTHENES IV.–VI: PRIVATE ORATIONS and IN NEAERAM. A. T. Murray.

DEMOSTHENES VII: FUNERAL SPEECH, EROTIC ESSAY, EXORDIA and LETTERS. N. W. and N. J. DeWitt.

DIO CASSIUS: ROMAN HISTORY. E. Cary. 9 Vols.

DIO CHRYSOSTOM. J. W. Cohoon and H. Lamar Crosby. 5 Vols.

DIODORUS SICULUS. 12 Vols. Vols. I.–VI. C. H. Oldfather. Vol. VII. C. L. Sherman. Vol. VIII. C. B. Welles. Vols. IX. and X. R. M. Geer. Vol. XI. F. Walton. Vol. XII. F. Walton. General Index. R. M. Geer.

DIOGENES LAERTIUS. R. D. Hicks. 2 Vols. New Introduction by H. S. Long.

DIONYSIUS OF HALICARNASSUS: ROMAN ANTIQUITIES. Spelman's translation revised by E. Cary. 7 Vols.

DIONYSIUS OF HALICARNASSUS: CRITICAL ESSAYS. S. Usher. 2 Vols. Vol. I.

EPICTETUS. W. A. Oldfather. 2 Vols.

EURIPIDES. A. S. Way. 4 Vols. Verse trans.

EUSEBIUS: ECCLESIASTICAL HISTORY. Kirsopp Lake and J. E. L. Oulton. 2 Vols.

GALEN: ON THE NATURAL FACULTIES. A. J. Brock.

GREEK ANTHOLOGY. W. R. Paton. 5 Vols.

GREEK BUCOLIC POETS (THEOCRITUS, BION, MOSCHUS). J. M Edmonds.

GREEK ELEGY AND IAMBUS with the ANACREONTEA. J. M. Edmonds. 2 Vols.

GREEK LYRIC. D. A. Campbell. 4 Vols. Vol. I.

GREEK MATHEMATICAL WORKS. Ivor Thomas. 2 Vols.

HERODES. Cf. THEOPHRASTUS: CHARACTERS.

HERODIAN. C. R. Whittaker. 2 Vols.

HERODOTUS. A. D. Godley. 4 Vols.

HESIOD AND THE HOMERIC HYMNS. H. G. Evelyn White.

HIPPOCRATES and the FRAGMENTS OF HERACLEITUS. W. H. S. Jones and E. T. Withington. 4 Vols.

HOMER: ILIAD. A. T. Murray. 2 Vols.

HOMER: ODYSSEY. A. T. Murray. 2 Vols.

ISAEUS. E. W. Forster.

ISOCRATES. George Norlin and LaRue Van Hook. 3 Vols.

[ST. JOHN DAMASCENE]: BARLAAM AND IOASAPH. Rev. G. R. Woodward, Harold Mattingly and D. M. Lang.

JOSEPHUS. 10 Vols. Vols. I.–IV. H. Thackeray. Vol. V. H. Thackeray and R. Marcus. Vols. VI.–VII. R. Marcus. Vol. VIII. R. Marcus and Allen Wikgren. Vols. IX.–X. L. H. Feldman.

JULIAN. Wilmer Cave Wright. 3 Vols.

LIBANIUS. A. F. Norman. 3 Vols. Vols. I.–II.

LUCIAN. 8 Vols. Vols. I.–V. A. M. Harmon. Vol. VI. K. Kilburn. Vols. VII.–VIII. M. D. Macleod.

LYCOPHRON. Cf. CALLIMACHUS.

Lyra Graeca, J. M. Edmonds. 2 Vols.

Lysias. W. R. M. Lamb.

Manetho. W. G. Waddell.

Marcus Aurelius. C. R. Haines.

Menander. W. G. Arnott. 3 Vols. Vol. I.

Minor Attic Orators (Antiphon, Andocides, Lycurgus, Demades, Dinarchus, Hyperides). K. J. Maidment and J. O. Burtt. 2 Vols.

Musaeus: Hero and Leander. Cf. Callimachus.

Nonnos: Dionysiaca. W. H. D. Rouse. 3 Vols.

Oppian, Colluthus, Tryphiodorus. A. W. Mair.

Papyri. Non-Literary Selections. A. S. Hunt and C. C. Edgar. 2 Vols. Literary Selections (Poetry). D. L. Page.

Parthenius. Cf. Daphnis and Chloe.

Pausanias: Description of Greece. W. H. S. Jones. 4 Vols. and Companion Vol. arranged by R. E. Wycherley.

Philo. 10 Vols. Vols. I.–V. F. H. Colson and Rev. G. H. Whitaker. Vols. VI.–IX. F. H. Colson. Vol. X. F. H. Colson and the Rev. J. W. Earp.

Philo: two supplementary Vols. (*Translation only.*) Ralph Marcus.

Philostratus: The Life of Apollonius of Tyana. F. C. Conybeare. 2 Vols.

Philostratus: Imagines; Callistratus: Descriptions. A. Fairbanks.

Philostratus and Eunapius: Lives of the Sophists. Wilmer Cave Wright.

Pindar. Sir J. E. Sandys.

Plato: Charmides, Alcibiades, Hipparchus, The Lovers, Theages, Minos and Epinomis. W. R. M. Lamb.

Plato: Cratylus, Parmenides, Greater Hippias, Lesser Hippias. H. N. Fowler.

Plato: Euthyphro, Apology, Crito, Phaedo, Phaedrus, H. N. Fowler.

Plato: Laches, Protagoras, Meno, Euthydemus. W. R. M. Lamb.

Plato: Laws. Rev. R. G. Bury. 2 Vols.

Plato: Lysis, Symposium, Gorgias. W. R. M. Lamb.

Plato: Republic. Paul Shorey. 2 Vols.

Plato: Statesman, Philebus. H. N. Fowler; Ion. W. R. M. Lamb.

Plato: Theaetetus and Sophist. H. N. Fowler.

Plato: Timaeus, Critias, Clitophon, Menexenus, Epistulae. Rev. R. G. Bury.

Plotinus: A. H. Armstrong. 7 Vols. Vols. I.–III.

Plutarch: Moralia. 16 Vols. Vols I.–V. F. C. Babbitt. Vol. VI. W. C. Helmbold. Vols. VII. and XIV. P. H. De Lacy and B. Einarson. Vol. VIII. P. A. Clement and H. B. Hoffleit. Vol. IX. E. L. Minar, Jr., F. H. Sandbach, W. C. Helmbold. Vol. X. H. N. Fowler. Vol. XI. L. Pearson and F. H. Sandbach. Vol. XII. H. Cherniss and W. C. Helmbold. Vol. XIII 1–2. H. Cherniss. Vol. XV. F. H. Sandbach.

Plutarch: The Parallel Lives. B. Perrin. 11 Vols.

Polybius. W. R. Paton. 6 Vols.

Procopius H. B. Dewing. 7 Vols.

Ptolemy: Tetrabiblos. F. E. Robbins.

Quintus Smyrnaeus. A. S. Way. Verse trans.

Sextus Empiricus. Rev. R. G. Bury. 4 Vols.

Sophocles. F. Storr. 2 Vols. Verse trans.

Strabo: Geography. Horace L. Jones. 8 Vols.

Theocritus. Cf. Greek Bucolic Poets.

Theophrastus: Characters. J. M. Edmonds. Herodes, etc. A. D. Knox.

Theophrastus: Enquiry into Plants. Sir Arthur Hort, Bart. 2 Vols.

Theophrastus: De Causis Plantarum. G. K. K. Link and B. Einarson. 3 Vols. Vol. I.

Thucydides. C. F. Smith. 4 Vols.

Tryphiodorus. Cf. Oppian.

Xenophon: Cyropaedia. Walter Miller. 2 Vols.

Xenophon: Hellencia. C. L. Brownson. 2 Vols.

Xenophon: Anabasis. C. L. Brownson.

Xenophon: Memorabilia and Oeconomicus. E. C. Marchant. Symposium and Apology. O. J. Todd.

Xenophon: Scripta Minora. E. C. Marchant. Constitution of the Athenians. G. W. Bowersock.